ANIMAL FACT•FILE

HEAD-TO-TAIL PROFILES OF MORE THAN 90 MAMMALS

ANIMAL FACT•FILE

HEAD-TO-TAIL PROFILES OF MORE THAN 90 MAMMALS

Dr. Tony Hare

Checkmark Books™

An imprint of Facts On File, Inc.

Animal Fact File

© 1999 Times Editions Pte Ltd

Published 1999 for Facts On File by
Marshall Cavendish Books
an imprint of Times Editions Pte Ltd
a member of the Times Publishing Group
Times Centre, 1 New Industrial Road
Singapore 536196
Tel: (65) 2848844 Fax: (65) 2854871
E-mail:te@corp.tpl.com.sg
Online Bookstore:
http://www.timesone.com.sg/te

For information contact:

Checkmark Books
An imprint of
Facts On File, Inc.
11 Penn Plaza
New York NY 10001

Library of Congress Cataloging-in-Publication Data
Hare, Tony Dr.
     Animal fact-file : head-to-tail profiles of over 90 mammals /
Dr. Tony Hare.
     p. cm.
Summary: Describes the physical features and behavior of over 90 mammals, including the elephant and polar bear.
    ISBN 0-8160-4016-8
     1. Mammals—Anatomy—Juvenile literature. [1. Mammals.]
I. Title.
QL739.W284 1999   98-42092
599—dc21

Checkmark Books are available at special discounts when purchased in bulk
quantities for businesses, associations, institutions or sales promotions. Please
call our Special Sales Department in New York at (212) 967-8800 or (800) 322-8755.

You can find Facts On File on the World Wide Web at http://www.factsonfile.com

Editorial and design
by Brown Packaging Books Ltd
Bradley's Close, 74-77 White Lion Street
London N1 9PF

Printed and bound in Singapore

10 9 8 7 6 5 4 3 2 1

Powerstock/Zefa (cover image of giraffe)
The Stock Market Photo Agency UK (cover image of whale)

Contents

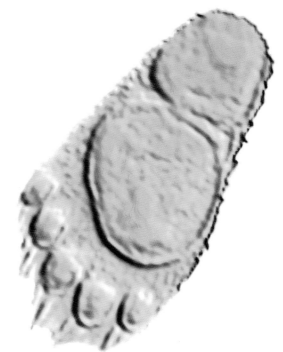

Orders of Mammals

There are over 4,000 species of mammals, covering animals from diverse corners of the globe: ranging from the trees of the Amazon basin to under the sea, the blazing floor of the desert to the freezing tundra of the Arctic.

Despite their diversity, all mammals share certain characteristics which, taken together, set them apart from other animals. They all have mammary glands, which are the organs used by the females to feed milk to their young, and from which they get their name. All mammals are 'warm-blooded', which means that they can maintain a regular internal body temperature using the heat generated in their muscles and other body tissues. Mammals have hair or fur to retain this heat and keep them warm in cold weather. Many have fur all over their body, and some over parts of their body, while some mammals, such as whales, have only a few hairs.

Mammals have four limbs (though in some sea mammals, such as dolphins, these have become flippers), well-developed brains and efficient hearts with four separate chambers, which keep apart oxygen-rich blood and blood from which most of the oxygen has been removed in its journey around the body.

All the mammals living today can be divided into 21 groups or orders (shown opposite).

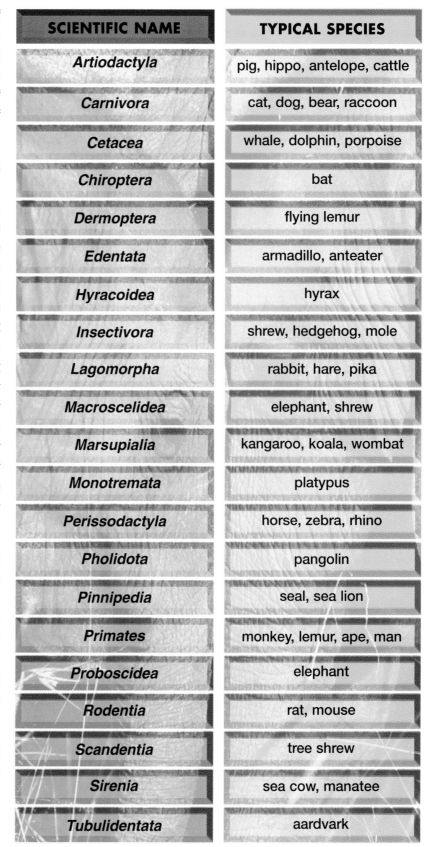

SCIENTIFIC NAME	TYPICAL SPECIES
Artiodactyla	pig, hippo, antelope, cattle
Carnivora	cat, dog, bear, raccoon
Cetacea	whale, dolphin, porpoise
Chiroptera	bat
Dermoptera	flying lemur
Edentata	armadillo, anteater
Hyracoidea	hyrax
Insectivora	shrew, hedgehog, mole
Lagomorpha	rabbit, hare, pika
Macroscelidea	elephant, shrew
Marsupialia	kangaroo, koala, wombat
Monotremata	platypus
Perissodactyla	horse, zebra, rhino
Pholidota	pangolin
Pinnipedia	seal, sea lion
Primates	monkey, lemur, ape, man
Proboscidea	elephant
Rodentia	rat, mouse
Scandentia	tree shrew
Sirenia	sea cow, manatee
Tubulidentata	aardvark

AARDVARK

HYRAX FOREFOOT   HIND FOOT

A hyrax walks on its soles. Naked toe pads, moistened by special glands, grip rocks or bark very tightly. A muscle in the center of each pad draws the center in so that it forms a suction cup.

The aardvark (above left) measures up to 63 in (160 cm) long and may weigh as much as 180 lb (82 kg), although most individuals weigh 110–154 lb (50–70 kg). Hyraxes (above right) measure 12–25 in (30–63 cm) from head to tail and weigh up to 12 lb (5.4 kg). The tail is only 0.4–1.2 in (1–3 cm) long, or is lacking altogether.

THE EARS

are long and tubelike, and the skin is smooth and waxy. The aardvark can move them independently of one another, and when it is digging it folds them back to keep dirt out.

EACH EYE

contains a special membrane—the umbraculum—that acts as a shade for the pupil and allows the animal to sit motionless on a rock apparently gazing directly at the sun.

NOSTRILS

On the tip of the snout are two circular nostrils from which grow a number of whitish, curved hairs, each 1–2 in (22–50 mm) long. The nostrils can be sealed shut to keep out soil when digging.

THE TONGUE

is long and tapering and is often left hanging outside the mouth, with the end coiled up like a clock spring.

X-RAY

AARDVARK SKELETON
The aardvark has a muscular, tapering tail up to 24 in (61 cm) long, and the legs are short and stocky.

vestigial tail

compact form

HYRAX SKELETON

deep rib cage

long skull

stocky limbs

The hyrax has a large stomach and two appendixes, and its rib cage is correspondingly expansive. Its body is characteristically compact.

X-ray illustrations Elisabeth Smith

HYRAX

TREE HYRAX HIND FOOT

The feet are well padded. The tree hyrax is a skilled climber, and its hind foot can be revolved on its axis.

THE CLAWS

are long, slightly curved, and spoon shaped, with sharp edges for digging. There are four claws on the forefeet and five on the hind feet.

AARDVARK

LOCATION: AFRICA (SOUTH OF THE SAHARA)

CLASSIFICATION

GENUS: *ORYCTEROPUS*

SPECIES: *AFER*

SIZE

HEAD–BODY LENGTH: 40–63 IN (100–160 CM)

WEIGHT: 110–155 LB (50–70 KG)

COLORATION

PINKISH GRAY SKIN WITH A SPARSE COVERING OF HAIR THAT VARIES IN COLOR FROM BROWN TO YELLOWISH GRAY

FEATURES

LONG SNOUT ENDING IN A PIGLIKE MUZZLE

LARGE, WAXY, NAKED EARS

LARGE HINDQUARTERS, SEEMINGLY OUT OF PROPORTION TO THE REST OF THE BODY

TAPERING TAIL

THE TAIL

tapers away from a stout base with a circumference of about 16 in (40 cm). It often leaves a distinctive trail on soft ground.

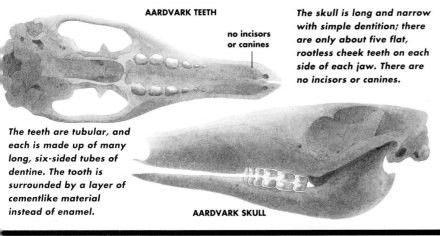

AARDVARK TEETH

no incisors or canines

The skull is long and narrow with simple dentition; there are only about five flat, rootless cheek teeth on each side of each jaw. There are no incisors or canines.

The teeth are tubular, and each is made up of many long, six-sided tubes of dentine. The tooth is surrounded by a layer of cementlike material instead of enamel.

AARDVARK SKULL

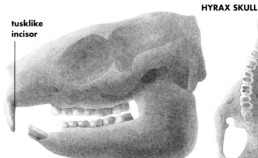

tusklike incisor

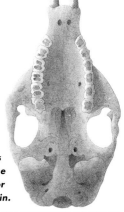

HYRAX SKULL

The hyrax first grows milk teeth—12 incisors and a canine tooth in the upper jaw. With the arrival of permanent molars, only one incisor is left in the upper jaw and no canines remain.

Main illustration Steve Kingston

AFRICAN BUFFALO

The African buffalo is the largest and most feared of the wild cattle. The mountain anoa (above right) is the smallest, measuring up to 5 ft (1.5 m) long and weighing up to 660 lb (300 kg).

AFRICAN BUFFALO HOOVES

The cloven hooves are exceptionally broad, with a wide spread for easy wading in swampy conditions. As in all artiodactyls, they have evolved to retain an even number of toes.

THE HEAD

is massive, with a prominent forehead. The broad muzzle is naked and permanently moist, and the nostrils are broad and flared. The eyes are comparatively small.

THE EARS

grow at right angles to the head, but hang droopily behind and below the horns. They are set far back and made to look even bigger by the fringe of soft hairs.

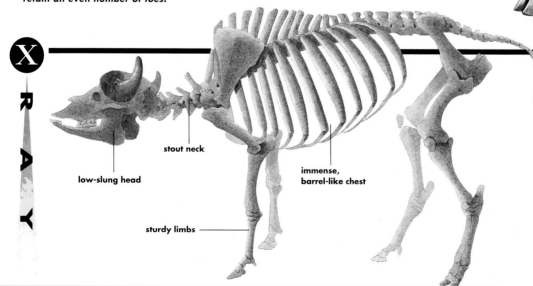

X RAY

low-slung head

stout neck

sturdy limbs

immense, barrel-like chest

BUFFALO SKELETON
The buffalo's body plan is characterized by its sheer sense of scale—there are massive, stout bones in the pelvis, limbs, and forequarters. Long fingers of bone extending from the upper vertebrae provide extra anchorage for the huge muscles that operate the shoulders and forelimbs. The skull is low-slung, enabling the embossed horns to serve as defensive weaponry.

X-ray illustrations Elisabeth Smith

YAK **WATER BUFFALO** **TAMARAU**

Horn shape and size vary widely among the wild cattle. Those of the yak grow to a length of 37 in (95 cm). The water buffalo's elegant, backswept horns are the longest of any bovid, and measure 48 in (122 cm) along the outside edge—the record length is 76 in (194 cm). By comparison, the tamarau's stout horns measure a mere 20 in (51 cm).

CLASSIFICATION

GENUS: *SYNCERUS*

SPECIES: *CAFFER*

SIZE

HEAD–BODY LENGTH: 6.8–11 FT **(2.1–3.4** M**)**

HEIGHT TO SHOULDER: 3.3–5.5 FT **(1–1.7** M**)**

AVERAGE LENGTH OF HORNS FROM ROOT TO TIP: 3.3 FT **(1** M**)**

TAIL LENGTH: 28 IN **(71** CM**)**

WEIGHT: 660–1,984 LB **(300–900** KG**)**

MALE IS 30–50 PERCENT LARGER THAN FEMALE

WEIGHT AT BIRTH: 88 LB **(40** KG**)**

COLORATION

ADULT BULLS ARE DARK BROWN TO BLACK. HAIR GRADUALLY THINS OUT AS ANIMALS MATURE, UNTIL LARGE PATCHES OF DARK HIDE ARE EXPOSED. THIS MAY BE ACCOMPANIED BY PATCHY MARKINGS ON THE FACE. COWS ARE PALER IN COLOR, AND CALVES ARE A REDDISH BROWN

FEATURES

MASSIVE, TYPICAL BOVINE APPEARANCE

LONG, SHALLOW CURVING HORNS, MEETING IN A HELMET, OR "BOSS," ON THE CROWN IN MALES

HORNS TAPER TO A POINTED TIP

LONG, DROOPING EARS FRINGED WITH HAIRS

PERMANENTLY MOIST MUZZLE

LONG TAIL ENDING IN A BUSHY TIP

THE BODY

is typically "cattle shaped," with a thick neck and strong shoulders. The humps of other cattle, such as the gaur and zebu, are formed from two massive muscles surrounded by fatty tissue.

THE TAIL

is slender, ending in a tuft of hairs. Of all the wild cattle, the kouprey's tail probably has the bushiest tip.

THE COAT

is dark brown to black in the male. The female's coat is paler in color. As animals mature, the coats become more sparse, particularly so in old bulls, when the dark brown hide often shows through. White patterns of grizzled hair may appear on the head.

BUFFALO SKULL
The horn helmet, or "boss," adds to the great size of the cranium. In spite of their size, the horns are surprisingly light and may help the animal to float in water.

tapering muzzle

large cranium

HORNS
The male's horns (below) are massive and spreading, and their central base forms a "boss" on the skull. Viewed from the front, they form a shallow W shape. The female's horns are similar but smaller, and there is no central boss.

central boss

Main illustration Kim Thompson. Heads Ruth Grewcock

AFRICAN CIVET

THE DORSAL CREST

of dark hairs up to 4.5 in (11 cm) long runs along the spine into the tail. The civet erects this when threatened. It will often also turn sideways to appear more impressive to its attacker.

THE COAT

is heavily marked with stripes, spots, and blotches, which vary according to location. They provide the civet with camouflage.

The African civet (above left) has an average head-and-body length of 34 in (86 cm) but may reach 42 in (107 cm) and weigh up to 31 lb (14 kg). The little African linsang (above right) has an average head-and-body length of 13 in (33 cm), and weighs 21–23 oz (595–652 g). The binturong (above center) reaches about 32 in (81 cm) from head to rump.

GENET FORE

CIVET FORE

GENET HIND

CIVET HIND

FEET

In all species of civet and genet each foot has five toes, with semiretractile, fairly blunt claws. The genet's soles are hairy, whereas the African palm civet has naked feet to provide a grip on branches.

THE HEAD

has blunt, raccoonlike features; the snout is white and there is a black mask around the eyes. The ears are oval and conspicuous.

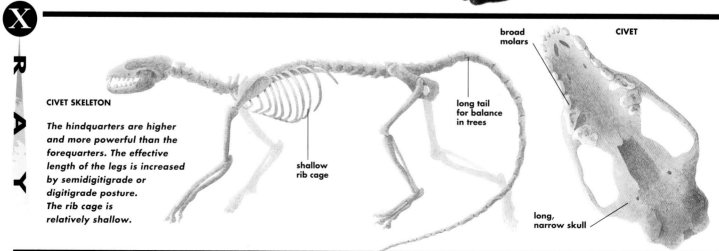

X

R A Y

CIVET SKELETON

The hindquarters are higher and more powerful than the forequarters. The effective length of the legs is increased by semidigitigrade or digitigrade posture. The rib cage is relatively shallow.

shallow rib cage

long tail for balance in trees

broad molars

CIVET

long, narrow skull

X-ray illustrations Elisabeth Smith

PALM CIVET

Sandy-brown coat with muted, indistinct dark blotches for camouflage.

BINTURONG

Dark, lustrous coat, often with gray, buff, or tawny tips to hairs.

BANDED LINSANG

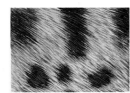

Pale, gray-brown coat with banded back and tail and spots on flanks.

AFRICAN CIVET
LOCATION: TROPICAL AFRICA

CLASSIFICATION

GENUS: *CIVETTICTIS*

SPECIES: *ČIVETTA*

SIZE

HEAD–BODY LENGTH: 26–35 IN (66–88 CM)

TAIL LENGTH: APPROX. 20 IN (51 CM)

HEIGHT TO SHOULDER: 13–15 IN (33–38 CM)

WEIGHT: 15–44 LB (7–20 KG)

MALES ARE LARGER THAN FEMALES

COLORATION

DARK SPOTS, STRIPES, AND BLOTCHES ON A GRAYISH OR TAWNY-BROWN BACKGROUND

LEGS AND TAIL ARE DARK

FACE HAS A RACCOONLIKE MASK, WITH WHITE MUZZLE AND SPECKLED GRAY FOREHEAD

FEATURES

RACCOONLIKE FACE MASK

HINDQUARTERS HIGHER THAN FOREQUARTERS

BLUNT, SEMIRETRACTILE CLAWS

DORSAL CREST OF ERECTILE, LONG DARK HAIRS

LARGE ANAL-SAC AND PERINEAL GLANDS UNDER TAIL

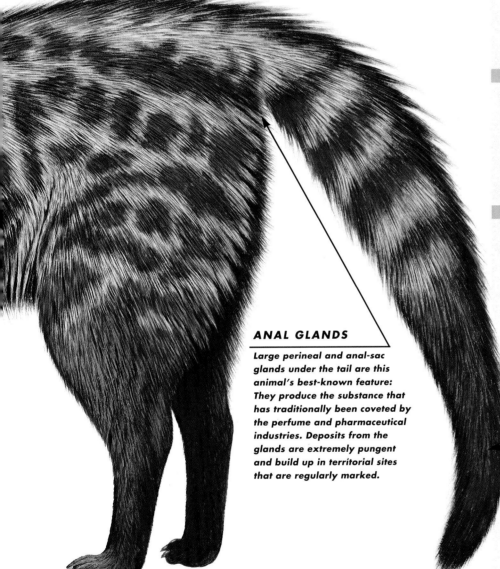

ANAL GLANDS

Large perineal and anal-sac glands under the tail are this animal's best-known feature: They produce the substance that has traditionally been coveted by the perfume and pharmaceutical industries. Deposits from the glands are extremely pungent and build up in territorial sites that are regularly marked.

THE TAIL

is broad at the base, tapering toward the tip. It measures perhaps a third of the animal's total length.

GENET

CIVET AND GENET SKULLS

The skull is remarkably strong and robust, although the cranium is long and narrow; it measures 6 in (15 cm) from front to back. The muzzle, too, is narrow. Civets have 40 teeth—10 more than is usual in cats; the molars are large and broad, similar to those of a dog.

robust cranium

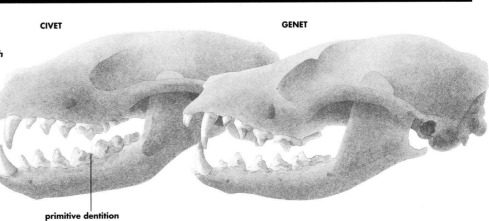

CIVET

primitive dentition

GENET

AFRICAN WILD DOG

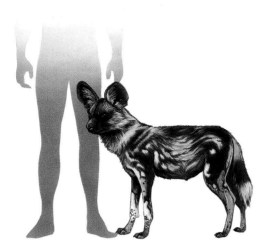

The African wild dog (above) is roughly the size of a wolf, but far more slender. Males and females are very similar in size, although males tend to be some 10 percent heavier than their sisters. For comparison, the Asian dhole has a similar build, while the bush dog of South America is barely the size of a badger (neither is shown above).

THE EARS

are mobile and unusually large, enabling the dog to use them for visual communication at long range. Well supplied with blood vessels, they act as heat radiators to help keep the dog cool in the tropical climate.

THE MUZZLE

is short and broad, and always black. The dog hunts mainly by sight and is less inclined to use scent signals than most canids, but despite this, its sense of smell is acute thanks to the large surface area of nasal membranes within its muzzle.

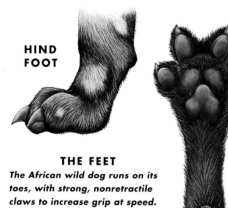

HIND FOOT

FOREFOOT

THE FEET

The African wild dog runs on its toes, with strong, nonretractile claws to increase grip at speed. Uniquely among canids, the wild dog has lost the dewclaw from each forefoot.

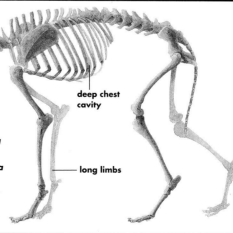

SKELETON

The African wild dog has a strong but relatively inflexible spine and a deep chest cavity to contain large-capacity lungs. Its limbs are specialized for running at speed, being elongated by extra long shoulder blades and a digitigrade stance. The collarbone, or clavicle, is redundant and has virtually disappeared.

deep chest cavity

long limbs

TEETH

The lower carnassial teeth have two knifelike cusps in line. These act against the upper carnassials like scissor blades to shear through tough hide, sinew, and flesh. In most other dogs, each lower carnassial has twinned rear cusps that form a flattened grinding surface for chewing tough vegetable food.

short, broad jaw

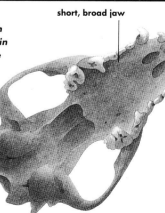

X-ray illustrations Elisabeth Smith

COAT PATTERN EXAMPLES

THE COAT

The fur is short and scant, and in older dogs it thins out even further to reveal the black skin beneath. The coat pattern is unique to each individual, but there are similarities between members of the same family.

THE BODY

is lean but wiry, like that of any endurance runner. A deep chest contains the big lungs needed to obtain the oxygen to fuel long chases. Its elastic stomach enables it to gulp down up to 11 lb (5 kg) of meat at a sitting.

THE TAIL

is tasseled, and always has a conspicuous white tip; it is used as a visual signal to other dogs in the pack.

THE LEGS

are long and slender, but well muscled to propel the dog at speeds of up to 40 mph (65 km/h) as it closes on its prey.

AFRICAN WILD DOG

LOCATION: FROM THE SAHARA TO SOUTH AFRICA

CLASSIFICATION

GENUS: *LYCAON*

SPECIES: *PICTUS*

SIZE

HEAD-BODY LENGTH: 30–40 IN (75–100 CM)

TAIL LENGTH: 12–16 IN (30–40 CM)

AVERAGE WEIGHT: 44–60 LB (20–27 KG)

MALES ARE SOME 10 PERCENT HEAVIER THAN FEMALES

COLORATION

SPARSE COAT OF RANDOM BUT WELL-DEFINED BLACK, TAN, YELLOW, AND WHITE BLOTCHES ON GRAYISH BLACK SKIN; IN OLDER ANIMALS THE SKIN IS CLEARLY VISIBLE. EACH INDIVIDUAL HAS A DIFFERENT COAT PATTERN, BUT THE MUZZLE IS ALWAYS BLACK AND THE TUFTED TAIL ALWAYS HAS A WHITE TIP

FEATURES

LITHE, SLENDER BUILD

LONG SLIM LEGS WITH FOUR TOES ON EACH FOOT

WHITE-TIPPED TAIL

BROAD, DARK MUZZLE WITH CONSPICUOUS TEETH

LARGE, ROUNDED EARS

SKULL

The jaw is broader and shorter than that of a more typical canid, such as a wolf. This increases the leverage that can be exerted on the long canine teeth by the big jaw muscles attached to the crest at the back of the skull, enabling the dog to hang on to powerful, struggling prey. The eyes face forward, giving the binocular vision essential for judging distances.

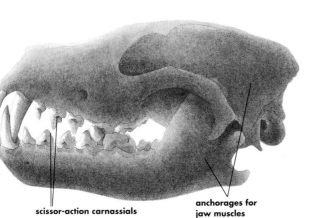

scissor-action carnassials

anchorages for jaw muscles

JAW MUSCLES

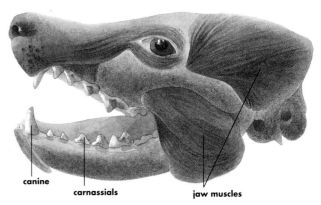

canine

carnassials

jaw muscles

AMERICAN BISON

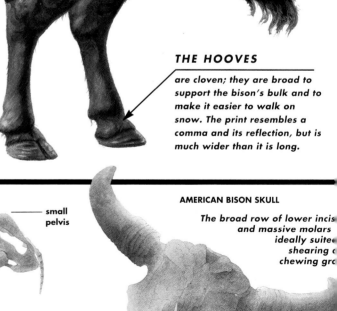

THE HUMP

that characterizes the American bison is a buildup of muscle and tissue over long bony outgrowths from the dorsal part of the spine.

Bulls of both species can attain shoulder heights of up to 6.6 ft (2 m). The massive forequarters and heavy mane of the American bison (above left) belie the fact that the European bison (above right) is actually larger.

THE HINDQUARTERS

are smallest in the plains bison, which has a relatively smaller pelvis than both the wood bison and the European bison.

THE TAIL

of the American bison is shorter than that of the European bison. Its short length limits its usefulness in fending off insects: Bison prefer to roll in dust or mud to rid themselves of insects.

PROTECTIVE FLEECE

A thick mantle of fur covers the bull's head and most of his forequarters. Apart from serving as winter insulation, the thick mane protects the bull's head from damaging horn thrusts in breeding battles with other males.

THE HOOVES

are cloven; they are broad to support the bison's bulk and to make it easier to walk on snow. The print resembles a comma and its reflection, but is much wider than it is long.

AMERICAN BISON SKELETON

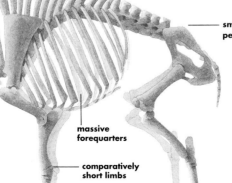

small pelvis

The American bison has far more massive forequarters, shorter legs, and a stockier appearance than the European bison. In effect, this species is more low slung and front heavy, qualities that are emphasized by the lower positioning of its head and its smaller pelvis.

massive forequarters

comparatively short limbs

AMERICAN BISON SKULL

The broad row of lower incis
and massive molars
ideally suite
shearing c
chewing gra

molars

X-ray illustrations Elisabeth Smith

AMERICAN BISON

EUROPEAN BISON

As a plains grazer, the American bison has evolved for a more herd-based lifestyle than its European counterpart.

AMERICAN BISON

LOCATION: NORTHERN PRAIRIES OF NORTH AMERICA

CLASSIFICATION

GENUS: *BISON*

SPECIES: *BISON*

SIZE

HEAD–BODY LENGTH: 7–11.5 FT (2.1–3.5 M)

TAIL LENGTH: 20–24 IN (50–60 CM)

HORN LENGTH/BULL: 26 IN (66 CM)

SHOULDER HEIGHT: 5–6.5 FT (150–200 CM)

WEIGHT/MALE: UP TO 2,200 LB (1,000 KG)

WEIGHT/FEMALE: 1,320 LB (600 KG)

WEIGHT AT BIRTH: 66 LB (30 KG)

COLORATION

THICK FUR ON HEAD, NECK, SHOULDERS, AND FORELEGS IS BROWNISH BLACK

SHORTER FUR ON REMAINDER OF BODY IS PALE IN COLOR

CALVES ARE REDDISH BROWN

FEATURES

"FRONT-HEAVY" APPEARANCE WITH LOW, BROAD SKULL, STOCKY FOREQUARTERS, AND COMPARATIVELY SMALL RUMP

THICK MANTLE OF HEAVY FUR ON THE HEAD AND FOREQUARTERS

HUMPED SHOULDERS

SHORT, SHARP HORNS

MALES CONSIDERABLY LARGER THAN FEMALES

HORNS

Both sexes have short, sharp horns that turn upward. They are effective in defense and are used, or at least brandished, by bulls in rivalry battles.

THE FACE

changes in shape as the bison grows, and is a good indicator of the animal's age. In bulls the jowls gradually fill out, while females retain a relatively slim muzzle even in maturity.

THE HAIR

on the body behind the mane is short and pale, although it often appears dark as the bison enjoys rolling in dust.

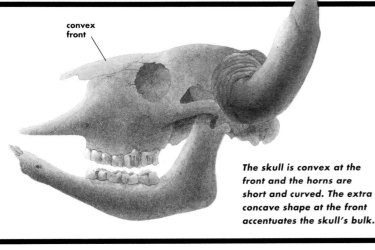

convex front

HORN STRUCTURE
Bison horns have a permanent bony core encased in a hardened sheath. These differ from antlers, which grow and are shed seasonally. There are distinct burrs on the bull's horns before they meet the skull; these are absent on the cow.

The skull is convex at the front and the horns are short and curved. The extra concave shape at the front accentuates the skull's bulk.

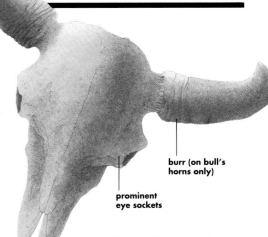

burr (on bull's horns only)

prominent eye sockets

Main illustration Rachel Lockwood/Wildlife Art Agency

ARCTIC FOX

THE EARS

are small and rounded to reduce heat loss and are probably less sensitive than the larger ears of southern species.

THE WINTER COAT

consists of 70 percent thick underfur and 30 percent long guard hairs—a combination that, for fur, provides a level of insulation unparalleled among animals, enabling the arctic fox to sleep on ice at –94°F (–70°C) for an hour before feeling chilled.

The smallest of all foxes—and the smallest canid—is the fennec (above right), which has a head-and-body length of 9.4–16 in (24–41 cm), an 7–12-in- (18–30-cm-) tail, and a weight of 1.8–3.3 lb (0.8–1.5 kg). The largest of the South American foxes is the small-eared dog (above left), which grows to a head-and-body length of 39 in (100 cm), with a 14-in- (35-cm-) tail and a weight of up to 20 lb (9 kg).

THE MUZZLE

is shorter than that of most foxes to reduce its surface area and heat loss, but it is still long enough to contain a multipurpose set of teeth and an extended nasal cavity to give an acute sense of smell.

PAWS

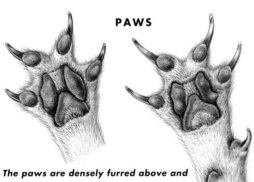

The paws are densely furred above and below to keep out the cold, enabling the arctic fox to range for hours over the ice without discomfort.

THE LEGS

are shorter than those of other foxes, reducing surface area and heat loss. The arctic fox lacks the lithe grace of species such as the red fox.

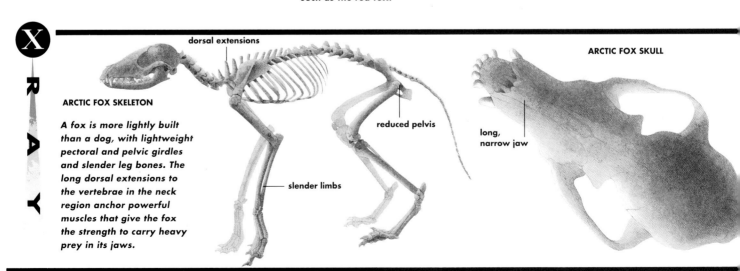

X RAY

ARCTIC FOX SKELETON

A fox is more lightly built than a dog, with lightweight pectoral and pelvic girdles and slender leg bones. The long dorsal extensions to the vertebrae in the neck region anchor powerful muscles that give the fox the strength to carry heavy prey in its jaws.

dorsal extensions

ARCTIC FOX SKULL

reduced pelvis

long, narrow jaw

slender limbs

X-ray illustrations Elisabeth Smith

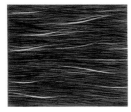

SUMMER COAT   **SUMMER COAT**   **BLUE COAT**

Most arctic foxes are pure white in winter, molting in summer to a smoky gray brown with white underparts; but in coastal areas where winter snow cover is patchy—particularly in Iceland—some individuals have bluish gray coats that molt to uniform chocolate brown in summer. This blue form has been cultivated in captivity but is relatively uncommon in the wild.

ARCTIC FOX
LOCATION: NORTHERN POLAR REGION

CLASSIFICATION

GENUS: *ALOPEX*

SPECIES: *LAGOPUS*

SIZE

HEAD–BODY LENGTH: 22 IN **(55** CM**)**

TAIL LENGTH: 12 IN **(30** CM**)**

AVERAGE WEIGHT/MALE: 8.3 LB **(3.8** KG**)**

AVERAGE WEIGHT/FEMALE: 6.8 LB **(3.1** KG**)**

COLORATION

THERE ARE TWO COLOR VARIETIES OF THE ARCTIC FOX. THE MOST COMMON AND WIDESPREAD IN THE FAR NORTH IS CREAMY WHITE IN WINTER, MOLTING IN PATCHES TO A SUMMER COAT OF GRAY BROWN ABOVE AND CREAM BELOW, WITH WHITE EYEBROWS AND EAR LININGS. THE LESS COMMON BLUE FORM IS ACTUALLY DEEP BROWN WITH A METALLIC BLUE-GRAY SHEEN IN WINTER, MOLTING TO BROWN IN SUMMER

FEATURES

EXTREMELY THICK, LUXURIANT WINTER COAT

BUSHY TAIL

SLIM LEGS

SHORT MUZZLE, COMPARED WITH OTHER FOXES

COMPARATIVELY SHORT, ROUNDED EARS

THE TAIL

is long and bushy, and the fox uses it like a fur stole to keep its face warm when it curls up to sleep on the ice. Tail gestures help foxes communicate when they are in sight of each other.

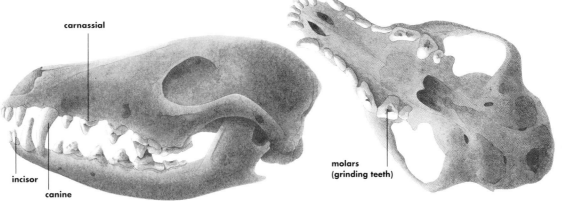

A typical fox has a long jaw with a varied array of teeth, including large, bladelike carnassials toward the back of the jaw; these act against each other like scissors to shear through skin, sinew, and flesh. The sideways movement of the jaw is restricted to keep these scissor blades in alignment, so the fox cannot grind its food like a dedicated plant-eater.

carnassial

incisor

canine

molars
(grinding teeth)

Main illustration Steve Kingston

ARMADILLO

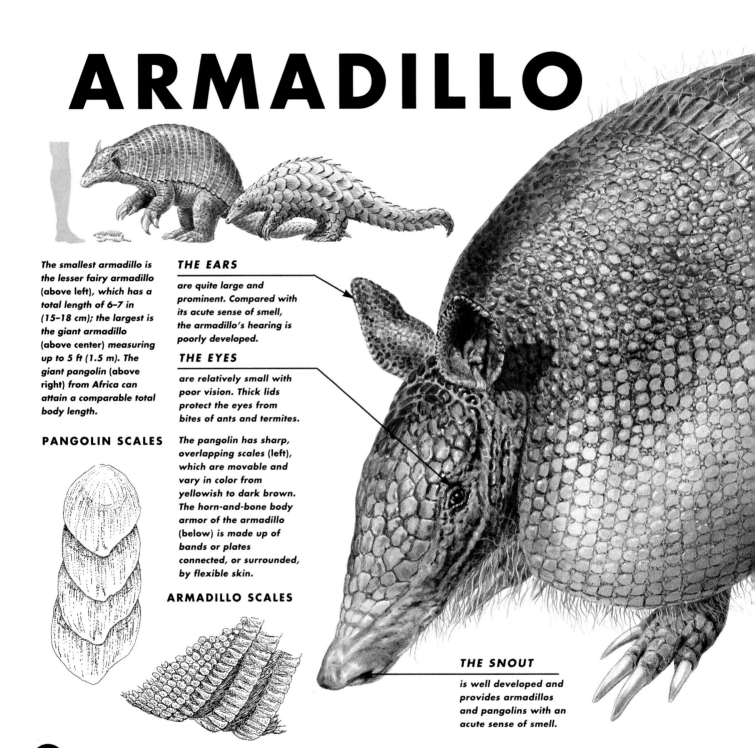

The smallest armadillo is the lesser fairy armadillo (above left), which has a total length of 6–7 in (15–18 cm); the largest is the giant armadillo (above center) measuring up to 5 ft (1.5 m). The giant pangolin (above right) from Africa can attain a comparable total body length.

PANGOLIN SCALES

THE EARS

are quite large and prominent. Compared with its acute sense of smell, the armadillo's hearing is poorly developed.

THE EYES

are relatively small with poor vision. Thick lids protect the eyes from bites of ants and termites.

The pangolin has sharp, overlapping scales (left), which are movable and vary in color from yellowish to dark brown. The horn-and-bone body armor of the armadillo (below) is made up of bands or plates connected, or surrounded, by flexible skin.

ARMADILLO SCALES

THE SNOUT

is well developed and provides armadillos and pangolins with an acute sense of smell.

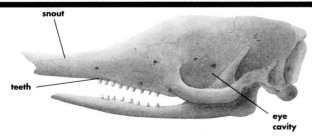

snout

teeth

eye cavity

ARMADILLO SKULL

The armadillo's skull is elongate and flattened, with a slim mandible (jawbone) and nearly cylindrical, peglike teeth. The skull provides a casing for the long tongue, which has a more important role to play in feeding than do the teeth.

PANGOLIN SKULL

The pangolin has a conical skull, devoid of teeth or chewing muscles. Its slender jawbones and long, thin, delicate mouthparts are an adaptation to a diet of ants and termites and act as a casing for the long, viscous tongue.

conical skull

slender bottom jaw

X RAY

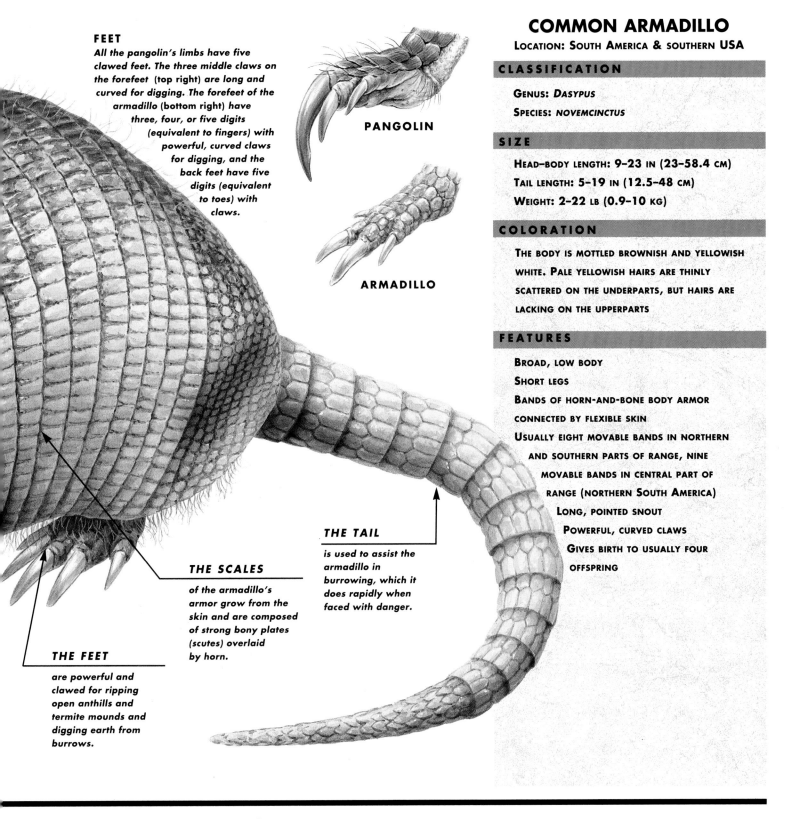

FEET

All the pangolin's limbs have five clawed feet. The three middle claws on the forefeet (top right) are long and curved for digging. The forefeet of the armadillo (bottom right) have three, four, or five digits (equivalent to fingers) with powerful, curved claws for digging, and the back feet have five digits (equivalent to toes) with claws.

PANGOLIN

ARMADILLO

THE SCALES

of the armadillo's armor grow from the skin and are composed of strong bony plates (scutes) overlaid by horn.

THE TAIL

is used to assist the armadillo in burrowing, which it does rapidly when faced with danger.

THE FEET

are powerful and clawed for ripping open anthills and termite mounds and digging earth from burrows.

COMMON ARMADILLO

LOCATION: SOUTH AMERICA & SOUTHERN USA

CLASSIFICATION

GENUS: *DASYPUS*

SPECIES: *NOVEMCINCTUS*

SIZE

HEAD–BODY LENGTH: 9–23 IN (23–58.4 CM)

TAIL LENGTH: 5–19 IN (12.5–48 CM)

WEIGHT: 2–22 LB (0.9–10 KG)

COLORATION

THE BODY IS MOTTLED BROWNISH AND YELLOWISH WHITE. PALE YELLOWISH HAIRS ARE THINLY SCATTERED ON THE UNDERPARTS, BUT HAIRS ARE LACKING ON THE UPPERPARTS

FEATURES

BROAD, LOW BODY

SHORT LEGS

BANDS OF HORN-AND-BONE BODY ARMOR CONNECTED BY FLEXIBLE SKIN

USUALLY EIGHT MOVABLE BANDS IN NORTHERN AND SOUTHERN PARTS OF RANGE, NINE MOVABLE BANDS IN CENTRAL PART OF RANGE (NORTHERN SOUTH AMERICA)

LONG, POINTED SNOUT

POWERFUL, CURVED CLAWS

GIVES BIRTH TO USUALLY FOUR OFFSPRING

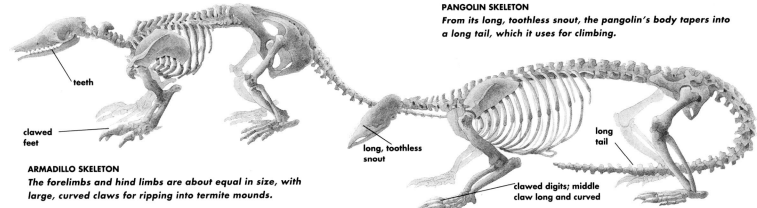

PANGOLIN SKELETON

From its long, toothless snout, the pangolin's body tapers into a long tail, which it uses for climbing.

teeth

clawed feet

ARMADILLO SKELETON

The forelimbs and hind limbs are about equal in size, with large, curved claws for ripping into termite mounds.

long, toothless snout

long tail

clawed digits; middle claw long and curved

Main illustration Robin Bouttell/Wildlife Art Agency

B A D G E R

hind foot   forefo

The European badger is a squat but stocky mammal, with a maximum weight of 35 lb (16 kg). The largest of all the badgers, it is about twice the size of the ferret badgers, which, at no more than 17 in (43 cm) long, is the smallest of all the species.

THE PADS

of the feet rest on the ground, but badgers walk on their toes. There are five fixed claws on each foot. The foreclaws are longer than the hind claws.

THE JAW

gives the badger its main means of attack and defense (see SKULL). The ratel will sink its teeth into adversaries many times its size— and when a badger bites, it hangs on with relentless determination.

THE SNOUT

is long, flexible, and muscular in all badgers and is used for probing the ground to find food. Long, sensitive whiskers grow from either side of the muzzle. Sense of smell is excellent.

THE LEGS

are relatively short and are very powerful to aid digging. Badgers move with a rather rolling gait but can run very quickly in short bursts.

All illustrations Guy Troughton/Wildlife Art Agency

X RAY

THE FOOT BONES

(the metacarpals and metatarsals) are elongated and slope upward, showing how the badger actually walks on its toes.

THE SKELETON

indicates a sturdy carnivore with plenty of strong, thick bone for the adherence of powerful muscles. Although the badger's head is quite small in comparison to its sturdy body, the skull itself is actually quite large— again to provide anchorage for the massive jaw muscles.

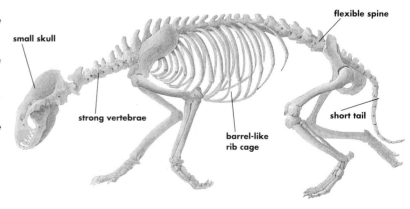

small skull

strong vertebrae

barrel-like rib cage

flexible spine

short tail

X-ray illustrations Elisabeth Smith

EUROPEAN BADGER

LOCATION: NORTHERN EUROPE & TEMPERATE ASIA

CLASSIFICATION

GENUS: *MELES*

SPECIES: *MELES*

SIZE

HEAD–BODY LENGTH: 27–31 IN (68–80 CM)

TAIL LENGTH: 5–7 IN (12–17 CM)

WEIGHT: 22–35 LB (10–16 KG)

WEIGHT AT BIRTH: 2.7 OZ (75 G)

COLORATION

BODY FUR IS GRIZZLED GRAY ON TOP AND BLACK UNDERNEATH. BLACK LIMBS. STRIKING WHITE STRIPES DOWN CENTER OF FACE AND ON EITHER SIDE OF CHEEKS, EXTENDING ALONG NECK. THROAT IS BLACK.

FEATURES

SHORT, POWERFUL LEGS

STURDY, ROUNDED BODY

THICKENED, MUSCULAR NECK AND SHOULDERS

SMALL, STRIPEY HEAD WITH LONG MUZZLE

SMALL, ROUNDED EARS EDGED WITH WHITE

SHORT TAIL

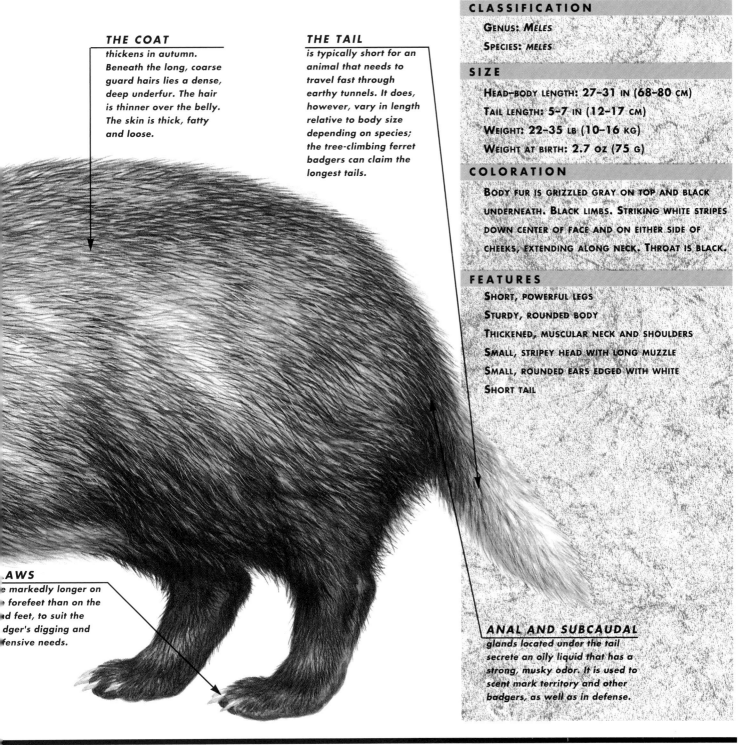

THE COAT
thickens in autumn. Beneath the long, coarse guard hairs lies a dense, deep underfur. The hair is thinner over the belly. The skin is thick, fatty and loose.

THE TAIL
is typically short for an animal that needs to travel fast through earthy tunnels. It does, however, vary in length relative to body size depending on species; the tree-climbing ferret badgers can claim the longest tails.

...AWS
...e markedly longer on ...e forefeet than on the ...d feet, to suit the ...dger's digging and ...fensive needs.

ANAL AND SUBCAUDAL
glands located under the tail secrete an oily liquid that has a strong, musky odor. It is used to scent mark territory and other badgers, as well as in defense.

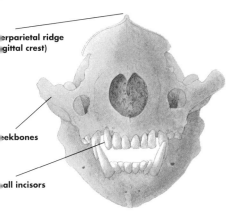

...erparietal ridge
...gittal crest)

...ekbones

...all incisors

THE SKULL
is about 5 in (12.7 cm) long. At ten months old the interparietal ridge arises along the crown, reaching 0.6 in (15 mm) high in mature badgers. Muscle tissue on either side of this connects with the lower jaw. The lower jaw is locked into sockets at the bases of the cheekbones. The lock is so powerful that one would have to fracture the skull to dislocate the badger's jaw.

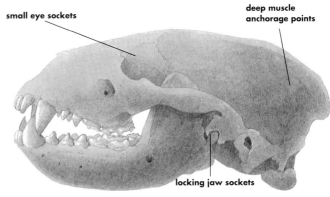

small eye sockets

deep muscle anchorage points

locking jaw sockets

BLACK BEAR

The American black bear varies in size but has a maximum head-and-body length of 6 ft (183 cm) and shoulder height of 3 ft (91 cm). That is much smaller than the polar bear, which may be up to 8 ft (243 cm) in length with a shoulder height of 5 ft (152 cm).

FOREFOOT

HIND FOOT

Anatomy illustrations Wayne Ford/Wildlife Art Agency

THE NOSE

is black and wet, giving an acute sense of smell. All bears sit back on their haunches and sniff the air. The muzzle is generally brown.

THE FEET

all have five toes, with the largest toe outermost. The claws are usually about 2.5 in (6.3 cm) long. The hind feet are more heavily padded than the forefeet.

TRACKS

typically show the heavily padded hind foot set in front of the forefoot.

X R A Y

BLACK BEAR SKELETON

The skeleton is characterized by a heavy bone structure. The spine is short and almost horizontal in profile. The rib cage is deep and barrel shaped. The bones of the feet are long, with pronounced heels, reflecting the bear's plantigrade (flat-footed) method of walking.

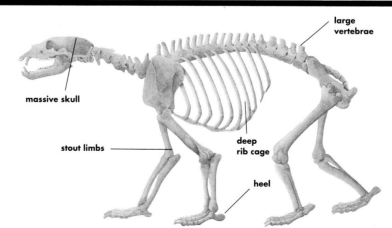

massive skull

stout limbs

large vertebrae

deep rib cage

heel

SKULL (RIGHT)

The big head of all bears comprises a skull that is the longest, with the most massive bone structure, of all carnivores. With plenty of bone to anchor on, powerful jaw muscles give a formidable bite.

X-ray illustrations Elisabeth Smith

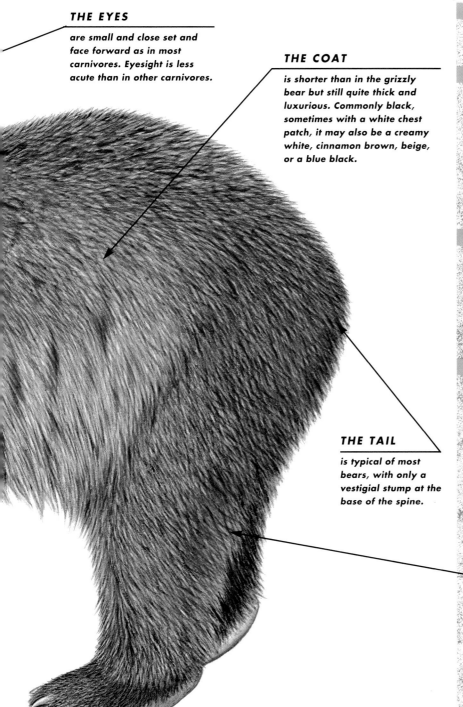

THE EYES

are small and close set and face forward as in most carnivores. Eyesight is less acute than in other carnivores.

THE COAT

is shorter than in the grizzly bear but still quite thick and luxurious. Commonly black, sometimes with a white chest patch, it may also be a creamy white, cinnamon brown, beige, or a blue black.

THE TAIL

is typical of most bears, with only a vestigial stump at the base of the spine.

THE LIMBS

are short and stocky but immensely powerful, enabling the bear to run at speed and also to deliver crushing blows to enemies.

AMERICAN BLACK BEAR
LOCATION: NORTHERN/WESTERN USA & CANADA

CLASSIFICATION

GENUS: *URSUS*

SPECIES: *AMERICANUS*

SIZE

HEAD–BODY LENGTH: 5–6 FT (152–183 CM)

SHOULDER HEIGHT: 3 FT (91 CM)

TAIL LENGTH: 5 IN (12.7 CM)

WEIGHT/MALE: 250–600 LB (113–272 KG)

WEIGHT AT BIRTH: 8–12 OZ (248–373 G)

THE ADULT MALE IS 10–50 PERCENT HEAVIER THAN THE FEMALE

COLORATION

COMMONLY JET-BLACK, OCCASIONALLY WITH A WHITE CHEST PATCH, BUT COAT COLOR MAY VARY FROM CREAMY WHITE, CINNAMON BROWN, AND BEIGE TO BLACK, OR BLACK WITH A PRONOUNCED BLUE SHEEN. MUZZLE IS USUALLY BROWN.

FEATURES

IN COMPARISON WITH THE GRIZZLY BEAR, THE FRAME IS SMALLER, THE COAT SHORTER, THE FACE MORE CONVEX IN PROFILE, THE MUZZLE MORE POINTED, THE EARS LARGER IN PROPORTION, THE BACK LESS SLOPING, AND THE CLAWS SHORTER.

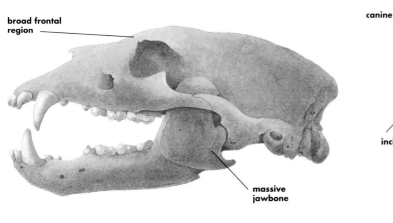

broad frontal region

massive jawbone

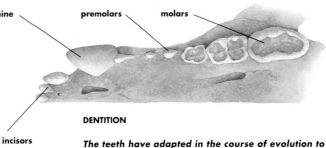

canine

premolars

molars

incisors

DENTITION

The teeth have adapted in the course of evolution to suit a more plant-based diet. The incisors are not specialized for tearing at flesh, the canines are short and strong, and the molars are broad and flat with rounded cusps—ideal for grinding plant material. The teeth grow slowly throughout the bear's life.

BLUE WHALE

THE FLIPPERS,

or pectoral fins, are supported by bones equivalent to those in your arm and hand but are used as paddles. They help with maneuvering at slow speeds.

In length, the blue whale is the equivalent of seventeen adult humans placed head to toe; its tongue alone weighs as much as an elephant. It is three times as long as the smallest rorqual in its family, the minke whale.

THROAT PLEATS

or grooves allow the slightly elastic skin to balloon out as the whale gulps in water. Then they fold back and retract as the water is expelled.

EYES AND EARS

are barely visible. The tiny eyes see only to the side. There are no external ears, although baleens hear very well.

THE BLOWHOLES

are the whale's nostrils, which have migrated during evolution from the front to the top of the head. There are two blowholes side by side, producing one blow of steamy, breathed-out air. The blowholes of baleen whales have some sense of smell.

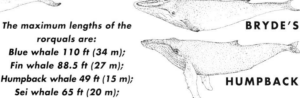

BLUE

FIN

SEI

The maximum lengths of the rorquals are:
Blue whale 110 ft (34 m);
Fin whale 88.5 ft (27 m);
Humpback whale 49 ft (15 m);
Sei whale 65 ft (20 m);
Bryde's whale 46 ft (14 m);
Minke whale 33 ft (10 m).

BRYDE'S

HUMPBACK

MINKE

X
R A Y

SKELETON
The typical mammal skeleton has been greatly modified to the totally aquatic lifestyle. The neck bones (cervical vertebrae) are short, thick, and fused together. The ribs are slim and delicate. The chest, hip, and tail sections of the backbone are hardly distinguishable from one another.

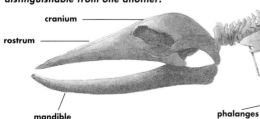

vertebrae

cranium

rostrum

mandible

phalanges

FRONT LIMBS
The shoulder and arm bones are short but wide and strong. The hand and finger bones splay out and support the flipper.

SKULL
Unlike the skulls of toothed whales, the baleen whale's skull is symmetrical. The upper part is extended into a long, beaklike rostrum that supports the upper mouth and baleen.

X-ray illustrations Elisabeth Smith. B/W illustrations Ruth Grewcock

BLUE WHALE HEAD

Like all rorquals, the blue whale has distinct throat grooves or pleats (below left), which distend when the huge mouth is full of water (below).

BLUE WHALE

LOCATION: ALL OCEANS

CLASSIFICATION

GENUS: *BALAENOPTERA*

SPECIES: *MUSCULUS*

SIZE

TOTAL LENGTH/MALE: AVERAGE 76 FT (23 M), EXCEPTIONALLY OVER 98 FT (30 M)

TOTAL LENGTH/FEMALE: AVERAGE 82 FT (25 M), EXCEPTIONALLY OVER 108 FT (33 M)

WEIGHT/MALE: 77–110 TONS

WEIGHT/FEMALE: 110–165 TONS, RECORD POSSIBLY 210 TONS

TOTAL LENGTH AT BIRTH: 23–26 FT (7–8 M)

COLORATION

GENERALLY BLUE-GRAY, VARYING FROM LIGHT BLUE TO SLATE GRAY, LIGHTER MOTTLED PATCHES AND FIN UNDERSIDES. MAY BE BLOTCHED YELLOWISH IN COLDER WATERS WITH ALGAL GROWTHS

FEATURES

LARGEST ANIMAL OF ALL TIME

VERY SLIM IN PROPORTION TO LENGTH COMPARED WITH MANY OTHER WHALES

AS HEAVY AS SIXTY TYPICAL ZOO ELEPHANTS OR FIVE TRACTOR TRAILERS

AS LONG AS SEVENTEEN ADULTS LYING HEAD TO TOE

STREAMLINING

means that the body and tail stock are smoothly contoured. Even the genitals and mammary glands are hidden in folds of skin.

THE SKIN

is smooth and hairless. This allows water to slip easily past it. Under the skin is a thick layer of fatty blubber, which acts as an insulating blanket to help retain body warmth.

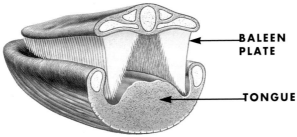

BALEEN PLATE

TONGUE

THE FLUKES

measure over 13 ft (4 m) from tip to tip, but they are relatively small for the blue whale's body size. They thrash up and down to power it through the water and are also used to smack the surface for sound-signaling.

FEEDING ACTION

The whale opens its mouth and water with plankton is drawn in (above). Then its tongue expands and water is extracted, leaving just the plankton (right).

BALEEN PLATE IN DETAIL

The above cross section shows the many layers of baleen plates in the whale's mouth. These are very effective in trapping tiny plankton.

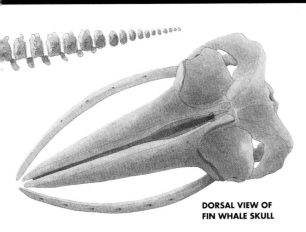

DORSAL VIEW OF FIN WHALE SKULL

LOWER JAW

The lower jawbones (mandibles) are set widely apart and loosely joined to the skull, so that they can move freely as the whale fills its mouth with water to take in tiny krill—its staple diet.

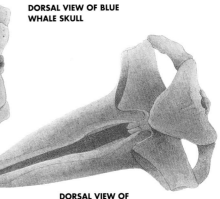

DORSAL VIEW OF BLUE WHALE SKULL

DORSAL VIEW OF HUMPBACK WHALE SKULL

BROWN HARE

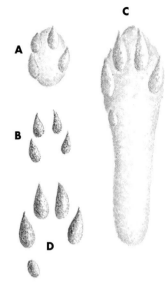

MOVEMENT

A hare uses the same running pattern whether it is simply hopping (top) or making an escape run (above). In each case, the long hind legs move beyond the forelegs, enabling the hare to make a powerful leap. The tighter crouch when running gives the hare even more propulsion.

FOOTPRINTS

There are four digits on the hare's forefeet, as shown here on snow (A) and hard ground (B). The five-toed hind feet, also shown on snow (C) and hard ground (D), are much larger than the forefeet; they are up to 4.3 in (11 cm) long, giving the hare a strong base for powerful leaps. A hare's footprints are much deeper than a rabbit's.

THE FUR

is long and soft, and even covers the feet. Some northern species molt to white during the winter.

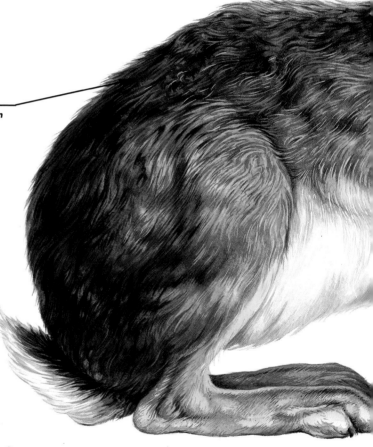

Lagomorphs range in size from the size of a small guinea pig to that of a large cat. The steppe pika (above right) is about 7 in (18 cm) long, while the brown hare (above left) measures 20–30 in (50–76 cm). The European rabbit (above center) has a head-body length of 10–11.5 in (25–29 cm).

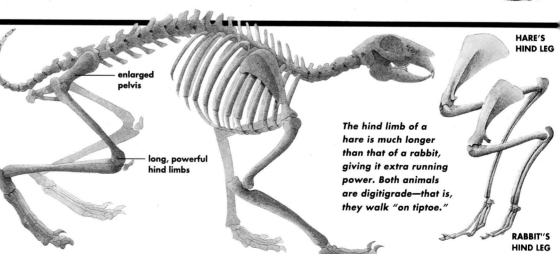

HARE SKELETON
The skeletons of pikas and hares are suited to different habitats. The hare (right), with its more lithe body and powerful legs, is built for speed on open ground. Its pelvic girdle is enlarged to deal with the force of the hind legs. Overall, the skeleton is light in order to aid running.

enlarged pelvis

long, powerful hind limbs

HARE'S HIND LEG

The hind limb of a hare is much longer than that of a rabbit, giving it extra running power. Both animals are digitigrade—that is, they walk "on tiptoe."

RABBIT'S HIND LEG

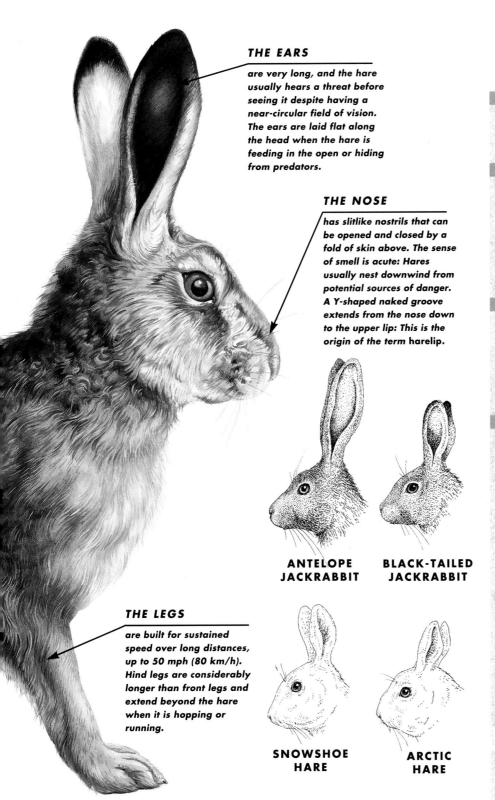

THE EARS

are very long, and the hare usually hears a threat before seeing it despite having a near-circular field of vision. The ears are laid flat along the head when the hare is feeding in the open or hiding from predators.

THE NOSE

has slitlike nostrils that can be opened and closed by a fold of skin above. The sense of smell is acute: Hares usually nest downwind from potential sources of danger. A Y-shaped naked groove extends from the nose down to the upper lip: This is the origin of the term harelip.

ANTELOPE JACKRABBIT

BLACK-TAILED JACKRABBIT

THE LEGS

are built for sustained speed over long distances, up to 50 mph (80 km/h). Hind legs are considerably longer than front legs and extend beyond the hare when it is hopping or running.

SNOWSHOE HARE

ARCTIC HARE

BROWN HARE
LOCATION: EUROPE, CENTRAL ASIA

CLASSIFICATION

GENUS: *LEPUS*

SPECIES: *EUROPAEUS*

SIZE

HEAD–BODY LENGTH: 20–24 IN (51–61 CM)

TAIL LENGTH: 4 IN (10 CM)

SHOULDER HEIGHT: 12–16 IN (30–41 CM)

WEIGHT: 8.8–13.2 LB (4–6 KG)

WEIGHT AT BIRTH: 4.6 OZ (130 G)

COLORATION

BROWN OR GRAYISH-BROWN UPPER PARTS AND YELLOWISH CHEEKS AND UNDERPARTS

BLACK TIPS TO EARS

BLACK STRIPE ON UPPER SURFACE OF TAIL

FEATURES

ELONGATED EARS

ROUNDED BACK LEADING TO POWERFUL HIND LEGS

GENITALS OF MALES AND FEMALES LARGELY HIDDEN AND DIFFICULT TO DISTINGUISH

SHORT EXTERNAL TAIL OR "SCUT"

EAR LENGTH (LEFT)

The ears vary among hare species, although most are long and all have a black tip at the end. The ears of the desert-dwelling antelope jackrabbit are up to 20 cm (8 in) long: The animal can control its temperature by regulating blood flow through vessels in its ears.

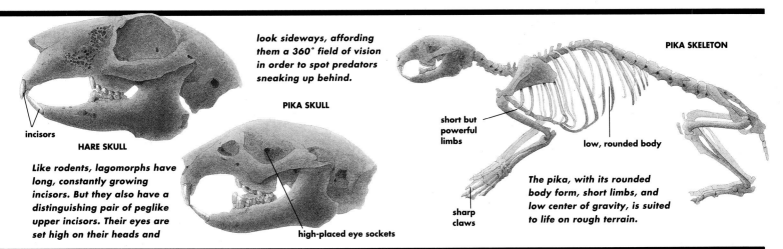

look sideways, affording them a 360° field of vision in order to spot predators sneaking up behind.

PIKA SKULL

incisors

HARE SKULL

Like rodents, lagomorphs have long, constantly growing incisors. But they also have a distinguishing pair of peglike upper incisors. Their eyes are set high on their heads and

high-placed eye sockets

PIKA SKELETON

short but powerful limbs

low, rounded body

sharp claws

The pika, with its rounded body form, short limbs, and low center of gravity, is suited to life on rough terrain.

BROWN RAT

BROWN RAT

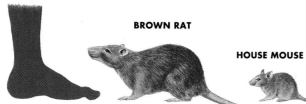

HOUSE MOUSE

THE RAT'S EARS

are large and prominent. Rats have a sharp sense of hearing, vital to a small animal hunted by larger predators.

The brown rat's body is about one foot long—a human foot, that is. Head-and-body length is 9–10.6 in (230–270 mm), and the tail is 7–8.7 in (180–220 mm). A house mouse is about one-third the size, or about 3.2–3.6 in (80–90 mm) long.

The muzzle of the brown rat is blunt and wedge-shaped, while that of the house mouse is pointed. Another difference: While a rat's ears sit neatly against its head, the ears of mice are more prominent and far larger in proportion to the head.

SENSITIVE SKIN

on the muzzle, and long whiskers that detect the slightest movement, allow the rat to feel its way in the darkness of night. The animal can assess the size of holes and cracks using its whiskers, and it can tell in advance whether they are wide enough to pass through.

THE FRONT, OR INCISOR, TEETH

are typical of any rodent. They are long and chisel-shaped, with strong, deep roots. The teeth grow continuously but are kept short and sharp by the animal's constant gnawing and biting.

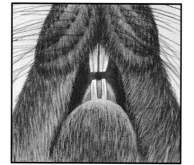

THE FRONT PAWS

are tipped with four claw-shaped nails. The toes can bend to cling when climbing and to hold and manipulate food. The feet are also used to dig holes, handle nesting material, and scratch enemies.

Illustrations Barry Croucher/Wildlife Art Agency

X

R A Y

The rat's skeleton is made up of relatively thin and light bones, which give the creature a flexible body that can squeeze through surprisingly small gaps and holes. The rear legs are slightly longer and stronger than the front ones, able to propel the rat quickly away from danger.

SKELETON

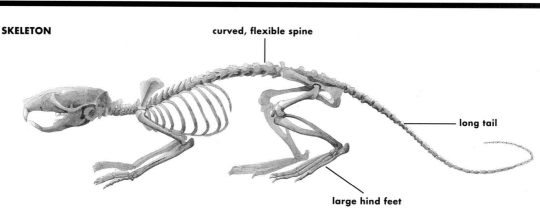

curved, flexible spine

long tail

large hind feet

X-ray illustrations Elisabeth Smith

BROWN RAT

LOCATION: WORLD OVER EXCEPT FOR POLAR REGIONS

CLASSIFICATION

GENUS: *RATTUS*

SPECIES: *NORVEGICUS*

SIZE

HEAD–BODY LENGTH/MALE: **9–10.6** IN (**230–270** MM)

WEIGHT/MALE: ON AVERAGE **7–14** OZ (**200–400** G),
ALTHOUGH **17.5** OZ (**500** G) IS NOT UNLIKELY

ADULT MALES ARE ABOUT **40** PERCENT LARGER THAN FEMALES

COLORATION

FUR VARIES FROM GRAY-BROWN TO BLACK OR, IN SOME
CASES, YELLOWISH

AT BIRTH RATS HAVE NO FUR—THEIR SKIN IS PINK AND
WRINKLED

FEATURES

COARSE, SHAGGY FUR

TAIL IS HAIRLESS AND COVERED WITH SMALL SCALES

HIGHLY SENSITIVE NOSE, LONG WHISKERS AND
PROMINENT EARS

BLACK, BEADY EYES THAT PROTRUDE FROM THE HEAD

PAW PRINTS
of a mouse (right) *and a rat* (far right)
*show the differences between the
forepaws, which have four toes, and the
hind paws, which have five.*

← *THE TAIL*

*is relatively thick and not as long
as its body (unlike that of the
black rat). The tail's scaly skin is
sensitive to touch, and the rat
uses it to feel surfaces and
textures and as a balancing aid.*

THE RAT'S HIND PAWS

*are longer and much stronger than
its forepaws. Some species of rats
are very capable swimmers and use
their hind paws like paddles.*

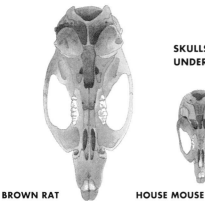

**SKULLS FROM
UNDERNEATH**

incisors

molars

diastema

BROWN RAT   HOUSE MOUSE   BROWN RAT   HOUSE MOUSE

*The skulls of both the
rat and the mouse
clearly display the
gnawing, ever-growing
incisors common to all
rodents. The molars are
used to grind and chew
food. There is a
considerable gap, or
diastema, between the
incisors and molars.*

CAMEL

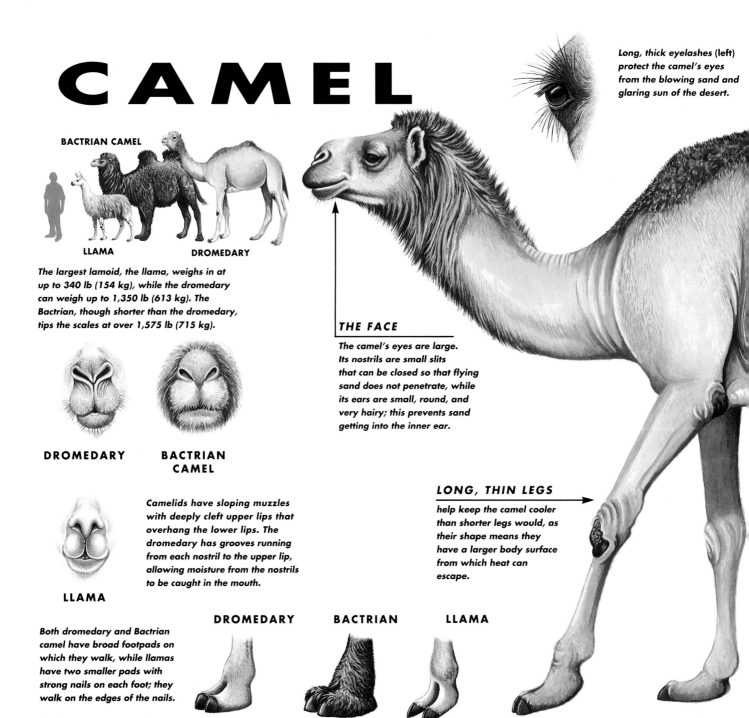

Long, thick eyelashes (left) protect the camel's eyes from the blowing sand and glaring sun of the desert.

BACTRIAN CAMEL

LLAMA

DROMEDARY

The largest lamoid, the llama, weighs in at up to 340 lb (154 kg), while the dromedary can weigh up to 1,350 lb (613 kg). The Bactrian, though shorter than the dromedary, tips the scales at over 1,575 lb (715 kg).

DROMEDARY

BACTRIAN CAMEL

LLAMA

Camelids have sloping muzzles with deeply cleft upper lips that overhang the lower lips. The dromedary has grooves running from each nostril to the upper lip, allowing moisture from the nostrils to be caught in the mouth.

THE FACE

The camel's eyes are large. Its nostrils are small slits that can be closed so that flying sand does not penetrate, while its ears are small, round, and very hairy; this prevents sand getting into the inner ear.

LONG, THIN LEGS

help keep the camel cooler than shorter legs would, as their shape means they have a larger body surface from which heat can escape.

DROMEDARY

BACTRIAN

LLAMA

Both dromedary and Bactrian camel have broad footpads on which they walk, while llamas have two smaller pads with strong nails on each foot; they walk on the edges of the nails.

Illustrations Kim Thompson

X

R A Y

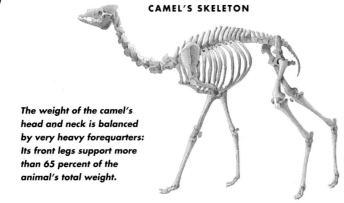

CAMEL'S SKELETON

The weight of the camel's head and neck is balanced by very heavy forequarters: Its front legs support more than 65 percent of the animal's total weight.

As camels evolved, the two long foot bones fused into one, the cannon bone.
    Present-day camels have two toes with very long bones on each foot. Because of this, they have increased strides and so can run faster.

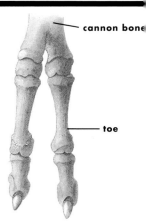

— cannon bone

— toe

CAMEL'S FOOT

X-ray illustrations Elisabeth Smith

DROMEDARY

LOCATION: SOUTH-WEST ASIA & NORTH AFRICA

CLASSIFICATION

GENUS: *CAMELUS*

SPECIES: *DROMEDARIUS*

SIZE

HEAD–BODY LENGTH: UP TO 10 FT (3M)

SHOULDER HEIGHT: 8 FT (2.4 M)

HEIGHT TO HUMP: UP TO 7.5 FT (2.3 M)

TAIL LENGTH: 14–22 IN (36–56 CM)

WEIGHT: 990–1,350 LB (450–613 KG)

WEIGHT AT BIRTH: 80 LB (36 KG)

COLORATION

USUALLY UNIFORM BEIGE OR PALE BROWN WITH SLIGHTLY LIGHTER UNDERSIDES; SOME ANIMALS ARE ENTIRELY BLACK OR WHITE.

FEATURES

VERY LONG LEGS

LONG, CURVED NECK

LOFTY HEAD CARRIAGE

ONE HUMP ON BACK

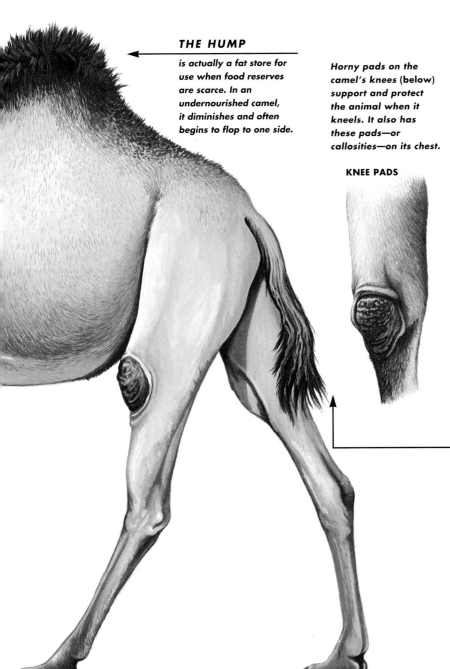

THE HUMP

is actually a fat store for use when food reserves are scarce. In an undernourished camel, it diminishes and often begins to flop to one side.

Horny pads on the camel's knees (below) support and protect the animal when it kneels. It also has these pads—or callosities—on its chest.

KNEE PADS

THE TAIL

is thick and fairly long, with a long tuft of hair at its end.

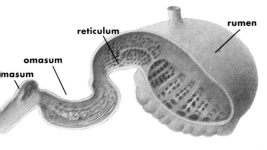

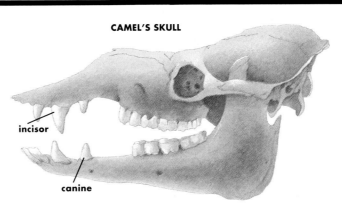

CAMEL'S SKULL

incisor

canine

rumen

reticulum

omasum

masum

The camel's stomach has four chambers (above). As food is broken down in the rumen, reticulum, and omasum, it releases protein that is digested in the abomasum. Digestive glands are found in sacs lining the rumen walls.

Members of the camel family have elongated skulls with very deep eye sockets. Unlike other ruminants—animals that chew the cud—camels have upper incisors. Young animals have three pairs, but in adults this is reduced to just one. They also have upper canine teeth, again possessed by few other ruminants.

CANADIAN BEAVER

THE FACIAL FEATURES

are all small. The ears and nostrils are protected underwater by valves that close to keep out the water, and the eyes are protected by a translucent "third eyelid."

With a head-and-body length of 35–47 in (89–119 cm), the Canadian beaver (above center) is generally a little larger than the European beaver, which tends to vary slightly in size according to location. In the rodent world, the Canadian beaver is second in size only to the capybara. However, a mature male beaver may weigh as much as a capybara. The mountain beaver (above right) is considerably smaller, reaching a maximum length of 18 in (46 cm) and a top weight of 3 lb (1.4 kg).

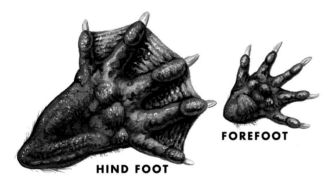

FOREFOOT

HIND FOOT

FOREFEET

The forefeet are considerably smaller than the hind feet, but remarkably dexterous. The beaver uses them to pick up and hold branches as it gnaws them, to dig its canals, and to scoop up mud from the bottom of the pond or lake. It also uses them to extract waterproofing oil from its sebaceous glands before rubbing its forefeet over its fur. All the front toes have claws.

TEETH

Lower and upper jaws each have a pair of chisel-like incisors, which are covered on their front surfaces with an extremely hard enamel. The inner part of each tooth is softer, so as the beaver gnaws at bark, the teeth are both worn and sharpened. The action of each pair of teeth against the other pair also helps to keep them sharp. The long roots of these teeth curve far back inside the bones of the skull and jaw; they have open roots so that they grow continuously, the upper pair over the lower pair.

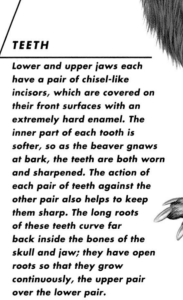

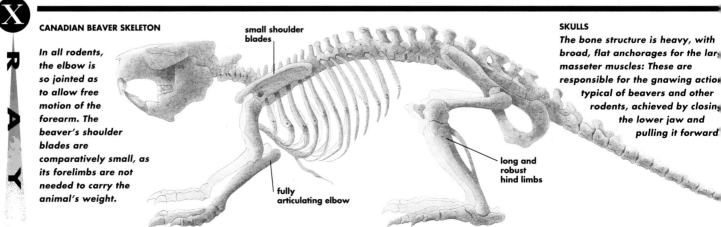

X

R A Y

CANADIAN BEAVER SKELETON

In all rodents, the elbow is so jointed as to allow free motion of the forearm. The beaver's shoulder blades are comparatively small, as its forelimbs are not needed to carry the animal's weight.

small shoulder blades

fully articulating elbow

long and robust hind limbs

SKULLS

The bone structure is heavy, with broad, flat anchorages for the larg masseter muscles: These are responsible for the gnawing action typical of beavers and other rodents, achieved by closin the lower jaw and pulling it forward

THE BODY

is compact and heavy. The beaver forms a sleek shape in the water, diving and swimming with grace and ease. A special respiratory and cardiovascular system enables large amounts of oxygen to be stored in the lungs, blood, and muscles; this enables the beaver to dive deep and stay underwater for up to 15 minutes if necessary.

THE FUR

is made up of two distinct layers; long guard hairs grow over a softer underfur. Both of these are remarkably dense— there are about 77,400 hair filaments per square inch (12,000 per square centimeter) on the back and almost double this number on the belly. The beaver constantly anoints the guard hairs with an oily secretion fro.n sebaceous glands on its underside to waterproof them.

THE TAIL

may measure 10–18 in (25–46 cm) long and 4–5 in (10–13 cm) wide. It is covered with thickened scaly skin; unlike true scales, they do not overlap, allowing for great flexibility. The tail acts as a rudder in the water and as a balancing prop on dry land. It can also be used to radiate excess heat from the body, and it stores fat for when food is scarce.

THE HIND FEET

are broad and fully webbed between the toes, improving the beaver's swimming skill. The claws on the first and second toes are cleft and are used in grooming the fur.

CLASSIFICATION

GENUS: CASTOR

SPECIES: CANADENSIS

SIZE

HEAD–BODY LENGTH: 35–47 IN (89–119 CM)

TAIL: 10–18 IN (25–46 CM)

WEIGHT: 45–60 LB (20.3–27 KG);
occasionally up to 66 LB (30 KG)

WEIGHT AT BIRTH: APPROX 1 LB (450 G)

COLORATION

RICH, GLOSSY, DARK BROWN WITH SLIGHTLY PALER UNDERPARTS. NO MARKINGS

FEATURES

THICKSET, ROUNDED BODY

VERY SMALL EARS AND EYES

SMALL FORELIMBS, WITH DEXTEROUS PAWS

LONGER AND STRONGER HIND LIMBS, WITH MUCH LARGER, FULLY WEBBED HIND FEET

OVAL, HORIZONTALLY FLATTENED TAIL, COVERED WITH SCALY SKIN

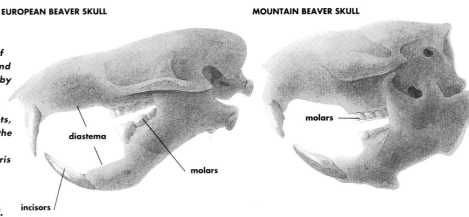

CANADIAN BEAVER SKULL

diastema

incisors

TEETH

The huge incisors dominate the muzzle area. In the absence of canines, the incisors and molars are separated by a gap called the diastema. The beaver, like many other rodents, can draw its lips into the diastema when gnawing, to keep debris out of its throat. The molars have efficient grinding surfaces for processing tough food.

EUROPEAN BEAVER SKULL

diastema

molars

incisors

MOUNTAIN BEAVER SKULL

molars

Main illustration Rachel Lockwood/Wildlife Art Agency

CAPUCHIN

The woolly spider monkey (above left) measures 18–25 in (46–63 cm) from head to rump, with a tail 25.5–29 in (65–74 cm) long. The squirrel monkey (above right) has a head-and-body length of 10–14.5 in (25–37 cm), and a tail length of 14.5–17.5 in (37–44.5 cm).

SQUIRREL MONKEY

MONK SAKI

RED HOWLER MONKEY

Some of the diversity within the cebid monkeys can be seen simply in a look at facial features. The neat little squirrel monkey has a facial "mask" on its short, broad muzzle; the monk saki's face is framed by full, shaggy hair and two white jaw streaks, while the red howler has a naked face.

THE ARMS

are lithe and short but well muscled. A young capuchin can grasp its mother's fur immediately after birth, and soon learns to use its limbs to swing about the branches.

HIND FOOT

Like many primates, capuchins have an opposable big toe, which improves their grip on branches. Despite this, capuchins are rarely seen seated in a tree without their tail tip locked around a branch to give a third point of contact and support.

SKELETON

The skeleton of a white-faced capuchin shows the slender form, long legs, and long balance-aiding tail typical of agile, tree-climbing monkeys, for whom maneuverability is key and great weight would be a distinct liability.

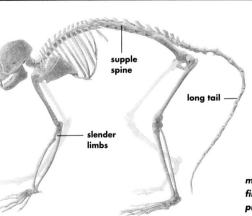

supple spine

long tail

slender limbs

CAPUCHIN HAND

long thumb

long, fine bones

Capuchins have nimble hands, and as such were widely used in the past in scientific research. Many apes, and New World monkeys too, have thumbs that are short in proportion to the fingers: This enables a strong "hook grip" on branches but provides little finesse when handling objects or using tools. The capuchin, however, has a comparatively functional thumb.

WHITE-FACED CAPUCHIN

FACE FUR

Capuchin monkeys have distinctive fur on the head and face. The brown capuchin is notable for developing prominent tufts or horns of fur over the eyes or on top of the head. The white-faced capuchin, by contrast, develops a ruff of long white hairs around the face. The name capuchin derives from the likeness of the monkey's black cap to the hood, or "capuche," of Franciscan monks.

THE BODY

is fairly small but robust. Cebid monkeys differ greatly not just in shape and coloration but also in body size. The largest of them—indeed, the largest primate in the Americas—is the woolly spider monkey or muriqui. The smallest are the dainty squirrel monkeys. A full-size woolly spider monkey may weigh twelve times as much as a typical squirrel monkey.

THE TAIL

is long and, to a moderate degree, prehensile; it lacks the naked undertip present on fully prehensile-tailed species. Capuchins often carry their tails curled tightly at the tip, which has earned them the alternative name of ring-tail monkeys.

CLASSIFICATION

GENUS: *CEBUS*

SPECIES: *CAPUCINUS*

SIZE

HEAD–BODY LENGTH: 12.5–18 IN (32–46 CM)

TAIL LENGTH: 16–20 IN (40–50 CM)

WEIGHT: 4.5–8.5 LB (2–3.8 KG)

COLORATION

FUR ON UNDERSIDES, UPPER LIMBS, AND FACE CREAM TO WHITE; ELSEWHERE, INCLUDING CAP, GRADING TO BLACK

FEATURES

ROUNDED HEAD

FORWARD-FACING EYES

SLENDER, AGILE BUILD

MEDIUM-SHORT LIMBS AND LONG, FLEXIBLE, SEMIPREHENSILE TAIL

MALE SLIGHTLY LARGER THAN FEMALE

DISTINCTIVE BLACK CAP

WHITE FACIAL RUFF ON OLDER INDIVIDUALS

CAPUCHIN SKULL AND JAW

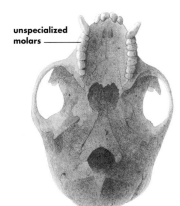

unspecialized molars

The teeth and jaws give strong clues to the diet of different monkeys. Large jaws and broad, flat teeth give the crushing power needed for chewing coarse plants. Those monkeys that eat insects have sharp, narrow teeth for piercing exoskeletons and cutting the prey up quickly.

CAPUCHIN SKULL

stout canines

large braincase

TITI SKULL

forward-facing eye sockets

WOOLLY MONKEY SKULL

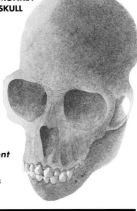

The skulls of cebid monkeys show the large braincase and forward-facing eye sockets typical of primates. These relatively intelligent animals rely on forward vision so that they can make accurate leaps from branch to branch.

CAPYBARA

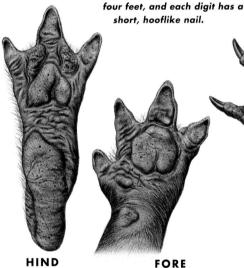

THE MORRILLO
GLAND

is a feature of adult male
capybaras. It is a dark,
mound-shaped scent
gland on the upper
surface of the snout. It
produces a white
secretion that serves
as a scent marker.

*The capybara (above left) is the world's largest living
rodent, approximately the size of a large dog. The
coypu (above right) is a robust rodent that weighs up
to 22 lb (10 kg).*

FRONT AND HIND FEET

*The undersides of coypu feet are hairless. Its hind feet
have webbed membranes between all the digits
except the fourth and fifth. This arrangement allows
for burrowing with the forefeet and swimming with
the hind feet. A capybara has four digits on the
forefeet and three on the hind feet. Short, webbed
membranes connect the digits on all
four feet, and each digit has a
short, hooflike nail.*

THE EYES

*are set high on a capybara's
snout, enabling it to see
above the water surface while
the rest of its body is
submerged and concealed.*

HIND　　　**FORE**　　　　**HIND**　　　**FORE**

CAPYBARA　　　　　　　**COYPU**

Both the capybara and
coypu have a stocky
body with short limbs.
This bulky appearance
is extreme in the
case of the
capybara (right),
which uses the natural
buoyancy of fatty
deposits to offset the
skeletal weight when it
swims. The long coypu
tail often falls victim to
frostbite in populations
outside South America.

CAPYBARA SKELETON

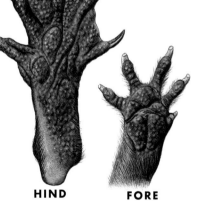

The incisors of the
coypu (right) are
proportionately larger
than those of the
capybara (far right),
indicating a diet
composed of tougher
fibers. The capybara's
teeth are well suited
to constant chewing
and grinding. Its
incisors have a
combined width of
0.75 in (2 cm). All the
cheek teeth are rootless
and ever-growing.

COYPU TEETH

large
incisors

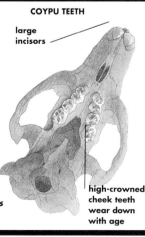

high-crowned
cheek teeth
wear down
with age

CAPYBARA

COYPU

HAIR

The capybara's hair (far left) is long and so sparsely distributed that the skin is visible. The coarse hair of a coypu (left) is also long, but it covers a layer of thick, soft underfur (nutria), which keeps the coypu from becoming waterlogged.

CAPYBARA

CLASSIFICATION

GENUS: *HYDROCHAERIS*

SPECIES: *HYDROCHAERIS*

SIZE

HEAD–BODY LENGTH: 41–53 IN (104–135 CM)

TAIL LENGTH: VESTIGIAL (A SMALL, HORNY LUMP)

HEIGHT: 20–24 IN (51–61 CM)

WEIGHT: 77–145 LB (35–66 KG)

WEIGHT AT BIRTH: 3.3 LB (1.5 KG)

FEMALES ARE ABOUT 10–15 PERCENT HEAVIER THAN MALES

COLORATION

REDDISH BROWN TO GRAYISH ON THE BACK AND UPPER PARTS; YELLOWISH BROWN ON THE UNDERPARTS. OCCASIONALLY SOME BLACK ON THE FACE, RUMP, AND FLANKS

FEATURES

FORELEGS SHORTER THAN HIND LEGS; SLIGHTLY WEBBED TOES

LARGE, BLUNT HEAD WITH PROMINENT MORRILLO SCENT GLAND ON TOP OF SNOUT; EYES, NOSTRILS, AND EARS TOWARDS TOP OF HEAD

VESTIGIAL TAIL

TWO PAIRS OF LARGE INCISORS

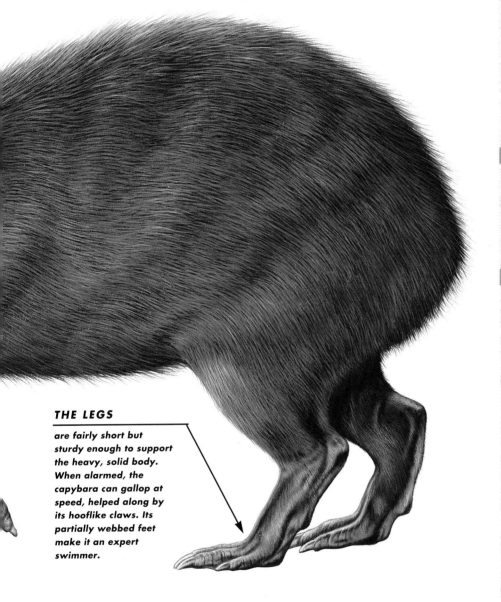

THE LEGS

are fairly short but sturdy enough to support the heavy, solid body. When alarmed, the capybara can gallop at speed, helped along by its hooflike claws. Its partially webbed feet make it an expert swimmer.

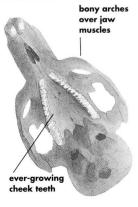

bony arches over jaw muscles

ever-growing cheek teeth

CAPYBARA TEETH

The capybara and coypu both have a large, broad skull with formidable incisors. Typical of the cavylike rodents are the bony arches in front of the eye sockets: These house extra jaw muscles. In addition, each species has a deep muzzle, and the eyes and nose are placed high to enable the animal to see and breathe while almost fully submerged.

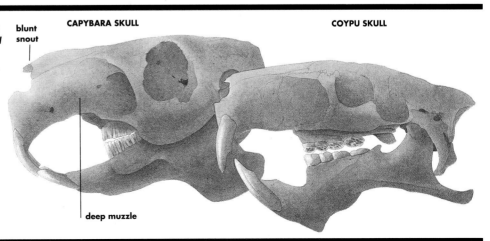

blunt snout

CAPYBARA SKULL

COYPU SKULL

deep muzzle

CHEETAH

THE EARS

are broad and sit fairly low on the head. They have black backs.

THE EYES

are well placed on the skull to give excellent binocular vision for judging distances—an essential ability for a high-speed hunter such as the cheetah. The black lines that resemble tear stains are a characteristic of all cheetahs and may be used to communicate mood.

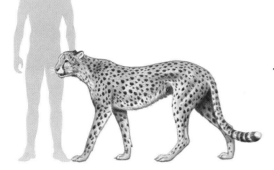

The cheetah is about the same length as the leopard but stands higher at the shoulder. It is lighter in weight, however, since it relies on speed rather than the ambush in its hunting technique.

STRIDE

The long, rapid stride of the cheetah is facilitated both by the animal's extremely supple spine and by remarkable freedom of movement in the hips and shoulders.

RUNNING

Pushing off first with one hind limb and then, as the body is propelled forward, with the other, the cheetah launches itself into the air in full extension. Next, touching down with one forelimb and then, as the body continues forward, with the other, the cheetah pulls itself into a fully flexed posture before the first of the hind limbs touches the ground again to complete the stride sequence. Loose joints and the arching ability of the flexible spine enable the cheetah to push and pull off the surface with its limbs stretched far out, adding greatly to the length of

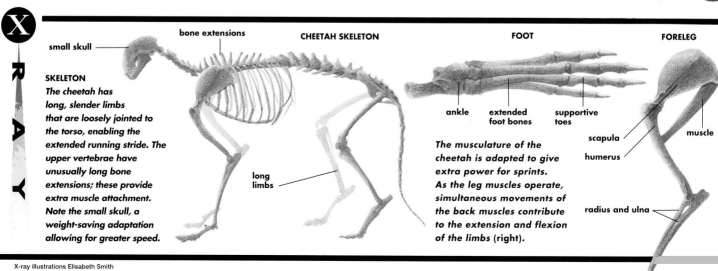

CHEETAH SKELETON   **FOOT**   **FORELEG**

small skull — bone extensions

SKELETON
The cheetah has long, slender limbs that are loosely jointed to the torso, enabling the extended running stride. The upper vertebrae have unusually long bone extensions; these provide extra muscle attachment. Note the small skull, a weight-saving adaptation allowing for greater speed.

long limbs

ankle   extended foot bones   supportive toes

The musculature of the cheetah is adapted to give extra power for sprints. As the leg muscles operate, simultaneous movements of the back muscles contribute to the extension and flexion of the limbs (right).

scapula   muscle
humerus

radius and ulna

X-ray illustrations Elisabeth Smith

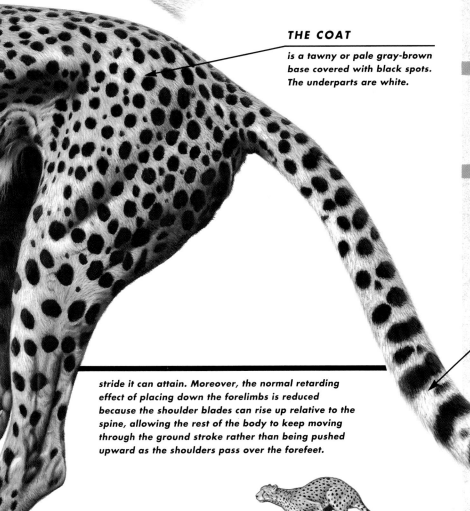

CHEETAH

LOCATION: AFRICA, SOUTH ASIA, MIDDLE EAST

dewclaw

FOREPAW

The cheetah cannot withdraw its claws fully since it lacks the protective sheaths present in the digits of other cats. The sharp "dewclaw" on the inside of the foreleg is used by the cheetah to help bring down running prey.

THE COAT

is a tawny or pale gray-brown base covered with black spots. The underparts are white.

CLASSIFICATION

GENUS: *ACINONYX*

SPECIES: *JUBATUS*

SIZE

HEAD–BODY LENGTH: 43–58 IN (110–150 CM)

SHOULDER HEIGHT: 27–35 IN (70–90 CM)

TAIL LENGTH: 23–31 IN (60–80 CM)

WEIGHT: 77–145 LB (35–66 KG)

WEIGHT AT BIRTH: 5–10 OZ (142–284 G)

COLORATION

TAWNY TO BUFF, WITH PALER UNDERPARTS; ROUND BLACK SPOTS ALL OVER WITH BLACK RINGS NEAR END OF TAIL

FEATURES

SLENDER BUILD

SMALL, ROUNDED HEAD

LONG LEGS

LONG TAIL

CLAWS NOT FULLY RETRACTILE

BLACK STRIPES FROM EYE TO MOUTH

THE TAIL

is long, improving steerage during fast chases. The bright white tip helps young cheetahs to keep track of their mother.

stride it can attain. Moreover, the normal retarding effect of placing down the forelimbs is reduced because the shoulder blades can rise up relative to the spine, allowing the rest of the body to keep moving through the ground stroke rather than being pushed upward as the shoulders pass over the forefeet.

SKULL

domed profile

short muzzle

LUMBAR VERTEBRAE

highly flexible joints

The cheetah has a distinctive skull, with the highest point above the eyes, while its canines are relatively small and its cheek teeth narrow. Sprinting requirements of reduced weight and enhanced air intake are at the root of some of these differences.

SKULL

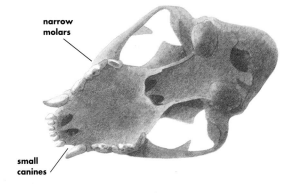

narrow molars

small canines

Color illustrations Steve Kingston

CHIMPANZEE

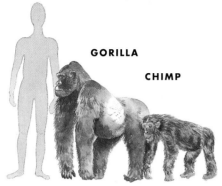

GORILLA

CHIMP

The head-and-body length of a male chimp measures about 30–36 in (76–91 cm), considerably smaller than a gorilla, the largest of the great apes, and smaller than some humans.

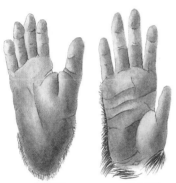

FOOT   **HAND**

Strong hands and feet provide a firm grip. When the chimp is climbing, the foot's big toe, which can be spread like a thumb, helps to push the animal upward.

The chimp's "opposable" thumb is a feature it shares with humans and other primates. It allows it to handle small objects such as this berry and to use a number of tools.

A CHIMP'S FACE

is very expressive, largely because of the animal's protruding muzzle and flexible lips.

THICK, MUSCULAR

arms are more flexible than the legs, and reach to just below knee level when the chimp stands erect.

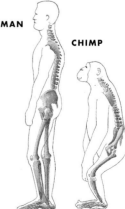

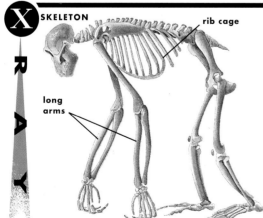

X **SKELETON**

rib cage

long arms

This view of a chimpanzee skeleton shows the very long limbs, hands, and feet, in the typical "knuckle-walk" position. In contrast, the trunk is relatively small. The rib cage, though short, is quite large, reflecting the chimp's broad, muscular chest and shoulders.

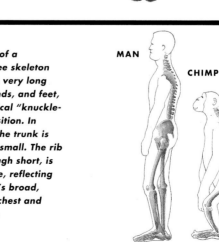

MAN

CHIMP

Although chimpanzees can stand upright for a short time, they can never stand erect in the way that humans do. This is because their spine and their legs are curved, and an upright stance causes too much strain on the spine and leg muscles to be permanent.

X-ray illustrations Elisabeth Smith

COMMON CHIMPANZEE

LOCATION: WEST & CENTRAL AFRICA

The cerebellum, that part of the brain which controls problem-solving activities, is highly developed among chimps. It is exceeded in its complexity only by that of humans.

CHIMPANZEE   MAN

cerebellum

LIKE HUMANS,
chimps are covered in hair, though theirs is thicker and covers their whole body apart from the genital area, palms, and soles.

CLASSIFICATION

GENUS: *PAN*

SPECIES: *TROGLODYTES*

SIZE

BODY LENGTH/MALE: 30–36 IN (76–91 CM)

BODY LENGTH/FEMALE: 28–33 IN (71–84 CM)

WEIGHT/MALE: 88 LB (40 KG)

WEIGHT/FEMALE: 66 LB (30 KG)

WEIGHT AT BIRTH: 2–4 LB (0.9–1.8 KG)

COLORATION

VARIES GEOGRAPHICALLY: MAINLY BLACK, THOUGH AFTER ABOUT 20 YEARS GRAY HAIR ON BACK IS COMMON. SKIN IS BLACK ON HANDS AND FEET. FACE CHANGES WITH AGE FROM PINK TO BROWN TO BLACK. BOTH SEXES OFTEN HAVE A SHORT WHITE BEARD, AND A BALD TRIANGLE ON THE FOREHEAD IS PARTICULARLY COMMON IN FEMALES

FEATURES

LONG, MUSCULAR LIMBS

STRONG, STOUT BODY

LARGE HEADS WITH PROMINENT MUZZLE, A STRONG BROW RIDGE, LARGE PROTRUDING EARS, AND DEEP-SET EYES

GRASPING FEET AND HANDS WITH OPPOSABLE THUMB

FLEXIBLE ANKLE
joints, muscular legs, and large feet with slender toes and an extended big toe combine to make the chimpanzee a strong tree-climber.

Main Illustration Barry Croucher/Wildlife Art Agency

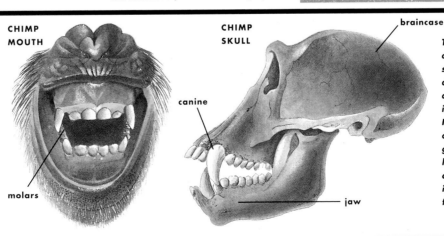

The chimpanzee's prominent mouth can make a considerable noise, though it is not capable of true speech. Its teeth, at least in comparison with those of humans, are rather large, though its molars are smaller than those of a gorilla. This reflects its largely fruit-based diet.

CHIMP MOUTH

molars

CHIMP SKULL

canine

braincase

jaw

The skull of an adult chimpanzee features strong projecting jaws, deep-set eye sockets, and a large cavity for its sizable brain. Note the extended canine teeth, which grow particularly long in adult males and are often used in vicious, sometimes fatal, fights.

COMMON SEAL

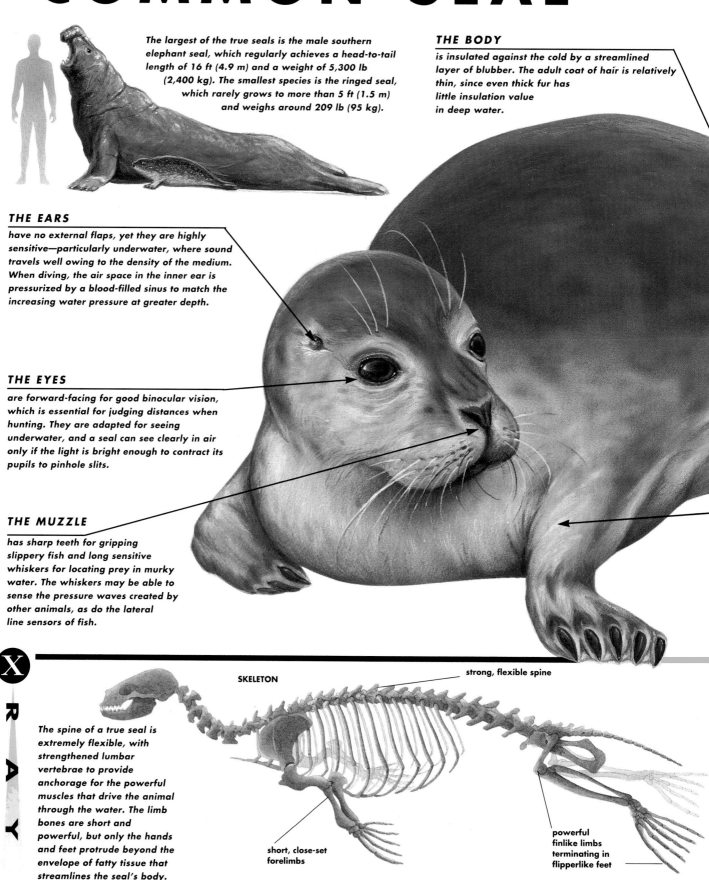

The largest of the true seals is the male southern elephant seal, which regularly achieves a head-to-tail length of 16 ft (4.9 m) and a weight of 5,300 lb (2,400 kg). The smallest species is the ringed seal, which rarely grows to more than 5 ft (1.5 m) and weighs around 209 lb (95 kg).

THE BODY

is insulated against the cold by a streamlined layer of blubber. The adult coat of hair is relatively thin, since even thick fur has little insulation value in deep water.

THE EARS

have no external flaps, yet they are highly sensitive—particularly underwater, where sound travels well owing to the density of the medium. When diving, the air space in the inner ear is pressurized by a blood-filled sinus to match the increasing water pressure at greater depth.

THE EYES

are forward-facing for good binocular vision, which is essential for judging distances when hunting. They are adapted for seeing underwater, and a seal can see clearly in air only if the light is bright enough to contract its pupils to pinhole slits.

THE MUZZLE

has sharp teeth for gripping slippery fish and long sensitive whiskers for locating prey in murky water. The whiskers may be able to sense the pressure waves created by other animals, as do the lateral line sensors of fish.

X RAY

SKELETON

strong, flexible spine

The spine of a true seal is extremely flexible, with strengthened lumbar vertebrae to provide anchorage for the powerful muscles that drive the animal through the water. The limb bones are short and powerful, but only the hands and feet protrude beyond the envelope of fatty tissue that streamlines the seal's body.

short, close-set forelimbs

powerful finlike limbs terminating in flipperlike feet

X-ray illustrations Elisabeth Smith

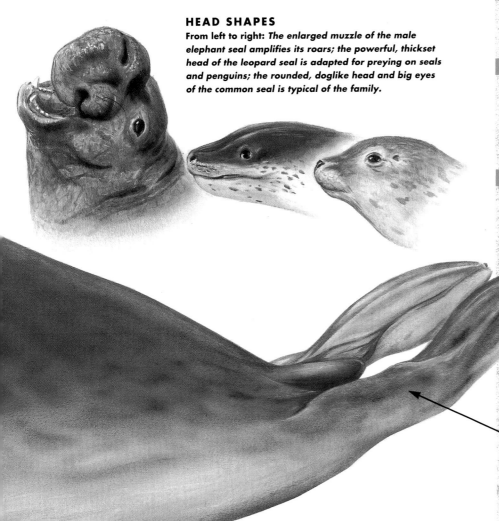

HEAD SHAPES

From left to right: *The enlarged muzzle of the male elephant seal amplifies its roars; the powerful, thickset head of the leopard seal is adapted for preying on seals and penguins; the rounded, doglike head and big eyes of the common seal is typical of the family.*

COMMON SEAL

CLASSIFICATION

GENUS: *PHOCA*

SPECIES: *VITULINA*

SIZE

HEAD–BODY LENGTH: 4.9–5.6 FT (1.5–1.7 M)

WEIGHT (MALE): 240–265 LB (109–120 KG)

WEIGHT (FEMALE): 175–200 LB (79–91 KG)

WEIGHT AT BIRTH: 22–26 LB (10–12 KG)

COLORATION

ADULT: PALE TO DARK GRAY, WITH A DENSE MOTTLING OF DARKER SPOTS OR RINGS

PUP: UNUSUALLY ITS FUR IS SIMILAR TO THE ADULT, FOR THE PALE, FURRY LANUGO IS SHED IN THE WOMB

FEATURES

BROAD, ROUNDED, DOGLIKE HEAD

NO VISIBLE EARS

LARGE EYES

SLEEK, STREAMLINED BODY

SHORT FLIPPERS

THE HIND LIMBS

project backward like the tail fin of a fish and provide most of the power that drives the seal forward through the water. The feet are elongated and flattened into flippers, but the rest of each limb is shortened and contained within the body.

HIND FLIPPERS

Like all true seals of the northern subfamily, the common seal has large claws on its hind flippers, although they have little function on limbs that are primarily adapted for swimming. On southern seals, such as the southern elephant seal, the claws are greatly reduced, and the toes are strongly webbed to increase their propulsive efficiency.

THE FORELIMBS

are formed into short flippers, which are held close to the flanks during fast swimming and used for maneuvering during slow swimming. A seal may also hold large prey between its forelimbs while it tears chunks off with its teeth, like an otter.

COMMON SEAL   **ELEPHANT SEAL**

FORELIMB AND HAND

The enlarged hand of a seal broadens the area of the limb to increase swimming performance. It also provides a degree of digital dexterity that some species find very useful when dealing with large prey.

SKULL

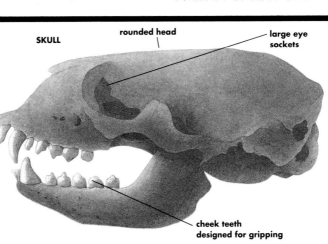

rounded head

large eye sockets

cheek teeth designed for gripping

Unlike land carnivores, the seal's cheek teeth are not differentiated into meat-slicing carnassials and bone-cracking molars. A typical seal uses its teeth to grip rather than slice or chew, and even the strongly predatory leopard seal is poorly equipped to process its prey. The eye sockets are large to accommodate big eyes for seeing in the submarine gloom.

Illustrations Lee Gibbons/Wildlife Art Agency

DEER MOUSE

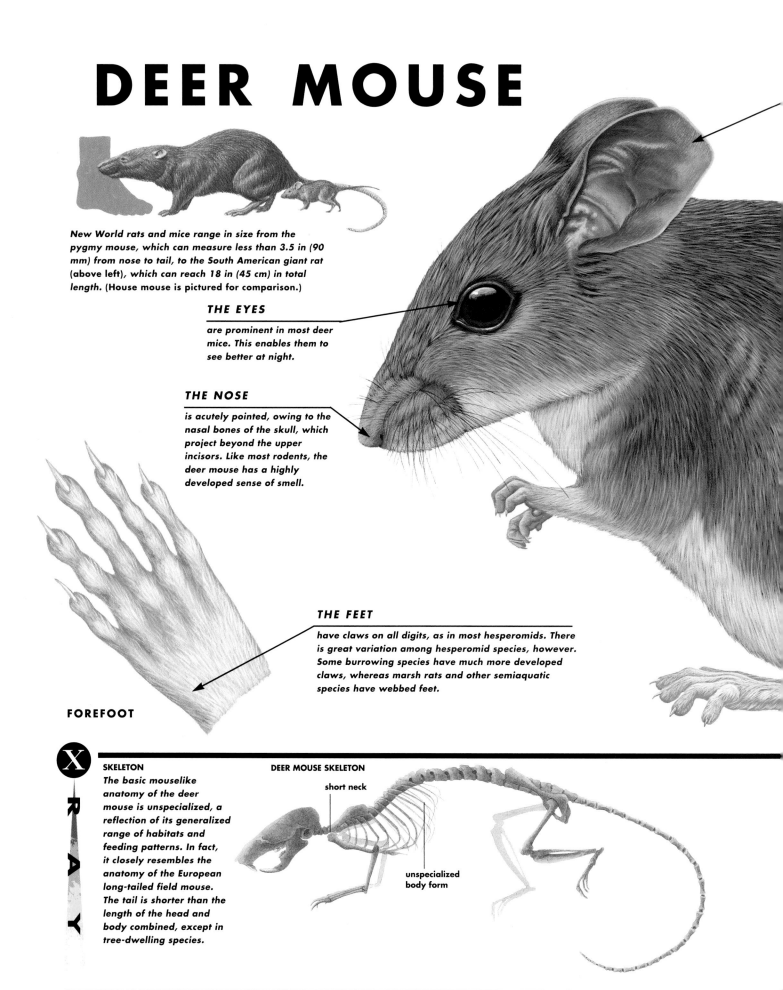

New World rats and mice range in size from the pygmy mouse, which can measure less than 3.5 in (90 mm) from nose to tail, to the South American giant rat (above left), which can reach 18 in (45 cm) in total length. (House mouse is pictured for comparison.)

THE EYES

are prominent in most deer mice. This enables them to see better at night.

THE NOSE

is acutely pointed, owing to the nasal bones of the skull, which project beyond the upper incisors. Like most rodents, the deer mouse has a highly developed sense of smell.

THE FEET

have claws on all digits, as in most hesperomids. There is great variation among hesperomid species, however. Some burrowing species have much more developed claws, whereas marsh rats and other semiaquatic species have webbed feet.

FOREFOOT

SKELETON

The basic mouselike anatomy of the deer mouse is unspecialized, a reflection of its generalized range of habitats and feeding patterns. In fact, it closely resembles the anatomy of the European long-tailed field mouse. The tail is shorter than the length of the head and body combined, except in tree-dwelling species.

DEER MOUSE SKELETON

short neck

unspecialized body form

X-ray illustrations Elisabeth Smith

THE EARS

provide extremely keen hearing, which is often used defensively. In common with many hesperomid species, deer mice also emit high-pitched squeaks as a territorial marking device or in alarm.

SPINY RICE RAT

Named after their bristly coats, these rats feed at night on seeds. Many island species are now close to extinction.

VESPER RAT

This long-tailed Central American species is an excellent climber. It nests in trees, where it feeds on fruit.

SOUTH AMERICAN FIELD MOUSE

These mice forage on the ground for insects, as well as fruit, seeds, and green plant matter. Some of them also burrow well.

CENTRAL AMERICAN WATER MOUSE

Equipped with webbed hind feet, water mice live in mountain streams, where they feed on snails and, perhaps, fish.

THE SOFT FUR

varies greatly in color among deer mice according to where they live. Those inhabiting temperate forests are usually camouflaged with a grayish-brown upper fur, whereas those living in more open terrain have a paler coloration.

DEER MOUSE

LOCATION: CIRCUMPOLAR (NORTH ATLANTIC & NORTH PACIFIC)

CLASSIFICATION

GENUS: *PEROMYSCUS*

SPECIES: *MANICULATUS*

SIZE

HEAD–BODY LENGTH: 2.8–6.7 IN (70–170 MM)

TAIL LENGTH: 1.6–8 IN (40–205 MM)

WEIGHT: 0.5–3.2 OZ (15–90 G)

WEIGHT AT BIRTH: 0.1 OZ (2.3 G)

COLORATION

GRAY OR SANDY TO GOLDEN OR DARK BROWN ON THE BACK AND UPPER PARTS; WHITE OR OFF-WHITE ON THE UNDERPARTS AND FEET SOME SPECIES ARE NEARLY ALL WHITE; OTHERS ARE NEARLY ALL BLACK

FEATURES

SPARSELY HAIRED TAIL IS AT LEAST ONE-THIRD OF TOTAL LENGTH; EYES AND EARS ARE LARGE IN RELATION TO BODY

THE TAIL

has only a thin coating of hair, like that of a house mouse or a wood mouse. Some deer mice can let the tip of the tail slip off the vertebrae as a way of escaping predators.

SKULL

The brain-to-body–weight ratio varies among deer mice species and is linked to habitat. Those facing upheavals of climate or food supply have smaller brains. Those in stable

lower incisors

MEXICAN DEER MOUSE SKULL

molars

upper incisors

habitats have larger brains, a trend that is linked to their increased longevity and smaller litter size. Burrowing species have thinner, more conical skulls and deeper eye sockets.

TEETH

Unlike Old World rats and mice, hesperomids have no rounded projections on the inner side of the upper molars. The teeth of some insect-eating hesperomids are greatly reduced—particularly molars.

cheek arch

Color illustrations Barry Croucher/Wildlife Art Agency

DHOLE

THE EARS

are large and sensitive, enabling the dhole to detect hidden prey and also keep track of its companions in dense undergrowth with its soft whistling calls.

THE EYES

have a wide field of view, which is essential for a hunter, but their frontal position also provides the binocular vision that enables distances to be judged accurately for the final strike. A reflective membrane behind the retina of each eye increases its sensitivity in low light.

Largest of the three, the dingo (above left) is slightly smaller than a typical gray wolf. The dhole (above center) stands almost as tall as the dingo, but is more compact in form. The raccoon dog (above right) is about the size and weight of a common raccoon.

THE MUZZLE

is shorter and broader than that of most dogs, but is still long enough to contain keen sensory apparatus. The damp, leathery surface moistens the inhaled air and increases the nose's scent-carrying capacity.

FOREFOOT

The dhole's feet are small and compact, with well-cushioned pads that act as shock absorbers when the animal is running fast on hard surfaces, and sturdy, blunt, nonretractable claws for improved traction. Dewclaws on the forelimbs stay sharp because they are not in contact with the ground, and may help the dhole subdue small prey. Only domestic dogs—and dingoes—have dewclaws on the hind limbs.

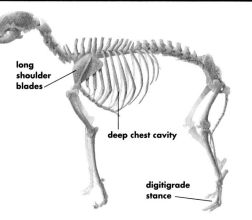

X RAY

DHOLE SKELETON
Like most dogs, the dhole has a strong but relatively inflexible spine and a deep chest cavity to contain capacious lungs for stamina. Its limbs are extended for speed by elongated shoulder blades and a digitigrade stance (it runs on its toes). The bones of the lower limbs are fused together for strength.

long shoulder blades

deep chest cavity

digitigrade stance

CARNASSIAL TEETH
The lower carnassials of the dhole have two sharp cusps in line. These act against the upper carnassials like scissor blades to shear through tough hide, sinew, and flesh. In most other dogs, such as the dingo, each lower carnassial has two rear cusps that form a grinding surface, suiting a broader diet.

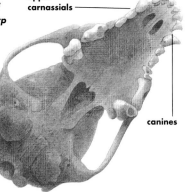

upper carnassials

canines

DHOLE
The dhole has a short, broad muzzle, and its ears have rounded tips.

DINGO
The dingo has the clean, elegant facial features characteristic of the lupine canids.

RACCOON DOG
The raccoon dog has a full, bushy coat, small, rounded ears, and a face mask—just like that of a real raccoon.

DHOLE
LOCATION: WEST & SOUTH EAST ASIA

CLASSIFICATION
GENUS: *CUON*

SPECIES: *ALPINUS*

SIZE
HEAD–BODY LENGTH: 35 IN (90 CM)

TAIL LENGTH: 16–18 IN (40–45 CM)

AVERAGE WEIGHT: 37 LB (17 KG)

NORTHERN ANIMALS ARE SOME 20 PERCENT LARGER THAN OTHERS

COLORATION
VARIES FROM BROWN GRAY TO MAHOGANY RED, OFTEN WITH BLACK-TIPPED FUR ON THE BACK. TAIL IS BLACK AND BUSHY, ALTHOUGH OCCASIONALLY THE TAIL HAS WHITE FUR. MANY INDIVIDUALS HAVE A WHITE THROAT PATCH THAT MAY EXTEND DOWN THE CHEST

FEATURES
LITHE, SLENDER BUILD

LONG, SLIM LEGS

DARK BUSHY TAIL

BROAD MUZZLE

ERECT, ROUNDED EARS

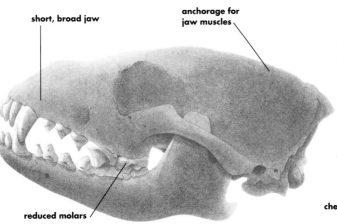

THE BUSHY TAIL
with its black-tipped fur is used like a semaphore flag to signal states of arousal and social submission. It also helps the dhole keep its balance when running fast.

THE THICK PELT
has a woolly undercoat to protect the dhole against the winter cold in the north of its range. The coat is less dense farther south, but often a deeper red: In India the dhole is sometimes known as the red dog.

THE SLENDER LEGS
are well muscled throughout their length to provide the strength for subduing prey as well as running.

SKULL
The dhole has a shorter, broader jaw than a wolf, so the canine teeth are nearer to the jaw hinge: This increases their biting power. The shortened jawline means that the dhole has lost one molar tooth on each side of the lower jaw, but since it rarely needs to chew its food into smaller, more manageable morsels, this is a small sacrifice.

short, broad jaw

anchorage for jaw muscles

reduced molars

JAW MUSCLES
One set of jaw muscles attaches to the large crest at the back of the skull, while the other set lies beneath the cheekbone.

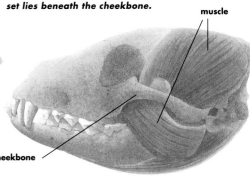

muscle

cheekbone

DOLPHIN

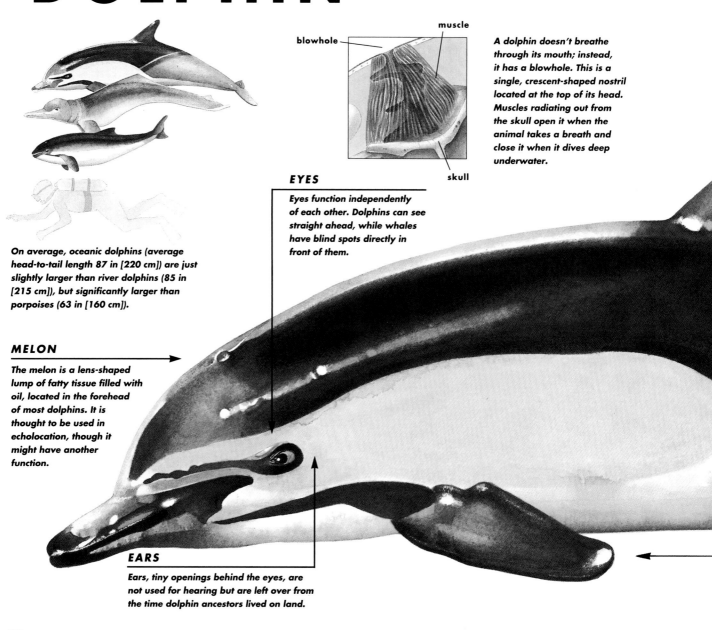

blowhole

muscle

A dolphin doesn't breathe through its mouth; instead, it has a blowhole. This is a single, crescent-shaped nostril located at the top of its head. Muscles radiating out from the skull open it when the animal takes a breath and close it when it dives deep underwater.

skull

On average, oceanic dolphins (average head-to-tail length 87 in [220 cm]) are just slightly larger than river dolphins (85 in [215 cm]), but significantly larger than porpoises (63 in [160 cm]).

EYES

Eyes function independently of each other. Dolphins can see straight ahead, while whales have blind spots directly in front of them.

MELON

The melon is a lens-shaped lump of fatty tissue filled with oil, located in the forehead of most dolphins. It is thought to be used in echolocation, though it might have another function.

EARS

Ears, tiny openings behind the eyes, are not used for hearing but are left over from the time dolphin ancestors lived on land.

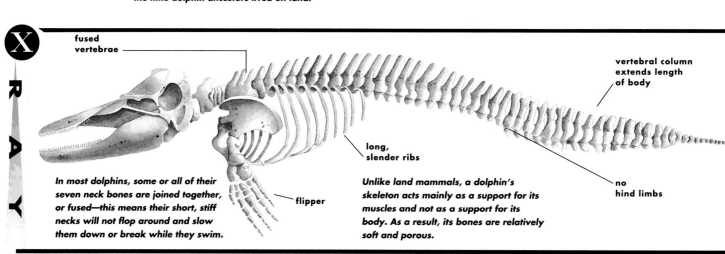

X

R A Y

fused vertebrae

vertebral column extends length of body

long, slender ribs

no hind limbs

flipper

In most dolphins, some or all of their seven neck bones are joined together, or fused—this means their short, stiff necks will not flop around and slow them down or break while they swim.

Unlike land mammals, a dolphin's skeleton acts mainly as a support for its muscles and not as a support for its body. As a result, its bones are relatively soft and porous.

X-ray illustrations Elisabeth Smith

COMMON DOLPHIN

LOCATION: TROPICAL, SUBTROPICAL & WARM TEMPERATE OCEANS

CLASSIFICATION

GENUS: *DELPHINUS*

SPECIES: *DELPHIS*

SIZE

HEAD–TAIL LENGTH/MALE: 87 IN (220 CM)

HEAD–TAIL LENGTH/FEMALE: 83 IN (210 CM)

WEIGHT/MALE: 190 LB (85 KG)

WEIGHT/FEMALE: 165 LB (75 KG)

HEAD–TAIL LENGTH AT BIRTH: 31 IN (80 CM)

COLORATION

VARIES GEOGRAPHICALLY: DARK BROWN OR BLACK ABOVE AND AROUND EYES, CREAM TO WHITE BELOW, WITH ELABORATE FIGURE-EIGHT PATTERN ON SIDES IN BUFF OR YELLOW AND LIGHT GRAY. SOME INDIVIDUALS HAVE WAVY GRAY LINES ON BELLY

FLIPPERS BLACK, LIGHT GRAY, OR WHITE

CALVES HAVE MORE MUTED COLOR PATTERNS

FEATURES

SLEEK, STREAMLINED BODY

TALL, SLENDER, POINTED FIN IN MIDDLE OF BACK; USUALLY CURVES BACKWARD

LONG, NARROW BEAK

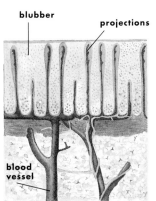

blubber | projections | blood vessel

A dolphin's skin, unlike that of most land mammals, is very smooth and more or less hairless: hair would only slow it down while it swims. Instead, the animal is kept warm by a thick layer of fat, called blubber, underneath the skin. Skin and blubber are attached to each other by small projections, and this allows the skin to ripple as the animal swims, thus reducing friction caused by turbulence.

FINS

Fins are made of firm fatty tissue. They are used for stabilization; some cetaceans, such as the finless porpoise, have no fins.

STREAMLINED SHAPE

A streamlined, torpedo-shaped body enables the dolphin to move quickly and easily through the water.

FLIPPERS

Flippers are paddle-shaped and used for steering. The flipper's skeletal structure with its five finger bones is similar to that of a shortened human arm.

FLUKES

Flukes are the two lobes of the powerful horizontal tail that propel the animal through the water. Made of a tough, fibrous material, they are broad and flat.

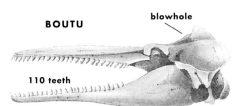

BOUTU

blowhole

110 teeth

The skulls of dolphins and porpoises are asymmetrical, with the blowhole located at the top and slightly to the left. The harbor porpoise has relatively few teeth, while the common dolphin has about 200.

HARBOR PORPOISE

92 teeth

200 teeth

COMMON DOLPHIN

One difference between dolphins and porpoises lies in the shape of their teeth: Dolphins (left) have sharp pointed teeth, while those of porpoises (right) are flattened into a spade or chisel shape at the tips.

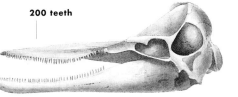

ELEPHANT

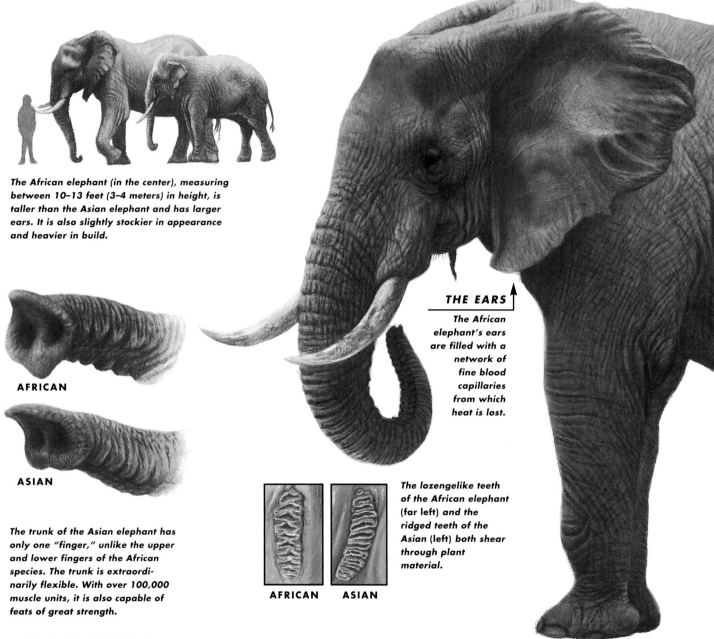

The African elephant (in the center), measuring between 10–13 feet (3–4 meters) in height, is taller than the Asian elephant and has larger ears. It is also slightly stockier in appearance and heavier in build.

AFRICAN

ASIAN

The trunk of the Asian elephant has only one "finger," unlike the upper and lower fingers of the African species. The trunk is extraordinarily flexible. With over 100,000 muscle units, it is also capable of feats of great strength.

THE EARS

The African elephant's ears are filled with a network of fine blood capillaries from which heat is lost.

The lozengelike teeth of the African elephant (far left) and the ridged teeth of the Asian (left) both shear through plant material.

AFRICAN   ASIAN

Illustrations Mathew Hillier/Wildlife Art Agency

X RAY

concave backbone

The most striking feature of the elephant's skeleton is its large skull, essential for supporting the animal's trunk and tusks. The African elephant has twenty-one ribs and a backbone that curves down, while the Asian species has one less rib and an upward-curving backbone.

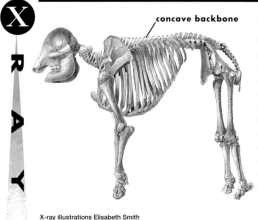

leg bone

SOLE OF FOOT

toes

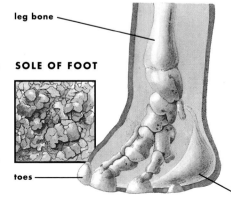

Despite appearances, the elephant walks on its toes like a horse, its "heel" being just a pad of tissues. This is why the elephant is so light on its feet. The sole of the elephant's foot (inset) is covered by a thick layer of skin, which constantly renews itself.

fatty tissue pad

X-ray illustrations Elisabeth Smith

AFRICAN ELEPHANT

LOCATION: AFRICA (SOUTH OF THE SAHARA)

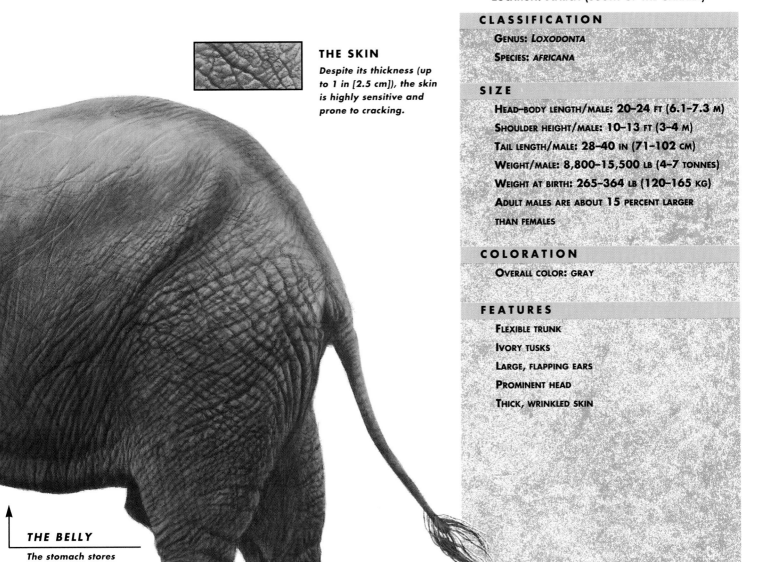

THE SKIN
Despite its thickness (up to 1 in [2.5 cm]), the skin is highly sensitive and prone to cracking.

CLASSIFICATION
GENUS: *LOXODONTA*

SPECIES: *AFRICANA*

SIZE
HEAD–BODY LENGTH/MALE: 20–24 FT (6.1–7.3 M)

SHOULDER HEIGHT/MALE: 10–13 FT (3–4 M)

TAIL LENGTH/MALE: 28–40 IN (71–102 CM)

WEIGHT/MALE: 8,800–15,500 LB (4–7 TONNES)

WEIGHT AT BIRTH: 265–364 LB (120–165 KG)

ADULT MALES ARE ABOUT 15 PERCENT LARGER THAN FEMALES

COLORATION
OVERALL COLOR: GRAY

FEATURES
FLEXIBLE TRUNK

IVORY TUSKS

LARGE, FLAPPING EARS

PROMINENT HEAD

THICK, WRINKLED SKIN

THE BELLY
The stomach stores huge quantities of cellulose–rich food, of which only about 44 percent is digested.

THE LEGS
The pillarlike limbs of the elephant provide strong support for its massive bulk. Elephants can run at speeds of up to 30 mph (48 km/h).

Common to all African elephants and some Asian males, tusks are incisor teeth that continue to grow throughout the animal's life. Elephants use them to break off tree branches, for digging, and for warding off would-be attackers. They are the one true major source of ivory.

AFRICAN ELEPHANT

ASIAN ELEPHANT

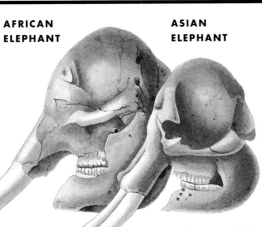

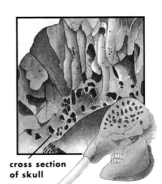

cross section of skull

The skull of the elephant is very large in comparison with its brain and is partly made up of a network of hollow cavities (left). These ensure that the skull is relatively light in weight. The jaws and teeth form the apparatus by which the elephant crushes the coarsest plant material.

EURASIAN WILDCAT

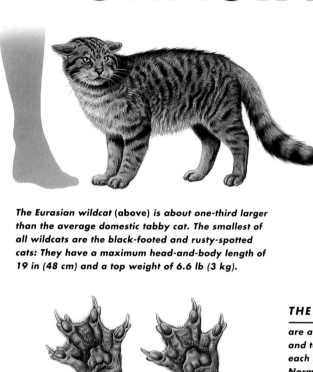

The Eurasian wildcat (above) is about one-third larger than the average domestic tabby cat. The smallest of all wildcats are the black-footed and rusty-spotted cats: They have a maximum head-and-body length of 19 in (48 cm) and a top weight of 6.6 lb (3 kg).

FOREFOOT   **HIND FOOT**

Like all small cats, the Eurasian wildcat (above) has five foreclaws and four hind claws; none of these claws leaves a print. The fishing cat (below) has partially webbed forefeet and its claws do not retract fully, so claw marks are visible in its footprints.

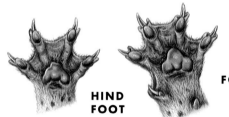

**HIND
FOOT**   **FOREFOOT**

THE WHISKERS

are arranged in four rows and total twenty-four on each side of the face. Normally they extend at right angles to the jaws to detect air currents and give a cat information about objects on either side. When hunting, they tend to be brought forward into a "net," pointing more in the direction of the mouth, where they help the cat position a fatal bite to prey. In a defensive posture, a cat usually angles the whiskers back to lie more alongside its face.

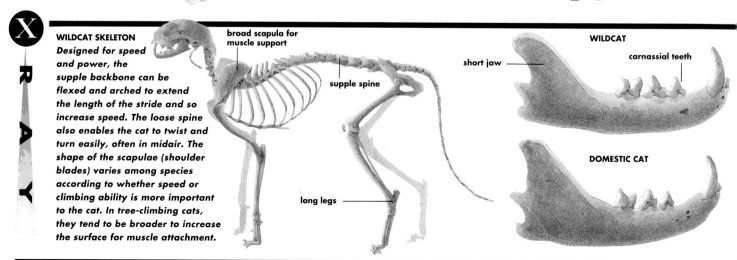

WILDCAT SKELETON
Designed for speed and power, the supple backbone can be flexed and arched to extend the length of the stride and so increase speed. The loose spine also enables the cat to twist and turn easily, often in midair. The shape of the scapulae (shoulder blades) varies among species according to whether speed or climbing ability is more important to the cat. In tree-climbing cats, they tend to be broader to increase the surface for muscle attachment.

broad scapula for muscle support

supple spine

long legs

WILDCAT

short jaw

carnassial teeth

DOMESTIC CAT

X-ray illustrations Elisabeth Smith

FACIAL EXPRESSION

When staring at prey, a cat pricks its ears forward and narrows its pupils (above left). Ears pricked and turned out (above center) denote aggression, while depressed ears and dilated pupils (above right) signify defensive submission.

EURASIAN WILD CAT

CLASSIFICATION

GENUS: *FELIS*

SPECIES: *SILVESTRIS*

SIZE

HEAD-BODY LENGTH: 19.5–29 IN (50–75 CM)

TAIL LENGTH: 8–14 IN (21–36 CM)

WEIGHT: 6.5–17.5 LB (3–8 KG)

SIZE VARIES ACCORDING TO LOCATION; MALES ARE LARGER THAN FEMALES

WEIGHT AT BIRTH: 1.4 OZ (40 G)

COLORATION

VARIES ACROSS RANGE: USUALLY A GRAY-BROWN BASE COLOR WITH INDISTINCT BUT COMPLETE STRIPES AROUND THE BODY; UNDERPARTS ARE PALER AND THERE IS A WHITE CHEST MARK LONGITUDINAL STRIPES OVER FACE MERGE AT BASE OF NECK INTO A DORSAL STRIPE THAT EXTENDS TO, BUT NOT ALONG, THE TAIL

FEATURES

EARS RESEMBLE THOSE OF THE DOMESTIC TABBY IN THEIR SHAPE AND SIZE RELATIVE TO THE BODY

TAIL IS SHORT AND THICK WITH BLUNT, BLACK TIP AND DARK RINGS

LEGS ARE LONGER THAN THOSE OF THE DOMESTIC CAT

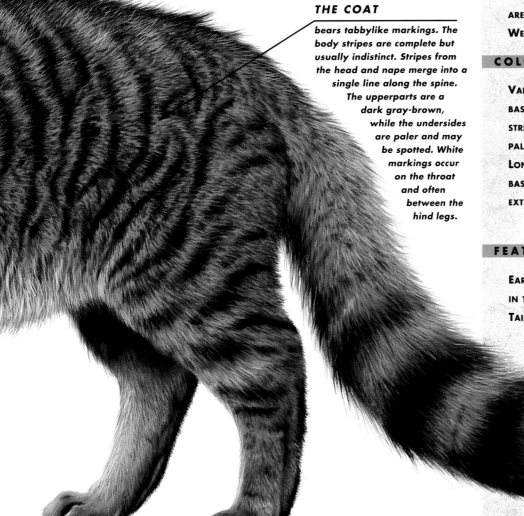

THE COAT

bears tabbylike markings. The body stripes are complete but usually indistinct. Stripes from the head and nape merge into a single line along the spine. The upperparts are a dark gray-brown, while the undersides are paler and may be spotted. White markings occur on the throat and often between the hind legs.

THE TAIL

is thicker and shorter than that of a domestic cat, with a blunt, black tip. Three to five complete rings encircle the lower part, and the hair is thick and long.

WILDCAT SKULL

The skull of the Eurasian wildcat is short and rounded, but it is larger and more robust than that of the domestic cat. The large eye sockets are positioned toward the front of the skull, reflecting the importance of vision and good distance judgment in cats. The jaws are scissor-hinged so that they move in one plane only; cats can deliver a very powerful bite but cannot chew effectively.

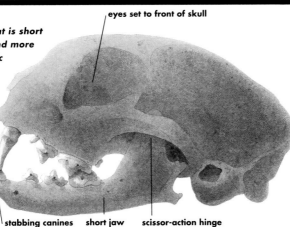

eyes set to front of skull

stabbing canines   short jaw   scissor-action hinge

The wildcat's braincase is larger and more robust than that of a domestic cat, with a volume of more than 2 cu in, as compared with around 1.95 cu in for the latter. Another aid to recognition lies in the the suture (joint) along the top of the crown, which in the wildcat is more convoluted.

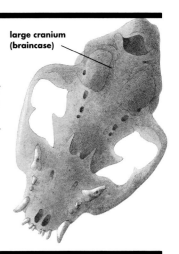

large cranium (braincase)

EUROPEAN MOLE

SIZE COMPARISON

The Russian desman (left) can reach 17 in (43 cm) from head to tail. The European mole (center) averages a head-to-tail length of 7 in (17.8 cm), while the shrew moles (right) may reach a total length of 6 in (15 cm).

THE EARS

have evolved without pinnae (external flaps) in order to minimize obstruction in the tunnel network. They are, however, fully functional.

THE EYES

are tiny and sunk deep into the fur. They enable the mole to distinguish between light and dark but are not much use for anything else.

THE SNOUT

is tipped with a set of several thousand touch-sensitive structures known as Eimer's organs. These structures, which are also a feature of desmans (see below), allow the animal to assess minute surface details of objects. Talpid moles have sensory hairs on and under the chin, on the muzzle, and in tufts behind the ears.

STAR-NOSED MOLE

A ring of 22 pink, fleshy tentacles form a star at the tip of the muzzle. This highly sensitive organ helps the animal to locate prey when hunting.

PYRENEAN DESMAN

The nostrils lie at the tip of a long snout extension. The tip is so sensitive that it can detect fissures as small as 0.0024 in (0.06 mm) deep and wide.

THE FOREPAWS

are formed in such a way that the palms face to the outside—ready to dig at a moment's notice.

X RAY

powerful shoulders lie close to the neck

reduced pelvic girdle

compact rib cage

SKELETON

The skeleton of the European mole reflects its digging ability. The close-set shoulders lie forward and low under the neck, and the forelimbs, which are massively reinforced, project almost at right angles to the body. The rib cage and pelvic girdle are greatly reduced in spread, to streamline the overall body shape.

X-ray illustrations Elisabeth Smith

FOREPAWS

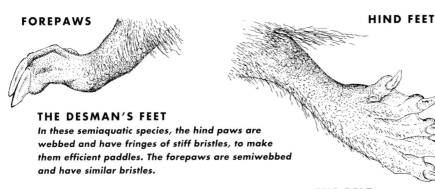

HIND FEET

THE DESMAN'S FEET
In these semiaquatic species, the hind paws are webbed and have fringes of stiff bristles, to make them efficient paddles. The forepaws are semiwebbed and have similar bristles.

EUROPEAN MOLE

CLASSIFICATION

FAMILY: TALPIDAE

GENUS: *TALPA*

SIZE

HEAD-BODY LENGTH: 4.3–6.7 IN (11–17 CM)

TAIL LENGTH: 0.8–1.3 IN (2–3.3 CM)

WEIGHT: 2.1–4.2 OZ (59.5–119 G)

WEIGHT AT BIRTH: 0.1–0.14 OZ (2.8–4 G)

COLORATION

THE VELVETY COAT IS BLACK, AND SOMETIMES SHOWS A SILVERY LUSTER

THE FUR OF THE UNDERSIDES IS PALER

FEATURES

CYLINDRICAL BODY

NO EXTERNAL EARS

LARGE, PINK FOREPAWS

DENSE, VELVETY COAT

TINY EYES

SHORT, CLUB-SHAPED TAIL

HAIRLESS, FLESHY, PINK SNOUT

BROAD, SPADELIKE FORELIMBS, DEVELOPED AS POWERFUL DIGGING AIDS; ATTACHED TO MUSCULAR SHOULDERS AND A DEEP CHEST BONE

SHORT, STURDY HIND LIMBS

THE PELT
is superbly adapted to the mole's lifestyle. Dense and velvety, it lies readily in any direction; this enables the mole to turn and reverse easily within a tunnel. The hairs are some 0.25 in (6.4 mm) long in summer, 0.35 in (8.9 mm) in winter, and are molted at least twice a year.

THE TAIL
is short, to suit the mole's burrowing habit, and is usually held erect. It is equipped with sensory bristles.

THE HIND FEET
are more delicate than the forepaws, but are similarly equipped with five stout claws. The hind feet help to brace the mole against tunnel walls while it digs with its forepaws.

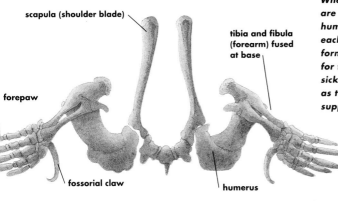

scapula (shoulder blade)

tibia and fibula (forearm) fused at base

forepaw

fossorial claw

humerus

FOREQUARTERS
Whereas the shoulder blades are slimmed down, the humerus (upper arm) on each forelimb is enormous, forming a broad anchorage for the digging muscles. A sickle-shaped bone known as the fossorial claw helps to support the broad forepaws.

TEETH
The crowns of the cheek teeth have W-shaped cusps for crushing insects.

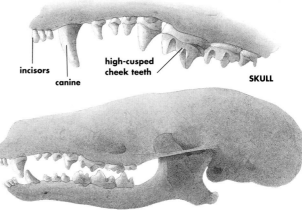

incisors

canine

high-cusped cheek teeth

SKULL

FUR SEALS

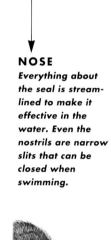

Eared seals (front) vary in length from 4–11.5 ft (120–350 cm) with the males usually being considerably larger and heavier than the females. At a length of 9–11.7 ft (275–355 cm), the walrus can be considerably larger.

NOSE

Everything about the seal is streamlined to make it effective in the water. Even the nostrils are narrow slits that can be closed when swimming.

WALRUS

The famous walrus tusks are actually the upper canine teeth, which grow throughout a walrus's life. They can grow to 22 in (55 cm) long in males and 16 in (40 cm) in females. Females' tusks are more slender and bend farther backward. They are mainly used to help pull the large body out of the water.

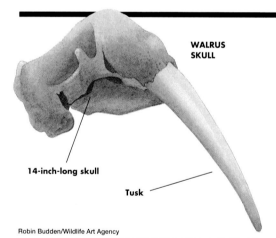

WALRUS SKULL

14-inch-long skull

Tusk

Robin Budden/Wildlife Art Agency

FRONT FLIPPERS

Front flippers are used for powering the seal in the water.

HIND FLIPPERS

The elongated digits of the hind flippers are clearly visible. The fact that they are slightly splayed helps give the seals some traction when they lumber across land. They are also able to turn these flippers forward, which makes them more effective in pushing them along.

The skeleton of eared seals reflectss both their swimming ability and their maneuverability on dry land. Vertebrae of the neck are enlarged to support powerful muscles used for swimming.

FUR SEAL SKELETON

FUR SEAL SKULL
(side view)

The flattened skull of an eared seal. The cheek teeth are simple and peglike and tend to drop out in advancing years.

canine teeth

X-ray illustrations Elisabeth Smith

EAR
Even though the ear is visible, it is very small.

EYES
The large round eyes give clear vision both in and out of the water. The retina is adapted for the low light conditions usually found underwater.

NORTHERN FUR SEAL
LOCATION: NORTH PACIFIC WATERS WEST OF ALASKA

CLASSIFICATION
GENUS: *CALLORHINUS*

SPECIES: *URSINUS*

SIZE
HEAD–TAIL LENGTH/MALE: 84 IN (213 CM)

HEAD–TAIL LENGTH/FEMALE: 56 IN (142 CM)

WEIGHT/MALE: 397–529 LB (180–240 KG)

WEIGHT/FEMALE: 95–110 LB (43–50 KG)

COLORATION
APPEARS VERY DARK OR BLACK WHEN THE COAT IS WET, BUT VARIOUS SHADES OF BROWN WHEN COAT IS DRY

WALRUS

CLASSIFICATION
GENUS: *ODOBENUS*

SPECIES: *ROSMARUS*

SOLE MEMBER OF GENUS

SIZE
HEAD–TAIL/MALE: 8.8–11.7 FT (268–356 CM)

HEAD–TAIL/FEMALE: 7.4–10.2 FT (226–311 CM)

WEIGHT/MALE: 1,764–3,748 LB (800–1,700 KG)

WEIGHT/FEMALE: 882–2,755 LB (400–1,250 KG)

TUSK LENGTH/MALE: 14–22 IN (36–56 CM)

TUSK LENGTH/FEMALE: 9–16 IN (23–41 CM)

COLORATION
FROM PALE TAWNY TO REDDISH BROWN. IMMATURE ANIMALS ARE DARKER THAN ADULTS

COAT IS DARKER ON UNDERSIDE

HAIRLESS SURFACES OF FLIPPERS ARE BLACK IN YOUNG ANIMALS, TURNING TO BROWN OR GRAY WITH AGE

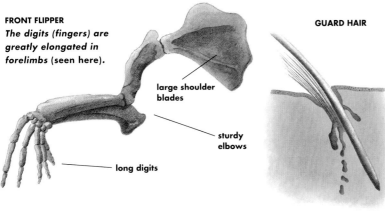

FRONT FLIPPER
The digits (fingers) are greatly elongated in forelimbs (seen here).

large shoulder blades

sturdy elbows

long digits

GUARD HAIR

PELT SECTION

Long guard hairs are interspersed through the coat with shorter, finer hairs, which comprise a dense covering of underfur. The fur is water-repellent and acts as insulation.

GIANT ANTEATER

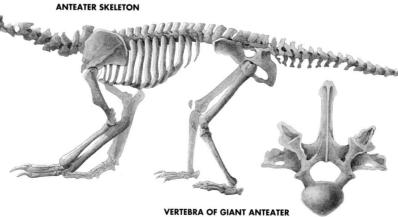

The giant anteater's shoulder height is about 2 ft (60 cm), and it weighs about 77 lb (35 kg). Its smallest relative, the silky anteater, by contrast, is only about 16 in (40 cm) long, including its long tail, and weighs a mere 10–18 oz (300–500 g).

Anatomy illustrations William Oliver/Wildlife Art Agency

THE SNOUT

The giant anteater's snout is long and tube shaped and ends in a tiny mouth opening. It contains the long, cylindrical nose; the anteater has an acute sense of smell, which is probably about 40 times more sensitive than a human's.

TONGUE

The tongue is worm-shaped and about 2 ft (60 cm) long. Huge glands beneath it keep the tongue coated with saliva, which enables the anteater to flick it in and out of its mouth at a rate of up to 150 times a minute and trap ants and termites on the sticky coating.

ANTEATER SKELETON

The giant anteater's skeleton is very elongated, with forelimbs adapted for breaking into ants' and termites' nests and for defense against predators. It also has expanded ribs, which help the animal maximize the striking force it can deliver when standing on its hind legs and slashing with its front claws at an enemy.

VERTEBRA OF GIANT ANTEATER

Unlike other mammals, anteaters and their relatives have extra jointlike projections on the rear vertebrae of their backs, making their lower backbone unusually rigid and able to cope with tearing into ants' nests and standing erect when defending themselves.

X-ray illustrations Elisabeth Smith

GIANT ANTEATER

LOCATION: SOUTH AMERICA EAST OF THE ANDES

CLASSIFICATION

GENUS: *MYRMECOPHAGA*

SPECIES: *TRIDACTYLA*

SIZE

HEAD–BODY LENGTH: 3–4 FT (100–120 CM)

SHOULDER HEIGHT: ABOUT 2 FT (60 CM)

TAIL LENGTH: 2–3 FT (65–90 CM)

WEIGHT: 48–86 LB (22–39 KG)

MALES ARE 10–20 PERCENT HEAVIER THAN FEMALES

WEIGHT AT BIRTH: 3.75 LB (1.7 KG)

COLORATION

BASIC COLOR: GRAYISH BROWN

MARKINGS: LONG, NARROW, BLACK TRIANGULAR BAND OUTLINED IN WHITE AND RUNNING BACKWARD ACROSS THE SHOULDERS

FEATURES

EYES: VERY SMALL FOR SIZE OF ANIMAL

SNOUT: VERY LONG

EARS: SMALL

GIANT ANTEATER

The front feet bear two extremely long claws, that of the third digit being 4 in (10 cm) long. When walking, the anteater tucks in these giant claws, moving on its knuckles and the sides of its forefeet.

TAMANDUA

In both species of tamanduas the three middle digits bear the sharp claws that they use to tear apart ants' and termites' nests.

SILKY ANTEATER

The first, fourth, and fifth digits of the silky anteater are much reduced. A long third digit extending into a fleshy pad, stiffened by a bone, acts as a "thumb" to aid grasping.

TAIL

The enormous, bushy tail measures 2–3 ft (65–90 cm) long and is covered in hairs up to 16 in (40 cm) long. It is held erect, like a flag, continuing the line of the mane along the anteater's back. When resting the anteater wraps its tail around itself, like a blanket.

HIND FEET

The anteater's hind feet have five toes of more or less equal length. It plants the soles of its feet firmly on the ground when it walks, like a bear or a human.

GIANT ANTEATER SKULL

The giant anteater has the most modified skull, almost tubular in shape. Like those of other anteaters, its jaws are completely toothless. The skull lacks the strong projections found in other mammals for the attachment of chewing muscles, and the tongue-retracting muscles are anchored to the animal's breastbone.

TAMANDUA SKULL

The tamandua has a much shorter snout than its larger relatives, with an even smaller opening for the mouth—it is only the diameter of a pencil.

SILKY ANTEATER SKULL

The silky anteater has a short, pointed, curved snout, with a much larger mouth opening than that found in its relatives.

GIANT PANDA

are short and rounded. They play an important role in communication.

GIANT PANDA

RED PANDA

The giant panda's shoulder height averages 35 in (90 cm) and it weighs about 245 lb (110 kg). The red panda, in contrast, is only abut 8 in (20 cm) high at the shoulder and weighs about 11 lb (5 kg).

The giant panda has excellent night vision. In the dark, the pupils of its eyes are large and round, but in bright light they are narrow slits, like those of a cat (top right). The pupils of the brown bear (bottom right) and other members of the bear family are more rounded.

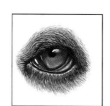

The forepaws of the giant panda (left) are larger than the hind paws. Both are covered with fur, except for a footpad and digits.

THEIR LEGS

are big and powerful. Pandas walk with a pigeon-toed, rolling gait. They usually walk slowly, though they are capable of running fast if the occasion demands it.

Illustrations Kim Thompson

X RAY

The giant panda's skeleton is very like that of other bears, although the head is extremely wide and round, and very big in relation to the rest of its body. Although it can stand on its hind legs—and frequently does so when feeding—it doesn't walk upright as other bears sometimes do.

The giant panda's "false thumb" is, in fact, a greatly enlarged wrist bone, called the radial sesamoid (RAY-dee-al SESS-a-moid). This bone does the work of a human thumb, enabling the panda to hold a bamboo stem in its forepaw and to feed with great speed.

BONES OF FOREPAW

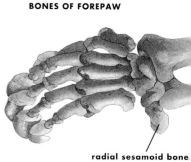

radial sesamoid bone

X-ray illustrations Elisabeth Smith

The red panda's paws are heavily furred, even on their undersides (above). Like the giant panda, the red panda's forepaw (left) has a modified wrist bone, which is used like a thumb, though it is not as developed as that of the giant panda.

THE THICK FUR

provides insulation from the cold. It is coated with an oil, which prevents the bear from getting wet in the always-soggy bamboo forest.

GIANT PANDA
LOCATION: SOUTH-WESTERN CHINA

CLASSIFICATION

GENUS: *AILUROPODA*

SPECIES: *MELANOLEUCA*

SIZE

HEAD–BODY LENGTH: 5–5.5 FT (1.5–1.7 M)

SHOULDER HEIGHT: 30–40 IN (80–100 CM)

TAIL LENGTH: 10 IN (25 CM)

WEIGHT: 200–285 LB (90–130 KG)

MALES ARE ABOUT 10 PERCENT HEAVIER THAN FEMALES

WEIGHT AT BIRTH: 3–3.5 OZ (90–100 G)

COLORATION

GROUND COLOR: WHITE, OFTEN WITH A DIRTY CREAMY OR YELLOWISH TINGE

MARKINGS: BLACK EARS, EYE PATCHES, MUZZLE, SHOULDERS, FORELIMBS, AND HIND LIMBS

CUBS: ALMOST BALD AT BIRTH, WITH ONLY SPARSE COAT OF WHITE HAIR GROWING FROM PINK SKIN; DARK MARKINGS GRADUALLY START TO SHOW THROUGH THICKENING WHITE FUR; BY ONE MONTH OLD, PATTERN RESEMBLES THAT OF AN ADULT

FEATURES

EYES: DARK BROWN; RELATIVELY SMALL FOR SIZE OF ANIMAL

NOSE AND LIPS: BLACK AND PROMINENT

WHISKERS: SHORT AND PALE

EARS: LARGE AND ALMOST ROUND

THE SHARP CLAWS

are used to help the panda manipulate bamboo stems and shoots, to grip the bark when climbing trees, and to strip the bark from tree trunks as a means of visual communication with other pandas.

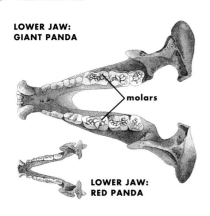

LOWER JAW: GIANT PANDA

molars

LOWER JAW: RED PANDA

Both pandas have the basic tooth pattern typical of carnivores, but modified to cope with a bamboo diet. They have lost the shearing carnassials, and the molars are broad, flattened, and have strongly ridged surfaces, enabling them to crush the toughest bamboo stems with ease. The skull's heavy bone structure allows for the attachment of massive chewing and crushing muscles.

GIANT PANDA

RED PANDA

GIBBON

HANDS & FEET
The long fingers of the hand (right) hook over the branches. The deeply cleft feet (far right) help the gibbon walk upright.

The siamang (above left) has a head-and-body length of some 3 ft (90 cm) and can weigh up to 28.5 lb (13 kg). The other species, including the lar (above right), are approximately half this size.

THE ARMS

are extremely long with highly mobile joints that help to propel the gibbon through the trees. Swinging from branch to branch is the the gibbon's specialty.

Despite the fact that on the ground the gibbon moves on its hind feet in a similar manner to humans, its skeleton is nowhere near as erect. The pelvis is lengthened to allow for muscle attachment that helps it stand erect when necessary. The scapulae (shoulder blades) are situated on the back of the thorax, as in humans, but this placement differs from that in the Old World monkeys.

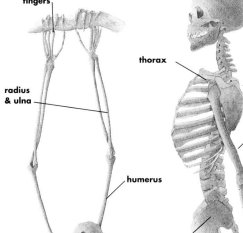

elongated fingers

thorax

scapula

radius & ulna

humerus

humerus

radius & ulna

scapula

pelvis

thorax

canines

elongated pelvis

GIBBON SKULL

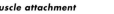

shallow lower jaw

THE SKULL
The skulls of gibbons differ from the great apes in having a much shallower lower jaw. Where the skulls of other apes show a considerable difference in size between males and females, this is not so among gibbons. Equally, the canine teeth are virtually the same size in both sexes.

ARMS AND SHOULDERS
With its extremely long arms and hooklike hands, the gibbon is the best adapted ape to move by brachiation—swinging from branch to branch by the arms. The shoulder joints are extremely mobile and possess very strong muscles.

THE LEGS

are long, although considerably shorter than the arms. The feet are also smaller than the hands. Gibbons are the only apes to stand upright and walk on their hind feet on the ground, their stance being plantigrade, that is, walking first on the heels then soles of the feet.

GIBBON SKELETON

HUMAN SKELETON

X-ray illustrations Elisabeth Smith

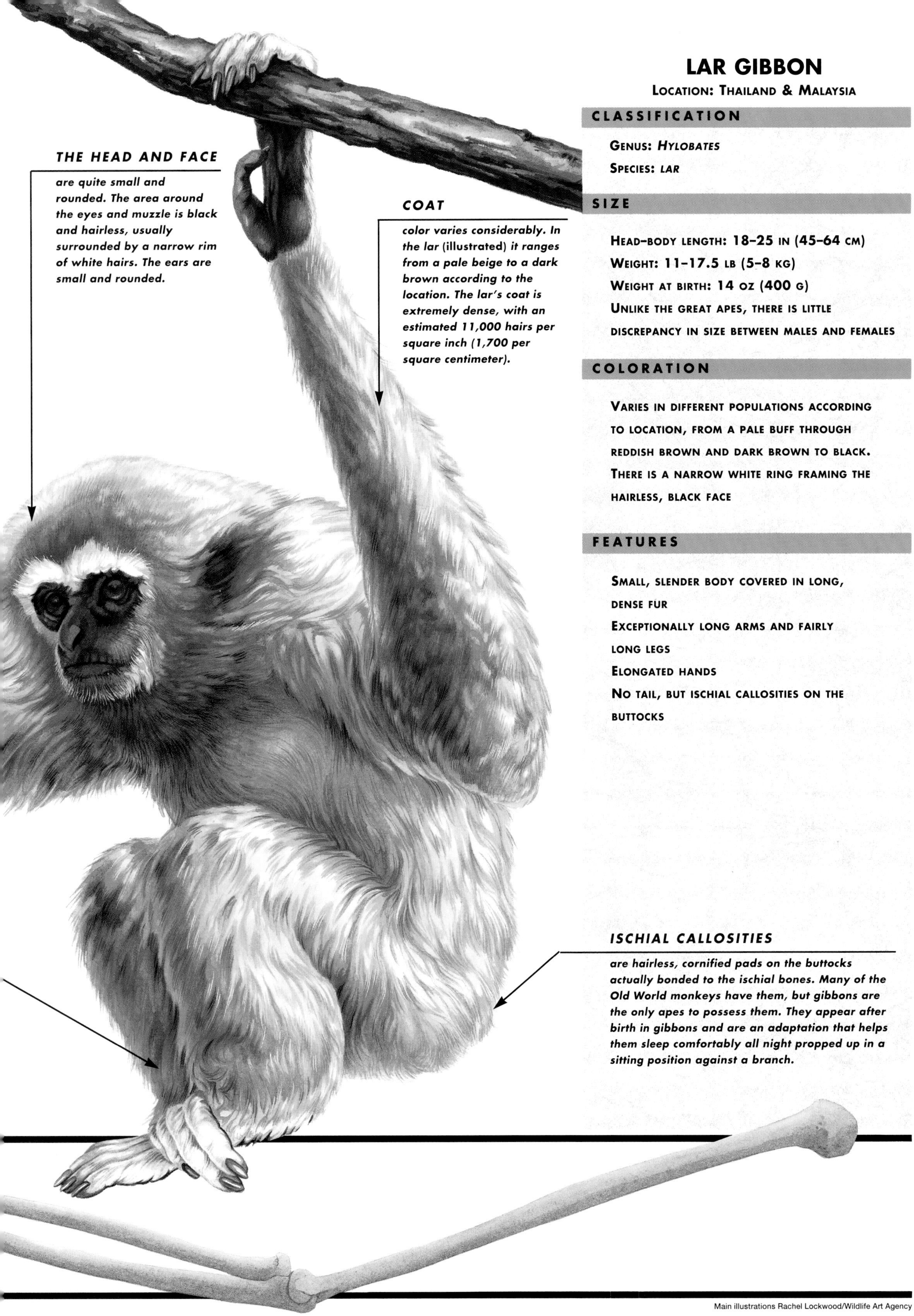

LAR GIBBON

LOCATION: THAILAND & MALAYSIA

CLASSIFICATION

GENUS: *HYLOBATES*

SPECIES: *LAR*

SIZE

HEAD-BODY LENGTH: **18–25** IN (**45–64** CM)

WEIGHT: **11–17.5** LB (**5–8** KG)

WEIGHT AT BIRTH: **14** OZ (**400** G)

UNLIKE THE GREAT APES, THERE IS LITTLE DISCREPANCY IN SIZE BETWEEN MALES AND FEMALES

COLORATION

VARIES IN DIFFERENT POPULATIONS ACCORDING TO LOCATION, FROM A PALE BUFF THROUGH REDDISH BROWN AND DARK BROWN TO BLACK. THERE IS A NARROW WHITE RING FRAMING THE HAIRLESS, BLACK FACE

FEATURES

SMALL, SLENDER BODY COVERED IN LONG, DENSE FUR

EXCEPTIONALLY LONG ARMS AND FAIRLY LONG LEGS

ELONGATED HANDS

NO TAIL, BUT ISCHIAL CALLOSITIES ON THE BUTTOCKS

THE HEAD AND FACE

are quite small and rounded. The area around the eyes and muzzle is black and hairless, usually surrounded by a narrow rim of white hairs. The ears are small and rounded.

COAT

color varies considerably. In the lar (illustrated) it ranges from a pale beige to a dark brown according to the location. The lar's coat is extremely dense, with an estimated 11,000 hairs per square inch (1,700 per square centimeter).

ISCHIAL CALLOSITIES

are hairless, cornified pads on the buttocks actually bonded to the ischial bones. Many of the Old World monkeys have them, but gibbons are the only apes to possess them. They appear after birth in gibbons and are an adaptation that helps them sleep comfortably all night propped up in a sitting position against a branch.

Main illustrations Rachel Lockwood/Wildlife Art Agency

65

GIRAFFE

X

X-RAY

The long neck of the giraffe has only seven vertebrae, the same as other mammals. However, each one is greatly elongated and articulated with ball-and-socket joints, allowing great flexibility. The size, together with the dorsal spines on the fourth and fifth vertebrae, give an anchorage for the large muscles that support the head and neck.

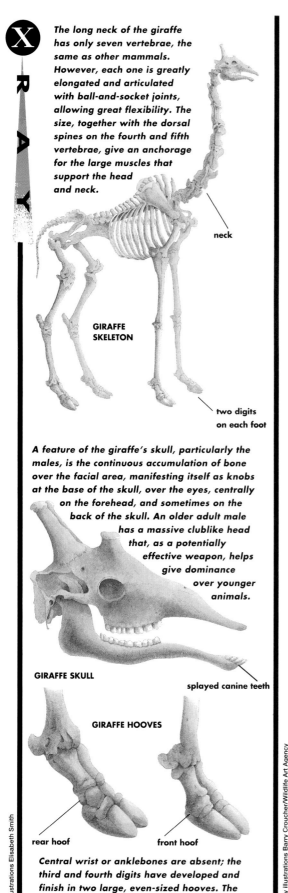

neck

GIRAFFE SKELETON

two digits on each foot

A feature of the giraffe's skull, particularly the males, is the continuous accumulation of bone over the facial area, manifesting itself as knobs at the base of the skull, over the eyes, centrally on the forehead, and sometimes on the back of the skull. An older adult male has a massive clublike head that, as a potentially effective weapon, helps give dominance over younger animals.

GIRAFFE SKULL

splayed canine teeth

GIRAFFE HOOVES

rear hoof

front hoof

Central wrist or anklebones are absent; the third and fourth digits have developed and finish in two large, even-sized hooves. The remaining digits have virtually disappeared during the course of evolution.

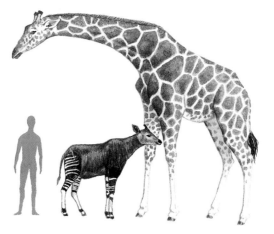

An adult male giraffe may stand up to 18 ft (5.4 m) high—almost twice the height of an elephant—and if he stretches his limbs and neck he can add another 18 in (45 cm) to this. The thicker-set okapi (above center) is considerably smaller at a maximum height of 7 ft (2.15 m).

THE TORSO

The torso is relatively small compared to the length of the legs and neck, with the shoulder much higher than the croup, so that the back slopes down to the tail. The additional height to the front of the body is mainly due to the heavy muscular development around the neck. The deep chest houses the enlarged lungs.

LEGS AND FEET

The giraffe's legs are extremely long, but in spite of the fact that the body slopes down toward the tail, the front legs are only fractionally longer than the hind. At a walk, in particular, there appears to be little flexion in each step, resulting in a somewhat stiff-legged gait. The feet are very large. In the giraffe the hooves are 6 in (15 cm) high in males and 4 in (10 cm) high in females. The okapi has scent-secreting glands in the hooves; these are absent in the giraffe.

BONY APPENDAGES

No other animal has horns like those of the giraffe and okapi. A calf is born with a pair of cartilaginous knobs, which initially are unattached to the skull. Later they begin to ossify (turn into bone), fusing with the skull. Although they grow slowly, they rarely exceed 5.3 in (13.5 cm). Throughout the life of the animal, the horns are covered with skin and hair, although the latter sometimes wears away from the apex. The okapi has one pair of horns, present in the male only.

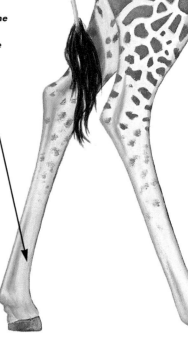

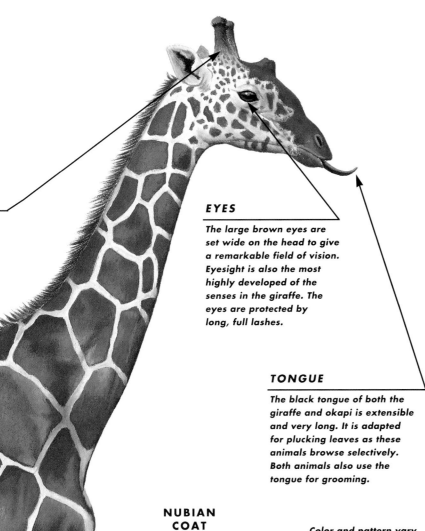

GIRAFFE

LOCATION: AFRICA (SOUTH OF THE SAHARA)

CLASSIFICATION

GENUS: *GIRAFFA*

SPECIES: *CAMELOPARDALIS*

SIZE

HEAD–BODY LENGTH/MALE: 12–15 FT (3.8–4.7 M)

HEIGHT/MALE: 15–18 FT (4.7–5.5 M)

WEIGHT/MALE: 1,764–4,255 LB (800–1,930 KG)

HEIGHT AT BIRTH/MALE: 6 FT 3 IN (1.9 M)

WEIGHT AT BIRTH/MALE: 225 LB (102 KG)

ADULT MALES ARE LARGER THAN FEMALES

COLORATION

BACKGROUND COLOR VARIES FROM PALE ORANGE TO ALMOST BLACK

COAT PATTERNS VARY FROM LARGE, REGULAR CHESTNUT SHAPES TO JAGGED PATCHES

BACKGROUND COLOR BROKEN BY NARROW, PURE WHITE LINES INTO IRREGULAR PATTERNS

FEATURES

LONG BLACK TONGUE THAT CAN BE EXTENDED TO 18 IN (46 CM)

BONY APPENDAGES ON HEAD THAT ARE MORE PRONOUNCED IN MALES

LARGE BROWN EYES

LONG TAIL OF ABOUT 30–40 IN (76–101 CM) WITH TASSEL ON TIP

SPLAYED CANINE TEETH TO HELP ANIMAL "COMB" FOLIAGE

EYES

The large brown eyes are set wide on the head to give a remarkable field of vision. Eyesight is also the most highly developed of the senses in the giraffe. The eyes are protected by long, full lashes.

TONGUE

The black tongue of both the giraffe and okapi is extensible and very long. It is adapted for plucking leaves as these animals browse selectively. Both animals also use the tongue for grooming.

NUBIAN COAT PATTERN

KENYAN COAT PATTERN

Color and pattern vary according to the subspecies and also to each individual, but they essentially comprise a latticework of pale hairs enclosing usually irregular-shaped blotches of a darker color. This may vary from golden to rich liver-red and tends to darken with age.

HOW A GIRAFFE MOVES

A giraffe appears stiff-legged when moving. Its pace can be described as a "rack," in that the front and back legs on each side of the body are moved almost in unison, the forefoot leaving the ground just in front of the hind one. This is an unusual gait, but one that works. A giraffe in full flight can run at 37 mph (60 km/h).

GOLDEN JACKAL

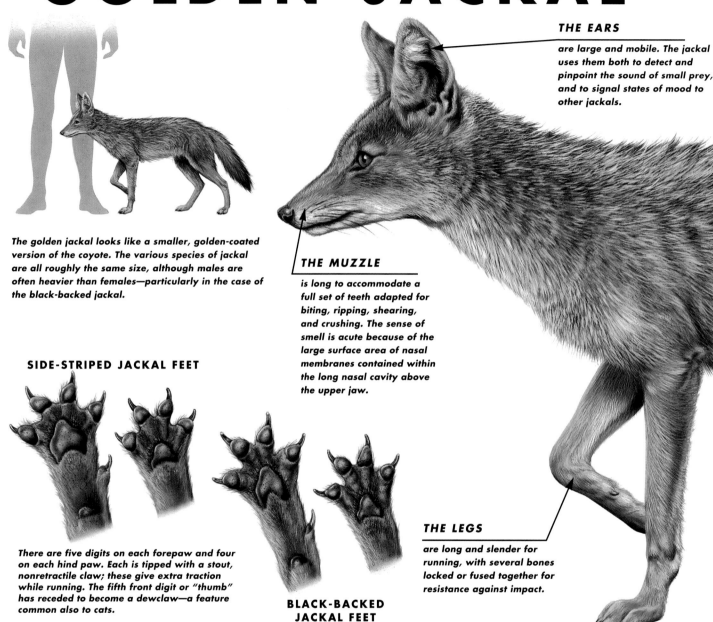

THE EARS

are large and mobile. The jackal uses them both to detect and pinpoint the sound of small prey, and to signal states of mood to other jackals.

The golden jackal looks like a smaller, golden-coated version of the coyote. The various species of jackal are all roughly the same size, although males are often heavier than females—particularly in the case of the black-backed jackal.

THE MUZZLE

is long to accommodate a full set of teeth adapted for biting, ripping, shearing, and crushing. The sense of smell is acute because of the large surface area of nasal membranes contained within the long nasal cavity above the upper jaw.

SIDE-STRIPED JACKAL FEET

There are five digits on each forepaw and four on each hind paw. Each is tipped with a stout, nonretractile claw; these give extra traction while running. The fifth front digit or "thumb" has receded to become a dewclaw—a feature common also to cats.

BLACK-BACKED JACKAL FEET

THE LEGS

are long and slender for running, with several bones locked or fused together for resistance against impact.

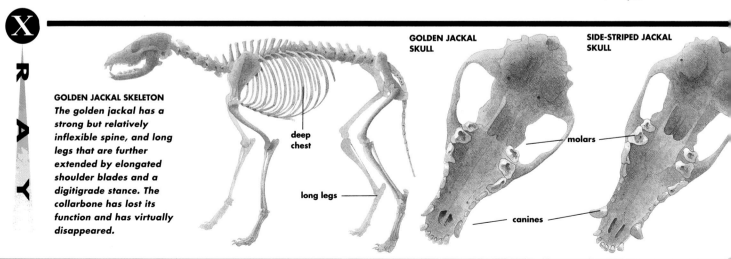

X

R A Y

GOLDEN JACKAL SKELETON
The golden jackal has a strong but relatively inflexible spine, and long legs that are further extended by elongated shoulder blades and a digitigrade stance. The collarbone has lost its function and has virtually disappeared.

deep chest

long legs

GOLDEN JACKAL SKULL

SIDE-STRIPED JACKAL SKULL

molars

canines

X-ray illustrations Elisabeth Smith

BLACK-BACKED JACKAL

SIDE-STRIPED JACKAL

SIMIEN JACKAL

The black-backed jackal's slate gray back contrasts strongly with the rusty brown underbelly. The side-striped jackal, not surprisingly, sports a pale stripe of guard hairs over its grayish fawn flanks—its species name adustus means "swarthy" or "sunburned." The Simien jackal has a reddish brown coat frosted with yellow.

GOLDEN JACKAL

LOCATION: NORTH & EAST AFRICA TO MYANMAR

CLASSIFICATION

GENUS: *CANIS*

SPECIES: *AUREUS*

SIZE

HEAD–BODY LENGTH: 24–41 IN (60–105 CM)

TAIL LENGTH: 10–12 IN (20–30 CM)

AVERAGE WEIGHT: 18–24 LB (8–11 KG)

MALES ARE HEAVIER THAN FEMALES

COLORATION

GENERALLY GOLDEN TO SILVER GRAY WITH DARKER, MORE REDDISH LEGS; PALE, OFTEN WHITE UNDERPARTS; BLACK TAIL TIP. OCCASIONAL BLACK-COATED (MELANISTIC) INDIVIDUALS HAVE BEEN REPORTED. THE EYES ARE AMBER

FEATURES

LITHE, SLENDER BUILD
LONG, SLIM LEGS
BUSHY, BLACK-TIPPED TAIL
POINTED MUZZLE
LARGE, POINTED EARS

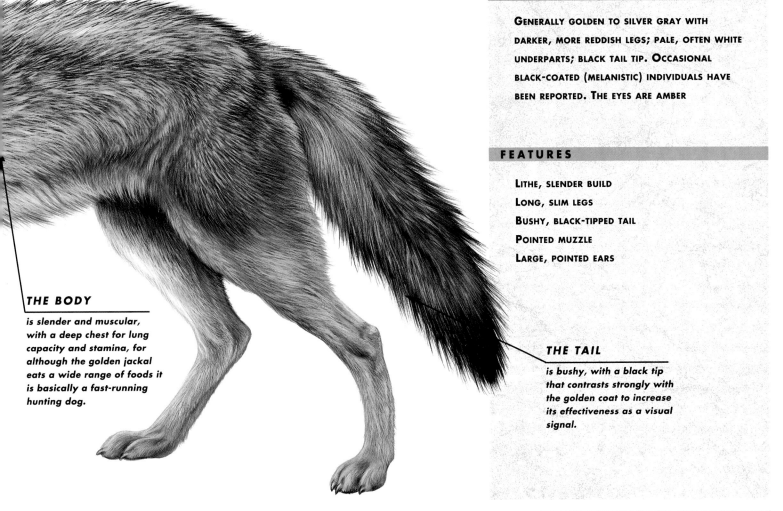

THE BODY

is slender and muscular, with a deep chest for lung capacity and stamina, for although the golden jackal eats a wide range of foods it is basically a fast-running hunting dog.

THE TAIL

is bushy, with a black tip that contrasts strongly with the golden coat to increase its effectiveness as a visual signal.

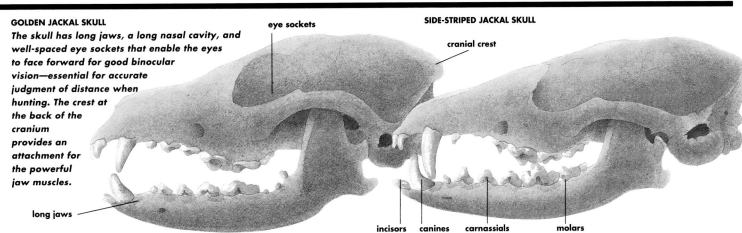

GOLDEN JACKAL SKULL
The skull has long jaws, a long nasal cavity, and well-spaced eye sockets that enable the eyes to face forward for good binocular vision—essential for accurate judgment of distance when hunting. The crest at the back of the cranium provides an attachment for the powerful jaw muscles.

eye sockets

SIDE-STRIPED JACKAL SKULL

cranial crest

long jaws

incisors   canines   carnassials   molars

Main illustration Steve Kingston

GORILLA

The gorilla often stands shorter than a tall adult man, let down mainly by its bandy-legged stance. The tallest gorilla subspecies is the eastern lowland (above left), which may reach 5.9 ft (180 cm) in height. The female (above right) can reach about 4.9 ft (150 cm). In weight and build, however, gorillas beat humans every time.

THE EYES

are small and deep-set beneath the prominent brow, and are a warm midbrown in color. They give good vision and can communicate the ape's moods and emotions very expressively.

THE NOSTRILS

are broad and flattened. The surrounding nasal wings are wrinkled and shaped in a highly personalized manner on each individual. The sense of smell is good; a gorilla can, for example, detect a human's presence at 65 ft (20 m) or more.

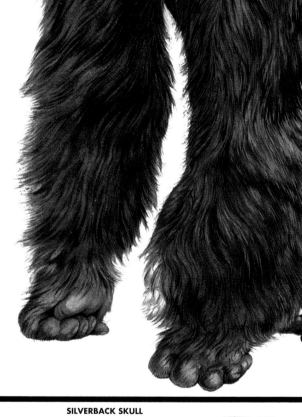

SILVERBACK KNUCKLE PRINT

SILVERBACK FOOTPRINT

JUVENILE KNUCKLE PRINT

FEMALE FOOTPRINT

TRACK IMPRINTS

Although the gorilla can easily walk upright like us, it prefers to amble on all fours, resting the weight of the forequarters on its knuckles. The impressions show up well on a muddy forest floor. The footprints look similar to ours, except that the gorilla's opposable big toe is visibly set apart from the rest of the foot.

SKELETON

The skeleton reflects a lifestyle more typical of the gibbon or even the orang. These are the experts at swinging through trees by their long arms, while an adult gorilla is more or less confined to the ground. As hangers and swingers, apes also need fewer lumbar vertebrae (the bones in the lower back), having only four or so compared with the six or seven in a monkey.

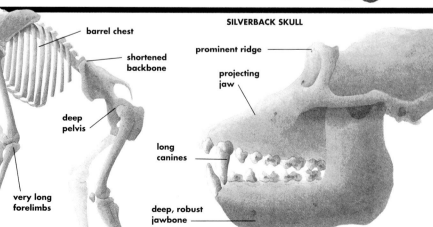

- barrel chest
- shortened backbone
- deep pelvis
- very long forelimbs

SILVERBACK SKULL

- prominent ridge
- projecting jaw
- long canines
- deep, robust jawbone

X-ray illustrations Elisabeth Smith

MOUNTAIN GORILLA

LOCATION: BORDERS OF ZAIRE, UGANDA & RWANDA

THE BODY

is huge and muscular, particularly in the male. The prominent rump and forequarters give the gorilla a slim-waisted profile when on all fours, but the torso slumps heavily when the animal sits down.

The female gorilla is not only smaller than a silverback but differs also in the shape of her head. She lacks the prominent sagittal crest—the keel of bone that supports some of the jaw muscles. Chewing power is less important to the female, as she does not have such a vast bulk to fuel each day.

ADULT FEMALE GORILLA

THE HAIR

grows longest and silkiest on the mountain subspecies—especially on the long forearms—to cope with the inclement weather conditions. An adult male is known as a silverback because the hair over his lumbar region turns a silver-gray.

THE HANDS

are huge, with thick fingers. The knuckles grow calloused with age, because the ape rests on them when on all fours. The thumbs are opposable, and each digit has a flattened nail.

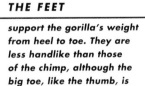

THE FEET

support the gorilla's weight from heel to toe. They are less handlike than those of the chimp, although the big toe, like the thumb, is capable of grasping.

CLASSIFICATION

GENUS: *GORILLA*

SPECIES: *GORILLA BERINGEI*

SIZE

STANDING HEIGHT/MALE: 4–5.7 FT (125–175 CM)

STANDING HEIGHT/FEMALE: AROUND 5 FT (150 CM)

ARM SPAN: 6.6–9 FT (2–2.75 M)

CHEST SPAN: UP TO 20 IN (50 CM)

WEIGHT/MALE: 365 LB (165 KG) ON AVERAGE

WEIGHT/FEMALE: 185 LB (85 KG) ON AVERAGE

WEIGHT AT BIRTH: 4.4 LB (2 KG)

COLORATION

THE MOUNTAIN GORILLA HAS LONG, SILKY BLACK HAIR OVER MOST OF THE BODY, WHILE THE EASTERN LOWLAND GORILLA HAS SHORTER HAIR OF SIMILAR COLOR. IN BOTH THESE SUBSPECIES THE SILVERBACK'S SADDLE IS RESTRICTED TO THE BACK THE WESTERN LOWLAND GORILLA HAS A BROWNISH-GRAY COAT; THE SILVERBACK'S SADDLE EXTENDS TO THE THIGHS AND RUMP

FEATURES

ADULT MALE IS MASSIVE, WITH MUSCULAR LIMBS AND A THICKSET, POT-BELLIED TORSO, AS WELL AS A HIGH-DOMED HEAD AND A SILVER-GRAY SADDLE

BOTH SEXES ARE LARGER THAN THE CHIMPANZEE, WHICH OTHERWISE LOOKS SIMILAR TO THE GORILLA

JUVENILE MALES LACK THE SILVER BACK

NEWBORN GORILLAS LOOK ALMOST HUMAN

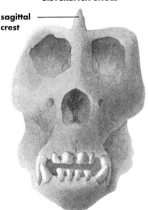

SILVERBACK SKULL

sagittal crest

SKULL

The gorilla's jaw projects less dramatically from the cranial mass than that of the chimpanzee. Nevertheless the jaw is deep and strong, providing extensive anchorage for operative muscles. In the silverback (left), these muscles are supported also by the sagittal crest—a long bony ridge similar to the keel of a boat. This crest grows as the male matures. The skull is clearly similar to that of humans, with the large braincase and forward-facing eyes typical of apes and hominids.

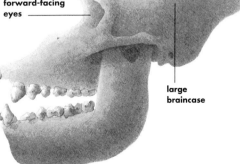

forward-facing eyes

large braincase

FEMALE GORILLA SKULL

Color illustrations Rachel Lockwood

GRAY-HEADED FRUIT BAT

The gray-headed fruit bat or flying fox displays most of the characteristics associated with the fruit bat family. It is one of the largest, with a wingspan of 4 ft (1.2 m). The largest fruit bat is the common fruit bat which has a wingspan of 5.5 ft (1.7 m) and weighs 3.3 lb (1,500 g). The smallest fruit bat, which belongs to the African long-tongued bat genus, has a wingspan of just 10 in (25 cm) and weighs little more than 0.5 oz (14 g).

WING MEMBRANE

The large surface area of the wing membrane is highly elastic and very thin. It is made up of two thin layers of skin. Blood vessels and nerves are sandwiched between these two layers.

FEET

The long claws provide such a secure grip that the fruit bat can hang upside down by one leg and use the other to groom itself. They are also used to grip on to fruit when they feed.

Anatomy illustrations Philip Hood/Wildlife Art Agency

FIVE DIGITS

The fruit bat's finger digits have evolved into long finger bones that support the large membranous wings in the same way as the spokes of an umbrella. Like all bats, fruit bats have a thumb claw; however, they also have a claw on their second finger. The thumb and extra finger claw help support the wing membrane in front of the forearm, which can be quite large in some fruit bats. In some species the males also use this claw to fight with.

THICK FUR

With a high metabolic rate and a vegetarian diet, fruit bats need a thick insulating layer of fur to keep their body heat in. For those fruit bats that live at high altitudes in mountains, this is especially important.

X RAY

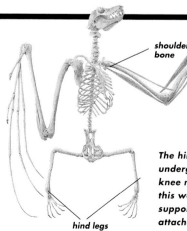

FRUIT BAT SKELETON

To keep the bat's body rigid in flight, several of its neck vertebrae have become fused together. Their ribs have also become flattened, giving the body a more stable and streamlined shape.

shoulder bone

finger bones

The hind limbs have undergone a rotation through 180°. The knee now bends outward and backward. In this way the wing membrane is given extra support during flight. Powerful tendons attached to the bones of the feet give the fruit bat a tight grip.

hind legs

The shoulder bones are considerably more developed than the pelvis. A large and solid collarbone, or clavicle, is fused to the shoulders, adding strength to the upper torso. The breastbone, or sternum, has a ridge running down its length that allows the powerful flight muscles to be attached firmly.

GRAY-HEADED FRUIT BAT
LOCATION: AUSTRALIA

CLASSIFICATION

GENUS: *PTEROPUS*

SPECIES: *POLIOCEPHALUS*

SIZE

HEAD-BODY LENGTH/MALE: 11.7 IN (30 CM)
HEAD-BODY LENGTH/FEMALE: 7.8 IN (20 CM)
WEIGHT/MALE: 2.6 LB (1.2 KG)
WEIGHT/FEMALE: 1.8 LB (0.8 KG)
WING SPAN/MALE: 4 FT (1.2 M)
WING SPAN/FEMALE: 2.6 FT (0.8 M)

COLORATION

GROUND COLOR VARIES FROM GRAYISH BROWN TO ALMOST BLACK

A PATCH OF FUR ON THE BACK BETWEEN THE WINGS IS GRAYISH YELLOW

EARS, WINGS, AND NOSE ARE BLACK

EYES ARE REDDISH BROWN

FEATURES

THICK FUR COVERS BODY AND HEAD

PROMINENT, HAIRLESS EARS

LARGE EYES

ELONGATED MUZZLE

FREE-TAILED BAT

MOUSE-TAILED BAT

MOUSE-EARED BAT

SHEATH-TAILED BAT

TUBE-NOSED FRUIT BAT

FLYING FOX

LARGE EYES

Fruit bats have excellent night vision. At the back of all mammalian eyes are special cells called rods. These are used for nighttime vision. Although they are not sensitive to colors, they are highly sensitive to light. In the fruit bat's eyes these rods have fingerlike projections that increase the surface area, enabling the bat's eyes to capture more of the available light. This gives the bat its sharp black-and-white vision in low light levels.

TELLTALE TAILS *(LEFT)*

Bats display a wide variety of tail shapes, and fruit bats are no exception. Usually they are short or nonexistent. Bats that belong to the flying fox genus Pteropus never have a tail. The rousette fruit bat, however, has a short stump of a tail that is rarely longer than 0.8 in (2 cm), while insectivorous bats, such as the mouse-tailed bats of the genus Rhinopoma, have long tails—up to 3.1 in (8 cm)—which hang freely. The lack of tails in fruit bats is another guide to their lifestyle. Because they do not need to chase after swiftly moving prey, they no longer need the rudderlike tail that gives other bats balance in flight.

FRUIT BAT SKULL

Fruit bats have varied skull shapes. Those that feed on flowers tend to have longer and thinner noses. Fruit bats also have many different patterns of teeth. The incisors are small as they have little use for them. Canine teeth are present even in those bats that have taken to a diet of pollen and fruit. The molar teeth are low and widely spaced. The crowns are long, flat, and grooved to help squash the ripe fruit and aid in the removal of seeds and the tough skin of some fruits.

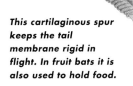

FRUIT BAT CLAW

This cartilaginous spur keeps the tail membrane rigid in flight. In fruit bats it is also used to hold food.

GREATER HORSESHOE BAT

THE WINGS

are used to scoop up the bat's insect prey rather than catching it directly with the mouth. The bat can manipulate the membrane like a hand to put food in the mouth.

THE EARS

are typically large. While in flight the bat can move its ears backward and forward as quickly as 60 times a second as it patrols the airwaves for sound signals.

THE EYES

are small, and the field of vision is reduced by the large nose leaf, indicating that sight is less important than sound.

THE "HORSESHOE"

is the fleshy middle section around the nose. Above the nose is the erect lancet, and between these two features is the sella. These features combine to act as a sonar megaphone, which can be adjusted to direct sound wherever the bat chooses.

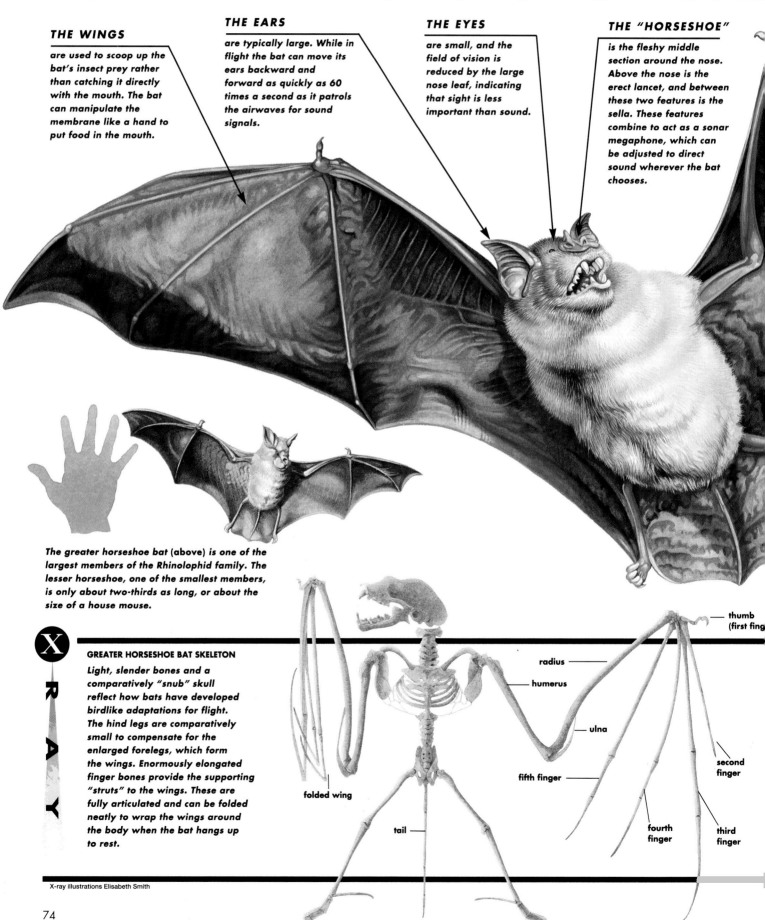

The greater horseshoe bat (above) is one of the largest members of the Rhinolophid family. The lesser horseshoe, one of the smallest members, is only about two-thirds as long, or about the size of a house mouse.

X RAY

GREATER HORSESHOE BAT SKELETON

Light, slender bones and a comparatively "snub" skull reflect how bats have developed birdlike adaptations for flight. The hind legs are comparatively small to compensate for the enlarged forelegs, which form the wings. Enormously elongated finger bones provide the supporting "struts" to the wings. These are fully articulated and can be folded neatly to wrap the wings around the body when the bat hangs up to rest.

thumb (first fing

radius

humerus

ulna

second finger

fifth finger

fourth finger

third finger

folded wing

tail

X-ray illustrations Elisabeth Smith

GREATER HORSESHOE BAT

CLASSIFICATION

GENUS: *RHINOLOPHUS*

SPECIES: *FERRUMEQUINUM*

SIZE

HEAD–BODY LENGTH: 4.5–5 IN (11–12.5 CM)

TAIL LENGTH: 1–1.5 IN (2.5–4 CM)

WINGSPAN: 13–14 IN (33–35 CM)

WEIGHT: 0.5–1.2 OZ (13–34 G)

WEIGHT AT BIRTH: 0.07–0.1 OZ (2–3 G)

COLORATION

PALE BROWN COAT WITH REDDISH TINT

FEATURES

LARGE EARS

MIDDLE RIDGE OF NASAL STRUCTURE IS CONCAVE WHEN SEEN FROM ABOVE

MUSCULAR LANCET ABOVE NOSTRILS AND SELLA BETWEEN THEM

TWO NONFUNCTIONING "DUMMY" TEATS ON FEMALE'S ABDOMEN

EARS AND NOSES

Ear size and shape range widely. Some species have an extra lobe called a tragus; others, such as the horseshoe bats, have extremely mobile ears capable of moving independently. The long ears of false vampire bats are connected by a membrane, whereas most species native to northern Europe have smaller, less mobile ears. Bats recognize sounds of 50,000–200,000 Hz (vibrations a second).

Most bats have elaborate, fleshy structures surrounding their noses. Muscular, and sensitive to the vibrations emitted from the nostrils, these nose leaves can assume grotesque shapes in some species. The nose leaves thereby provide easy means of distinguishing different bat species.

FALSE VAMPIRE BAT

MOUSE-TAILED BAT (SUPERFAMILY EMBALLONUROIDEA)

OLD WORLD LEAF-NOSED BAT

THE WINGS

are broad with rounded ends. The greater horseshoe is rather slow and fluttering in flight, but swoops down like a hawk on ground-dwelling beetles. Like other horseshoe bats, it wraps its wings around its body when roosting rather than folding them.

TEETH
Most insect-eaters have sharp-edged molars with a W-shaped pattern of ridges. The upper and lower ridges meet rather like scissor blades to grind the tough shells of insects.

scissor-action teeth

large brain-case to cope with sound analysis

WING MUSCLES
The various sections of the patagium are controlled by finger flexing and by muscles set within the membrane itself. An important muscle from the shoulder to the wrist controls the leading-edge patagium section; contraction of this muscle, for example, adjusts the curve of the wing surface. Limb muscles act to contract the skeleton (right).

shoulder blade

humerus

radius

wrist (fingers not shown here)

muscle

contracted limb

wrist

Main illustration Rachel Lockwood/Wildlife Art Agency

GRIZZLY BEAR

The grizzly bear is huge. With a head-body-and-leg length of 5.5–9.2 ft (1.7–2.8 m), when standing upright on its hind legs, it can tower over a man. Its cousin the Kodiak bear may stand more than 12 ft (3.6 m) tall on its hind legs.

THE FOREHEAD

is wide, contrasting with the long muzzle. The small, rounded ears give surprisingly acute hearing.

THE BODY

is extremely heavy and stocky. A hump between the shoulders, made up of fat and muscle, gives added power to the forelimbs.

The grizzly has the most impressive claws of all bears—up to 4 in (10 cm) long on its forefeet. It uses these for digging, scratching, and slashing. The black bear uses its short, stout, curved claws in climbing trees, as well as foraging; surprisingly for a climbing bear, it has thick fur between the foot and toe pads. In the wholly terrestrial grizzly, the soles are only sparsely haired.

HIND FOOT   **FOREFOOT**

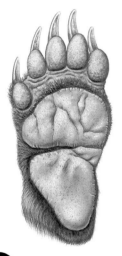
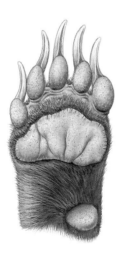

X

R A Y

As with all bears, the shape of the brown bear's skeleton shows that it is built for strength rather than speed. The limb bones are stout and short in relation to body size when compared, for example, to cats or dogs. The limbs are anchors for thick muscles all along their length, giving power through a wide range of body movements. The hind feet are plantigrade (the soles are placed flat on the ground). The bear's femur strongly resembles that of humans.

BROWN BEAR SKELETON

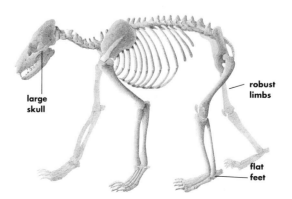

large skull

robust limbs

flat feet

The brown bear's forefeet are remarkably dextrous—the five long fingers enable it to pluck foliage and fruit with ease. The five nonretractile claws on the forefeet are particularly long and curved but are subject to a lot of wear throughout the bear's life.

FOREFOOT

X-ray illustrations Elisabeth Smith

GRIZZLY BEAR

LOCATION: CANADA, ALASKA & THE BALKANS

CLASSIFICATION

GENUS: *URSUS*

SPECIES: *ARCTOS HORRIBILIS*

SIZE

HEAD–BODY LENGTH: 5.9–7 FT (180–213 CM)

HEIGHT TO SHOULDER: 4.3 FT (131 CM)

TAIL LENGTH: 3 IN (7.6 CM)

HINDFOOT LENGTH: 10 IN (25 CM)

FOREFOOT CLAW LENGTH: UP TO 4 IN (10 CM)

WEIGHT: 300–860 LB (136–390 KG)

WEIGHT AT BIRTH: 12–24 OZ (340–680 G)

COLORATION

VARIES FROM LIGHT CREAMY BROWN TO BROWN BLACK BUT TYPICALLY IS DARK BROWN, WITH THE LONG GUARD HAIRS "GRIZZLED" WITH WHITE TOWARD THEIR TIPS. COLORATION TENDS TO BE UNIFORM OVER THE WHOLE BODY.

FEATURES

WIDE FOREHEAD, SMALL EYES, SLIM MUZZLE. CONCAVE FACIAL PROFILE. SMALL, ROUNDED EARS, OFTEN OBSCURED BY FUR, BUT MORE VISIBLE IN SPRING AND EARLY SUMMER AFTER MOLT. CHARACTERISTIC HUMP BETWEEN SHOULDERS. LONG FORECLAWS AND CURVED TAIL. SMELL IS MOST HIGHLY DEVELOPED SENSE, BUT HEARING IS ALSO QUITE ACUTE.

THE LIPS

are quite separate from the gums, as in all bears, rendering them highly mobile.

THE FUR

varies in color but is longer and more shaggy than that of the American black bear, particularly before the spring molt. The long guard hairs on the back and shoulders of the grizzly are frosted with white at the tips, giving it the "grizzled" look that earns the bear its name.

THE LIMBS

are stocky and immensely strong. Usually the bear walks in a slow, ambling gait on all fours, but it can move at a fast, if somewhat cumbersome, gallop when necessary.

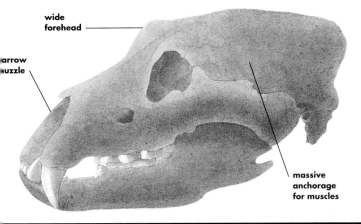

WHO'S GOT THE HUMP?
Silhouettes of the grizzly (left) and American black bear (right) reveal the grizzly's distinguishing dorsal hump.

Illustrations Steve Kingston

SKULL

All bears have long skulls when compared, for example, with cats. Bears need the extra room to accommodate grinding teeth (molars) for processing their broad diet, whereas cats, being wholly flesh-eaters, need only a few slicing teeth. To support the grinding process, a bear's skull has a heavy build on which to anchor the jaw-closing muscles.

wide forehead

narrow muzzle

massive anchorage for muscles

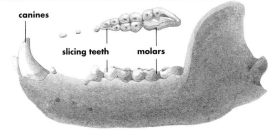

canines

slicing teeth   molars

JAWBONE
The brown bear's jawbone is heavy and powerful. Its teeth, in particular the flat-crowned molars, reflect its omnivorous diet. Its impressive upper and lower canines are used occasionally to bite and kill prey, but serve mainly in threat displays.

HAMSTER

The smallest hamster is the Dzungarian dwarf hamster at 2–4 in (5.1–10.2 cm). The largest is the common or black-bellied hamster (above left) at 7.8–11 in (20–28 cm). Dormice (above center) range in size from 2.5 in (6.4 cm) to 7.5 in (19 cm). They are compared with a house mouse (above right).

FOOT PATTERNS

Hamsters and dormice have four digits on the front feet and five on the back. In both species the front paws are extremely dexterous.

OTHER FOOT PATTERNS

Some rodents have four digits on both front and back feet. These include rock rats and gundis.

Hands & feet illustration Elisabeth Smith

EYES

Although hamsters have large eyes, their eyesight is poor. They are burrowers that spend most of the day underground where they rely more on their keen sense of smell.

PAWS AND CLAWS

The paws of the front legs are modified hands, giving greater dexterity in the manipulation of food. Hamsters use a characteristic squeezing movement when emptying their pouches.

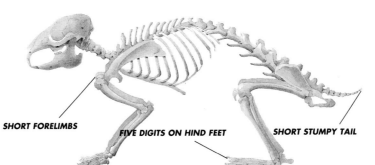

Main illustration & sizes Simon Turvey/Wildlife Art Agency

X

R A Y

THE HAMSTER SKELETON

The skeleton of the hamster shows a thick-set body and strong hind leg bones, which support the hamster when sitting up during feeding. The shorter forelimbs facilitate burrowing, foraging, and climbing.

SHORT FORELIMBS

FIVE DIGITS ON HIND FEET

SHORT STUMPY TAIL

Molar teeth have protuberances that always occur in two parallel, longitudinal lines.

X-ray illustrations Elisabeth Smith

EARS

Hamsters have acute hearing and communicate with ultrasounds as well as with squeaks audible to the human ear.

SCENT GLANDS

Territories are marked with secretions from scent glands. Hamsters also rely on scent to tell them when the females are in heat.

TAIL

The tail is short, or no more than a stump. This suits the hamster's burrowing lifestyle. A long, bushy tail would attract damp soil.

COMMON HAMSTER

LOCATION: CENTRAL EUROPE & RUSSIA

CLASSIFICATION

GENUS: *CRICETUS*

SPECIES: *CRICETUS*

SIZE

HEAD AND BODY: **8–13** IN **(20–33** CM**)**

TAIL: **1.5–2.4** IN **(3.8–6.1** CM**)**

WEIGHT: **4–32** OZ **(113–907** G**)**

WEIGHT AT BIRTH: **0.3** OZ **(8.5** G**)**

COLORATION

REDDISH- AND YELLOW-COLORED FUR WITH A BLACK UNDERBELLY. USUALLY HAS WHITE ON SIDES, MUZZLE, AND PAWS

FEATURES

BRIGHT, BEADY EYES

SMALL, ROUNDED, FUR-COVERED EARS

COMMON DORMOUSE

CLASSIFICATION

GENUS: *MUSCARDINUS*

SPECIES: *AVELLANARIUS*

SIZE

HEAD AND BODY: **2.4–3.5** IN **(6–9** CM**)**

TAIL: **2–3** IN **(5.1–7.6** CM**)**

WEIGHT: **0.5–1.5** OZ **(14.2–42.5** G**)**

WEIGHT AT BIRTH: **0.4–0.5** OZ **(11.3–14.2** G**)**

COLORATION

RICH, GOLDEN-COLORED COAT ON BACK. THE THROAT AND CHEST ARE CREAMY WHITE AND ITS BELLY IS PINKISH BUFF

FEATURES

BRIGHT, BEADY, BLACK EYES

SMALL, ROUNDED EARS

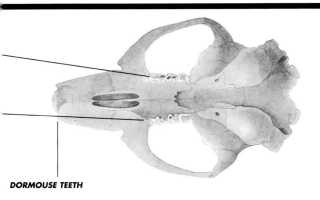

DORMOUSE TEETH

Hamsters have developed very strong jaws because much of their diet consists of nuts and seeds that have to be cracked open. This also equips them with a fierce bite for use in aggressive confrontations. Prominent incisors and premolars extend along the outside of the lower jaw.

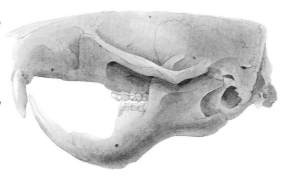

UPPER AND LOWER JAWS OF A HAMSTER

H E D G E H O G

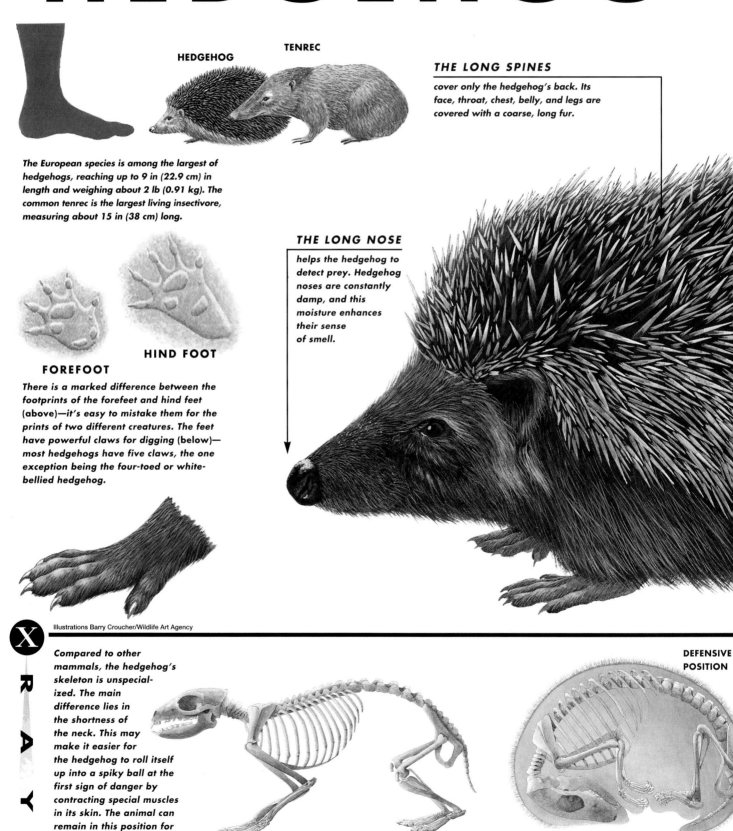

HEDGEHOG   **TENREC**

The European species is among the largest of hedgehogs, reaching up to 9 in (22.9 cm) in length and weighing about 2 lb (0.91 kg). The common tenrec is the largest living insectivore, measuring about 15 in (38 cm) long.

HIND FOOT

FOREFOOT

There is a marked difference between the footprints of the forefeet and hind feet (above)—it's easy to mistake them for the prints of two different creatures. The feet have powerful claws for digging (below)—most hedgehogs have five claws, the one exception being the four-toed or white-bellied hedgehog.

THE LONG SPINES

cover only the hedgehog's back. Its face, throat, chest, belly, and legs are covered with a coarse, long fur.

THE LONG NOSE

helps the hedgehog to detect prey. Hedgehog noses are constantly damp, and this moisture enhances their sense of smell.

Illustrations Barry Croucher/Wildlife Art Agency

X R A Y

Compared to other mammals, the hedgehog's skeleton is unspecialized. The main difference lies in the shortness of the neck. This may make it easier for the hedgehog to roll itself up into a spiky ball at the first sign of danger by contracting special muscles in its skin. The animal can remain in this position for hours, if necessary.

DEFENSIVE POSITION

X-ray illustrations Elisabeth Smith

EUROPEAN HEDGEHOG

LOCATION: WEST & NORTH EUROPE,
& NEW ZEALAND

CLASSIFICATION

GENUS: *ERINACEOUS*

SPECIES: *EUROPAEUS*

SIZE

HEAD–BODY LENGTH: 9 IN (22.9 CM)

WEIGHT: 3 LB (1.4 KG)

TAIL LENGTH: 0.75 IN (2 CM)

SPINE LENGTH: 1 IN (2–3 CM)

WEIGHT AT BIRTH: 1 OZ (28 G)

A HEDGEHOG MAY DOUBLE ITS WEIGHT AS IT LAYS

DOWN FAT IN PREPARATION FOR HIBERNATION

COLORATION

PALE TO DARK BROWN UNDERNEATH, WITH SPINES THAT
ARE SHADED WHITE TO BROWN. NEWBORNS HAVE WHITE
SPINES THAT SOON TURN BROWN

FEATURES

SMALL EARS

LARGE, BRIGHT DARK BROWN OR BLACK EYES THAT
PROTRUDE SLIGHTLY

LONG LEGS

SHORT, SPINELESS TAIL

**CROSS SECTION
THROUGH SKIN**

neck of spine

Each spine has its narrowest section—or "neck"—just above the point at which it ends, in a bulb shape, buried in the skin (right). If the hedgehog falls or is hit by something, the spine necks bend and thus absorb the force of the blow.

The spines (left), which are hollow and made of modified hair, measure about 1 in (25 mm) long. Some hedgehogs have as many as 7,000.

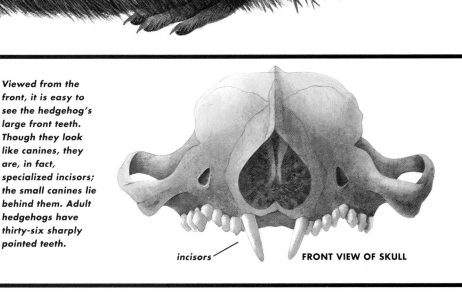

Viewed from the front, it is easy to see the hedgehog's large front teeth. Though they look like canines, they are, in fact, specialized incisors; the small canines lie behind them. Adult hedgehogs have thirty-six sharply pointed teeth.

incisors

FRONT VIEW OF SKULL

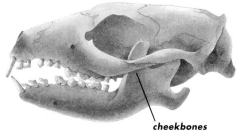

SIDE VIEW OF SKULL

cheekbones

Hedgehogs, like other insectivores, have elongated, flattened skulls with small braincases. Unlike the shrews and moles, though, hedgehogs have fully formed cheekbones.

HIPPOPOTAMUS

The pygmy hippo is roughly the size and shape of a prize pig; it may reach a length of 5.7 ft (1.75 m), stand up to 3.3 ft (1 m) at the shoulder, and weigh up to 600 lb (275 kg). The hippo is closer in length and weight to a small truck (see Fact File): An adult bull may weigh over three tons. Female hippos are smaller than the males.

THE SKIN

in both species is protected from infection and sunburn by the secretion of a pink, viscous fluid that hardens to a lacquer when exposed to the air. The outer skin is thin and loses moisture rapidly when not immersed in water.

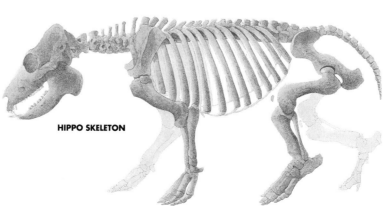

FEET

On both species, each foot has four spreading, conical toes connected by small webs. A pad of tissue on the heel helps to brace the structure. The pygmy hippo's toes are smaller and more slender than those of its relative. The feet suit soft soil or mud and are not very useful for walking great distances on firm ground.

PYGMY HIPPO

HIPPO

THE EARS

constantly waggle to flick away flies. The hippo can tuck them down to keep water out when submerged.

THE EYES

give good vision both in and out of the water. Night vision is adequate. Placed high on the skull, the eyes act as "periscopes" when the hippo's torso is immersed.

X
R
A
Y

The sturdy spine and stout legs form a crude arch, which supports the immense weight of the body. The neck vertebrae take the tension produced by the weight of the head; the spinal/cranial link in particular is heavily reinforced. The hippo's bulk obliges it to take the weight off its feet regularly—either by immersion or by lying prone.

HIPPO SKELETON

The hippo's dentition is dominated by the curving, tusklike lower canines, which can grow up to 20 in (50 cm) in length. They grow constantly, but their tips are honed by constant jawing. Of the four incisors in the lower jaw, the inner pair are particularly long and peglike. The canines and incisors are smaller in the upper jaw. The molars are simple and low-crowned, for grinding food.

X-ray illustrations Elisabeth Smith

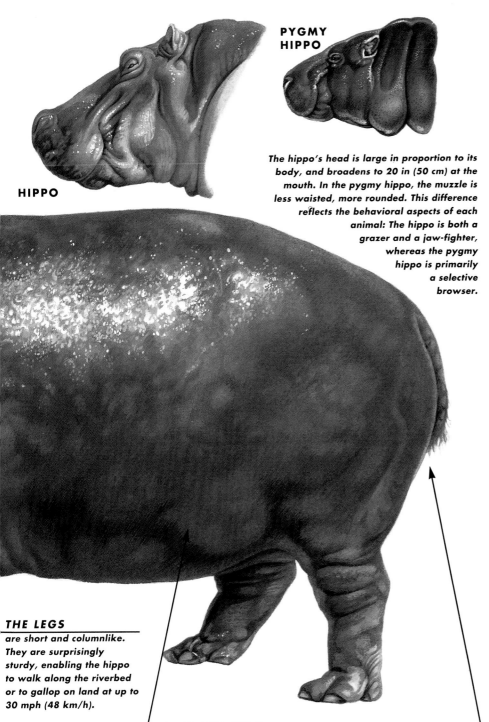

PYGMY HIPPO

HIPPO

The hippo's head is large in proportion to its body, and broadens to 20 in (50 cm) at the mouth. In the pygmy hippo, the muzzle is less waisted, more rounded. This difference reflects the behavioral aspects of each animal: The hippo is both a grazer and a jaw-fighter, whereas the pygmy hippo is primarily a selective browser.

HIPPOPOTAMUS
LOCATION: AFRICA (SOUTH OF THE SAHARA)

CLASSIFICATION

GENUS: *HIPPOPOTAMUS*

SPECIES: *AMPHIBIUS*

SIZE

HEAD–BODY LENGTH/MALE: 10–16.4 FT (3–5 M)

HEAD–BODY LENGTH/FEMALE: 9.5–14 FT (2.9–4.3 M)

TAIL LENGTH: 15 IN (40 CM)

SHOULDER HEIGHT: 4.9–5.4 FT (150–165 CM)

WEIGHT/MALE: 1,100–7,000 LB (500–3,200 KG)

AVERAGE: 3,250 LB (1,475 KG)

WEIGHT/FEMALE: 1,450–5,170 LB (650–2,350 KG)

AVERAGE: 3,000 LB (1,360 KG)

COLORATION

PURPLE-GRAY TO BLUE-BLACK ABOVE, BROWNISH PINK BELOW AND AROUND EYES AND EARS. OCCASIONALLY PARTIAL ALBINO (BRIGHT PINK WITH LIVER BLOTCHES). FACIAL PIGMENTATION MAY VARY AMONG INDIVIDUALS

FEATURES

MASSIVE, BARREL-LIKE TRUNK, HAIRLESS AND OFTEN HEAVILY SCARRED FROM FIGHTS

SHORT LEGS WITH SPREADING, FOUR-TOED FEET

STUMPY, ALMOST HAIRLESS TAIL

LARGE, HOURGLASS HEAD WITH WIDE, FLESHY SNOUT

EYES, EARS, AND NOSTRILS POSITIONED HIGH ON HEAD

DISTINCTIVE PINK SECRETION OVER HIDE, PARTICULARLY DURING TIMES OF HIGH EXCITEMENT

THE LEGS
are short and columnlike. They are surprisingly sturdy, enabling the hippo to walk along the riverbed or to gallop on land at up to 30 mph (48 km/h).

BODY AND HIDE
Characteristically barrel-shaped body. The hide is up to 2.5 in (6 cm) thick around the hindquarters but is much thinner around the forequarters.

THE TAIL
is short, stumpy, and almost hairless. The hippo wags it rapidly when defecating to scatter dung over a 6.5 ft (2 m) area.

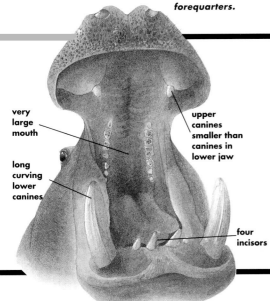

very large mouth

upper canines smaller than canines in lower jaw

long curving lower canines

four incisors

Although the braincase itself is small, the bony masses around the base of the skull are heavily reinforced. They are uniquely formed to make a sturdy lock with the first neck vertebra when the skull is fully raised, for example when the teeth are exposed in combat. The narrow "waist" of the skull accommodates the cheek teeth, while the front section is widened to hold the incisors and canines.

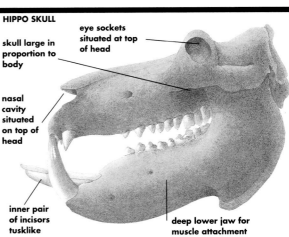

HIPPO SKULL

eye sockets situated at top of head

skull large in proportion to body

nasal cavity situated on top of head

inner pair of incisors tusklike

deep lower jaw for muscle attachment

HYENAS

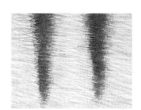

AARDWOLF COAT
The striped coat may have developed in mimicry of the bigger striped hyena, but it more probably represents a form of ancestral hyenid coat pattern.

MANE
Under threat, the thick mane of coarse hair can be bristled up to make the striped hyena seem much bigger and more dangerous than it actually is.

Hyenas range in size from the aardwolf, with a head-and-body length of 22–32 in (55–80 cm), to the spotted hyena, with a head-and-body length of 47–55 in (120–140 cm).

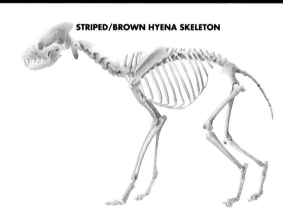

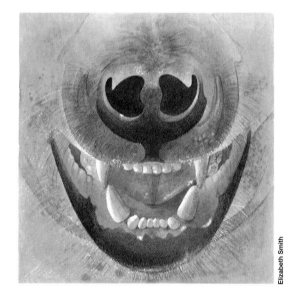

Elizabeth Smith

MUZZLE
The strong jaws have powerful muscles attached to a crest on top of the skull. These give the spotted hyena a bone-crushing biting pressure of 11,400 lb/sq in (800 kg/sq cm).

FEET
The strong feet have sturdy, nonretractile claws like those of a dog, adapted for running fast over grassland.

X
R
A
Y

Hyenas have long, powerful, mobile necks, massively developed forequarters and front limbs, sloping backs, and relatively lightly built hindquarters and hind limbs. The emphasis on the front end is reflected in their skeletons.

SPOTTED HYENA SKELETON

STRIPED/BROWN HYENA SKELETON

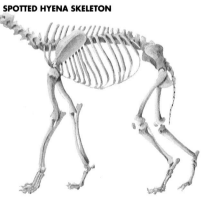

X-ray illustrations Elizabeth Smith

SPOTTED HYENA

LOCATION: AFRICA (SOUTH OF THE SAHARA)

STRIPED HYENA
In the striped hyena the black stripes on a background of gray or beige may have developed as a form of camouflage.

BROWN HYENA
The white mane of the brown hyena forms a striking contrast with the dark brown hair on its body. The coat is long and coarse.

SPOTTED HYENA
In the spotted hyena the striped coat pattern has become broken up into irregular spots of dark brown on a yellow-white background.

CLASSIFICATION
GENUS: *CROCUTA*
SPECIES: *CROCUTA*

SIZE
HEAD-BODY LENGTH: 4–4.5 FT (120–140 CM)
TAIL LENGTH: 9–12 IN (25–30 CM)
HEIGHT: 2.2–2.9 FT (70–90 CM)
WEIGHT: 110–175 LB (50–80 KG)
WEIGHT AT BIRTH: 3.5 LB (1.5 KG)
ON AVERAGE, FEMALES ARE 12 PERCENT HEAVIER THAN MALES

COLORATION
GRAYISH YELLOW WITH IRREGULAR DARK BROWN SPOTS ON THE BODY. MUZZLE, LOWER LIMBS, AND TAIL BRUSH DARKER
CUBS: DARK GRAYISH BROWN

FEATURES
POWERFUL BUILD, ESPECIALLY FOREQUARTERS
LONG NECK AND SLOPING BACK
HEAVY MUZZLE WITH MASSIVE TEETH
GENITALS OF FEMALE RESEMBLE THOSE OF MALE

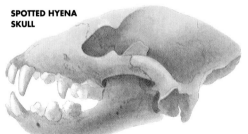

↑ UNDERBELLY
A hyenid's stomach is very efficient. Scavenging hyenas can digest bones and teeth, and the aardwolf can neutralize the poisonous secretions that make its termite prey inedible to most animals.

THE TAIL ←
Hyena tails are medium length and bushy (less so in the spotted hyena). The tail hides the anal pouch that lies between the tail and the rectum.

Anatomy illustrations Guy Troughton

SPOTTED HYENA SKULL

The spotted hyena has an immensely strong skull and jaw; long canines at the front of its mouth are used for ripping and killing, while massive bone-crushing premolars and scissorlike carnassials at the back slice through hide and flesh.

STRIPED HYENA SKULL

The striped hyena has a less massive jaw and a shallower skull crest than the spotted hyena. The premolars and carnassials are adapted for bone cracking, so it is less well equipped for shearing the flesh of live prey.

AARDWOLF SKULL

The termite-eating aardwolf has retained its long canine teeth for fighting, but its redundant cheek teeth have become mere pegs. It uses its lower front incisors as a spade for digging termites out of the earth.

IBEX

Goat antelope range in size from the Arabian tahr (above right), which often measures less than 40 in (100 cm) from head to tail, to the musk ox (above left), which can reach a length of almost 8 ft (240 cm).

THE HORNS

are the showpieces of the male ibex. Extravagantly long, they are used in ceremonial combat with other males, usually during the breeding season. Those of the female are far shorter and lack the frontal ridges.

DEWCLAW RAISED

Caprines are even-toed ungulates, a reference to the number of digits on each foot. Evolutionary reduction in the number of toes has left only two—the third and fourth—comprising a "cloven hoof." Many, such as the ibex, retain toes at the back of the foot called dewclaws. On level, easy terrain, the ibex holds its dewclaws aloft, but on slippery slopes it drops these natural crampons to the ground for extra grip.

DEWCLAW LOWERED

DEWCLAW

THE BEARD

may be barely noticeable in the Alpine ibex; it rarely grows longer than 2.5–3 in (6–7 cm). In the Ethiopian ibex, however, the beard may be more than twice this length.

FORELEGS

Like the hind legs, these are sturdy enough to absorb the repeated shocks sustained on the rocky crags. Permanent knee calluses are a feature of many caprines.

SKELETON

Strong leg bones support a stout, stocky body. Surefootedness and a low center of gravity combine to give the ibex an advantage in its mountain habitat.

HOOVES

The second and fifth digits of the hooves are made of rough, rounded horns that are detached from the cannon bone at the base of the leg. "Shod" with rubbery soles, these dewclaws help the ibex gain footholds on steep mountain slopes.

short tail

stout neck

sturdy legs

FOREFOOT

tibia

cannon bone

HIND FOOT

dewclaw

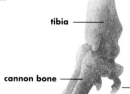

MARKHOR **SAIGA** **BIGHORN**

Horns vary widely among caprines. Resource defenders such as gorals, serows, and saigas have short, sharp horns for piercing attackers. Females usually have similar horns. Elaborate display horns such as those of the markhor or argalis are designed more for dominance rituals between males, although those of the American bighorn can inflict fatal injuries. Female bighorns have very short horns.

ALPINE IBEX
LOCATION: ALPS OF CENTRAL EUROPE

CLASSIFICATION

GENUS: *CAPRA*

SPECIES: *IBEX*

SIZE

HEAD-BODY LENGTH: 2.5–5.6 FT (75–170 CM)

TAIL LENGTH: 6–11.5 IN (15–29 CM)

SHOULDER HEIGHT: 2.3–3.1 FT (70–94 CM)

WEIGHT: 88–264 LB (40–120 KG)

WEIGHT AT BIRTH: 4.4–7.7 LB (2–3.5 KG)

HORN LENGTH/MALE: 40 IN (100 CM)

HORN LENGTH/FEMALE: 14 IN (35 CM)

THE MALE IS MARKEDLY LARGER THAN THE FEMALE

COLORATION

FEMALES AND VERY YOUNG MALES ARE A MID-OCHRE-BROWN. IN SUMMER, ADULT MALES ARE AN OCHRE-TAN OVERALL WITH PALER NECK, FOREHEAD, AND FLANKS, DARK LEGS, AND WHITE BELLY AND TAIL

IN LATE SUMMER, ADOLESCENT MALES DARKEN, WHILE OLDER MALES TURN GRAY

THE COAT FADES DURING WINTER, REPLACED WITH A NEW "SUMMER" GROWTH IN SPRING

FEATURES

STOCKY BODY

BROAD HOOVES WITH RUBBERY SOLES

HORNS OF MALE ARE SCIMITAR-SHAPED AND LONG; FEMALE HAS SMALLER, THINNER HORNS

SHORT BEARD IN MALE ONLY

THE COAT,

like the horns, is more spectacular in the male. It is molted in spring and replaced each year. In autumn and winter, the coat is thickened with extra woolly underhairs and long guard hairs.

THE LIMBS

of all caprid mountain goats are characteristically sturdy and powerful. The typical "mountaineering" technique involves thrusting strongly from one rock face to the other, relying on the keen edges of the hooves to find a grip. During the breeding season, rival male ibex rear up on their hind legs in display.

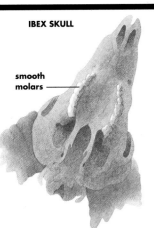

IBEX SKULL

smooth molars

TEETH
The array of teeth sheds light on the feeding habits of wild goats, and of most goat antelope. The upper canines are absent and molar surfaces are smooth, indicating a diet weighted predominantly toward tough, fibrous plant material.

upper canines absent

HORNS
Male wild goats have much longer horns than females. These horns are curved sharply backward, with sharp edges to the front. Ridges commonly form on the horns, appearing at irregular intervals. Horns differ from antlers in that they have a permanent bony core encased in a hardened sheath, whereas antlers are fully shed.

JAGUAR

Despite their stocky build and great physical strength, jaguars may be smaller than other, less powerful cats, such as the leopard.

CAMOUFLAGE

The irregular pattern of dark spots and blotches on the jaguar's coat serve as camouflage on the forest floor, breaking up the animal's outline as it stalks its prey through sun-dappled vegetation and shade.

THE EARS

are rounded and fully furred inside and out. As in all cats, they are highly mobile and sensitive to the slightest sound.

THE JAWS

have such powerful biting muscles, and are armed with such stout, pointed canine teeth, that the jaguar is said to possess the most lethal bite of any big cat.

SMALL CATS

PANTHERINE CATS

NOSES

In small cats, the fleshy speculum between the nostrils is proportionately wider, and the nostrils tend to be more rounded, than those of the pantherine cats. In big cats like the jaguar, moreover, the coat of hair on the face extends farther forward—as far as the front edge of the nose.

THE CLAWS

are long, curved, and retractile, enabling the jaguar to climb well and to bring down large prey.

X RAY

SKELETON

Power and flexibility are the hallmarks of the jaguar's build. Robust limbs and highly developed muscles enable the animal to unleash explosive attacks and pin down victims, while its flexible torso helps it grapple with large prey, as well as climb, leap, run, and swim.

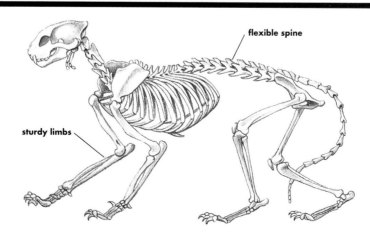

flexible spine

sturdy limbs

CANINES

The massive, curved canine teeth (see right) of the jaguar are not used for eating but for killing. The jaguar uses them first to grasp prey and then to deliver a lethal bite that crushes the windpipe, severs the spine at the neck, or even punctures through an animal's skull—a technique used particularly often by jaguars.

Skull illustrations Elisabeth Smith. Full skeleton Sean Milne

EYES

The forward-facing eyes of cats give excellent binocular vision. They function well by both day and night, owing to a highly sensitive retina at the back of each eye. At night a cat's pupils open wide, almost to the edges of the large iris, to gather as much light as possible (left). In brighter conditions, the pupils contract to prevent glare, becoming narrow slits in small cats (center) or circular dots in pantherine cats such as the jaguar (right).

JAGUAR

LOCATION: SOUTH & CENTRAL AMERICA

CLASSIFICATION

GENUS: *PANTHERA*

SPECIES: *ONCA*

SIZE

HEAD–BODY LENGTH: **43–72** IN (**110–185** CM)

TAIL LENGTH: **18–30** IN (**45–75** CM)

WEIGHT/MALE: **120–265** LB (**55–120** KG)

WEIGHT/FEMALE: **77–200** LB (**35–90** KG)

WEIGHT AT BIRTH: **1.5–2** LB (**700–900** G)

COLORATION

BACKGROUND COLOR OF YELLOWISH TO REDDISH BROWN WITH WHITISH UNDERSIDES

IRREGULAR DARK SPOTS AND BLOTCHES ALL OVER BODY, TYPICALLY FORMING LARGE ROSETTE SHAPES ENCLOSING DARK DOTS

FEATURES

ROBUST HEAD AND BODY

FORWARD-FACING EYES

LARGE CANINE AND CARNASSIAL TEETH

BROAD PAWS WITH SHARP, RETRACTILE CLAWS

PROPORTIONS

Along with the clouded leopard, the jaguar has the shortest forelegs, in proportion to its spinal column, of any big cat. This compact form suits it to life in the trees. The leggy cheetah, by contrast, is built for speed over the open savanna.

THE TAIL

provides the jaguar with extra balance when clambering among the branches.

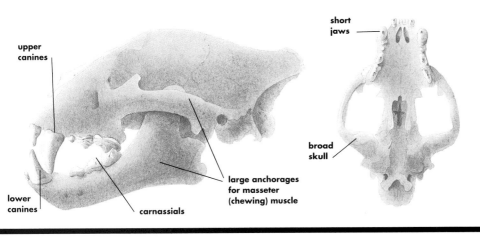

SKULL

The skull is particularly rounded and broad, providing for powerful jaw muscles. Because cats have short muzzles, they can deliver greater force in the bite. To allow for a shortened jaw they have lost their rear molar teeth, but the cheek teeth that exist are modified into bladelike carnassials for shearing flesh into manageable strips.

upper canines

lower canines

carnassials

large anchorages for masseter (chewing) muscle

short jaws

broad skull

Main illustration Kim Thompson

KANGAROO

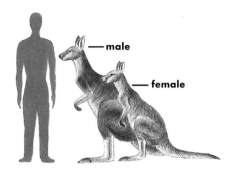

— male
— female

At two years of age, male red kangaroos are up to 50 percent bigger than the females of the species. In Australia, adult male kangaroos are commonly called "boomers," while young females are referred to as "blue fliers."

WALLAROO

RED KANGAROO

GRAY KANGAROO

The nose area of the red kangaroo is quite distinctive—the bare black area is larger than that of a gray but smaller than that of a wallaroo. The gray has a hairier muzzle.

THE EARS

The size, shape, and flexibility of the ears help pick up faint or distant sounds such as the approach of an enemy.

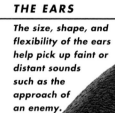

THE NOSE

A keen sense of smell is very important to the nocturnal kangaroo. Urine, feces, and secretions from glands are used to mark important sites.

THE FOREARMS

are much smaller than the hind limbs. They have five digits, and are used almost like human arms.

Illustrations Barry Croucher/Wildlife Art Agency

X

R A Y

The stance of the kangaroo is upright, so the skeleton is "bottom heavy" for stability; there are strong bones in the long, thick tail—which acts as a fifth leg for balancing—and in the large hind limbs that are used for leaping.

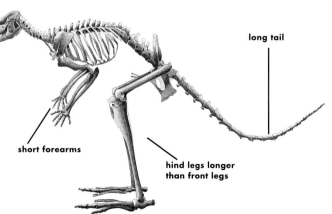

long tail

short forearms

hind legs longer than front legs

The pelvic bone of the female features two protrusions that act as support for the pouch. This avoids unnecessary strain on her spine when she is carrying her infant or joey in her pouch.

X-ray illustrations Elisabeth Smith

kangaroo foot, from below

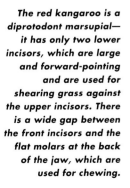

The feet are long and narrow, and their size gives stability to the upright kangaroo. They act like springs as the animal bounds, and are useful to males in trials of strength.

RED KANGAROO

CLASSIFICATION

GENUS: *MACROPUS*

SPECIES: *RUFUS*

SIZE

HEAD–BODY LENGTH/MALE: 65 IN (165 CM)

TAIL LENGTH/MALE: 42 IN (107 CM)

WEIGHT/MALE: 200 LB (90 KG)

WEIGHT AT BIRTH: LESS THAN 0.03 OZ (1 GRAM)

ADULT FEMALES ARE ABOUT 50 PERCENT SMALLER THAN ADULT MALES

COLORATION

MALES RUSSET TO BRICK RED ON BACK; PALER ON THE THROAT, BELLY, AND LIMBS; FEMALES AND YOUNG BLUISH GRAY

FEATURES

UPRIGHT STANCE

LARGE, POINTED EARS

SHORT FOREARMS

VERY LARGE, POWERFUL HIND LEGS

FEMALES HAVE POUCH IN WHICH TO CARRY YOUNG

THE TAIL

is thick and muscular. Outstretched, it acts as a counterbalance when the animal is running and as a stabilizer or third leg when it is grazing.

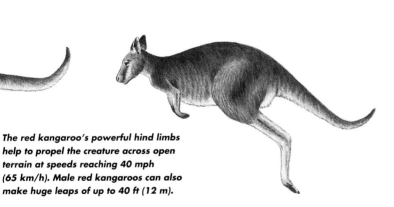

The red kangaroo's powerful hind limbs help to propel the creature across open terrain at speeds reaching 40 mph (65 km/h). Male red kangaroos can also make huge leaps of up to 40 ft (12 m).

The red kangaroo is a diprotodont marsupial—it has only two lower incisors, which are large and forward-pointing and are used for shearing grass against the upper incisors. There is a wide gap between the front incisors and the flat molars at the back of the jaw, which are used for chewing.

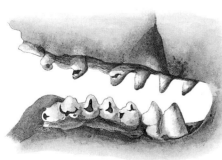

The skull of the red kangaroo is quite small in relation to its body size. The muzzle is long and narrow, and the face quite large, though the braincase is relatively small.

premolars   molars

KILLER WHALE

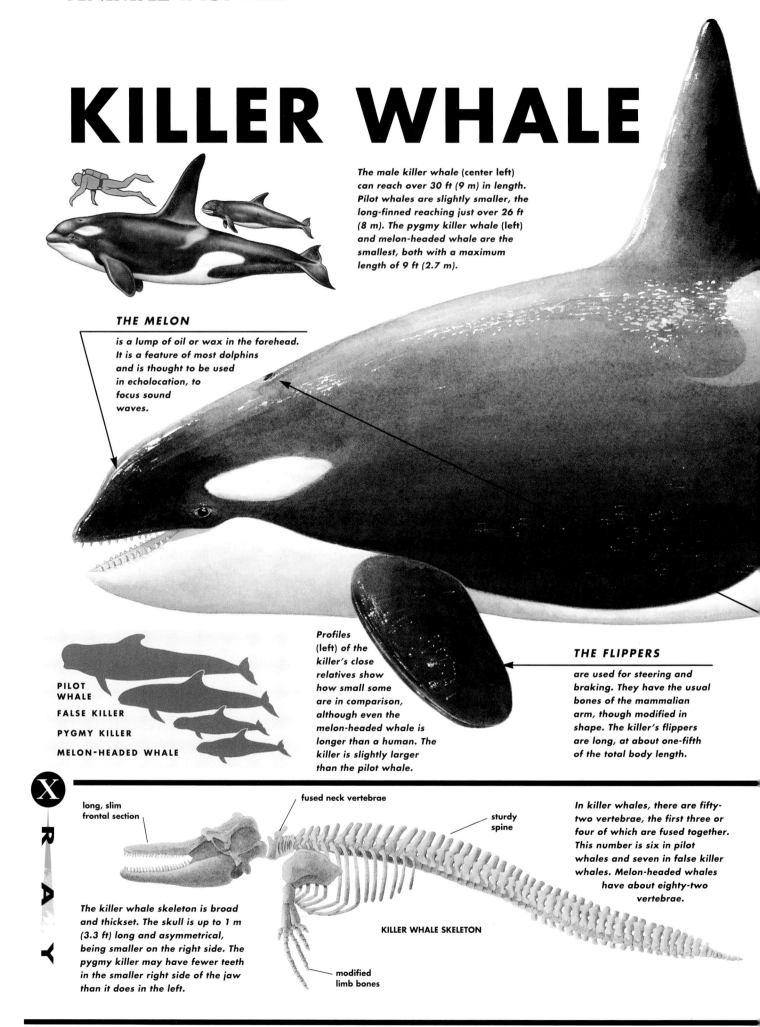

The male killer whale (center left) can reach over 30 ft (9 m) in length. Pilot whales are slightly smaller, the long-finned reaching just over 26 ft (8 m). The pygmy killer whale (left) and melon-headed whale are the smallest, both with a maximum length of 9 ft (2.7 m).

THE MELON

is a lump of oil or wax in the forehead. It is a feature of most dolphins and is thought to be used in echolocation, to focus sound waves.

PILOT WHALE

FALSE KILLER

PYGMY KILLER

MELON-HEADED WHALE

Profiles (left) of the killer's close relatives show how small some are in comparison, although even the melon-headed whale is longer than a human. The killer is slightly larger than the pilot whale.

THE FLIPPERS

are used for steering and braking. They have the usual bones of the mammalian arm, though modified in shape. The killer's flippers are long, at about one-fifth of the total body length.

X

R A Y

long, slim frontal section

fused neck vertebrae

sturdy spine

The killer whale skeleton is broad and thickset. The skull is up to 1 m (3.3 ft) long and asymmetrical, being smaller on the right side. The pygmy killer may have fewer teeth in the smaller right side of the jaw than it does in the left.

KILLER WHALE SKELETON

modified limb bones

In killer whales, there are fifty-two vertebrae, the first three or four of which are fused together. This number is six in pilot whales and seven in false killer whales. Melon-headed whales have about eighty-two vertebrae.

All illustrations Elisabeth Smith except silhouettes and dorsal fins by Steve Kingston

DORSAL FINS

KILLER WHALE | FALSE KILLER WHALE | PYGMY KILLER WHALE | MELON-HEADED WHALE | LONG-FINNED PILOT WHALE | SHORT-FINNED PILOT WHALE

The killer's dorsal fin is the largest and most upright of any dolphin or whale, up to 6.5 ft (2 m) tall in some

mature males. This has led to common names such as épée de mer ("sword of the sea") in

French and swaardvis ("swordfish") in Dutch. The female's fin is smaller and more curved.

KILLER WHALE

CLASSIFICATION

GENUS: *ORCINUS*

SPECIES: ORCA

SIZE

FULL LENGTH/MALE: 21–32 FT (6.5–9.8 M)

FULL LENGTH/FEMALE: 20–26 FT (6–8 M)

WEIGHT/MALE: 4–9 TONS

WEIGHT/FEMALE: 2.5–3.5 TONS

COLORATION

BLACK BACK, SIDES, DORSAL FIN, FLIPPERS, AND UPPER FLUKES; WHITE CHIN, THROAT, BELLY, AND UNDER-FLUKES. TWO WHITE LOBES ALONG THE LOWER FLANKS BEHIND THE DORSAL FIN, TWO WHITE OVAL FLASHES BEHIND AND SLIGHTLY ABOVE THE EYES (THESE VARY IN POSITION WITH THE GEOGRAPHICAL LOCATION), AND GRAY SADDLE BEHIND DORSAL FIN. OCCASIONALLY PURE BLACK ALL OVER, OR EVEN ALBINO WHITE

FEATURES

SLEEK, MUSCULAR, THICKSET SHAPE

BLUNTISH HEAD WITH PROTRUDING FOREHEAD LUMP OR MELON

THE SADDLE

is a paler, grayish patch on the back just behind the dorsal fin.

THE BODY SHAPE

may not look very streamlined, but this natural torpedo is superbly designed for moving rapidly through the water.

THE BLOWHOLE

represents the nostrils, through which the whale breathes. The whale can expel stale air from its lungs and take in fresh air when almost all of its body is under water. Odontocetes have a single blowhole, while mysticetes have a double hole.

THE SKIN

is virtually hairless to improve streamlining. The insulating function of fur, to keep in body warmth, is taken over by a thick layer of fat, called blubber, underneath the skin.

THE FLUKES

are broad lobes filled with muscle and fibrous tissue. Powerful muscles pulling on the backbone swish the flukes up and down, to propel the whale. (Fishes' tails move from side to side.)

There are usually 11 teeth in each half of each jaw, though the number varies from 10 to 14. They are cone-shaped and pointed, oval in cross section, and angle back a little down the gullet. They interlock when the jaws close. The melon-headed whales have up to 100 teeth.

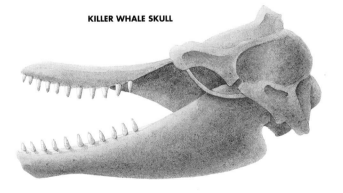

KILLER WHALE SKULL

Cross section of a whale tooth. From the lines on the tooth, scientists are able to tell the age of the animal.

KOALA

THE HEAD

is broad and large, with food-storing cheek pouches and big fluffy ears, but the koala's brain is relatively small.

In the south of their range, male koalas grow to an average head-body length of 31 in (78 cm); females grow to an average of 28 in (72 cm). Males average 26 lb (11.8 kg) while females average 17.4 lb (7.9 kg). Northern koalas are significantly smaller and lighter.

THE NOSE

is naked and leathery, and extremely sensitive. A koala can detect the type of eucalypt it prefers simply by sniffing the tree trunk at ground level.

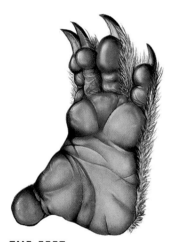

THE HANDS

each have "two thumbs" that act in opposition to the other fingers to give a secure grip on branches, reinforced by sharp, sturdy claws and granular, nonslip pads.

THE FEET

are big and strongly clawed, with granular, nonslip pads. The second and third toes are joined and the koala uses the twin claws as a grooming comb.

The massive skull is broad and flattened at the sides, with a shallow braincase and a deep, strong jaw. The front incisor teeth are separated from the grinding molars by a gap (diastema) that is used to form wads of foliage for chewing; the lower canines have been lost and the upper canines are much reduced.

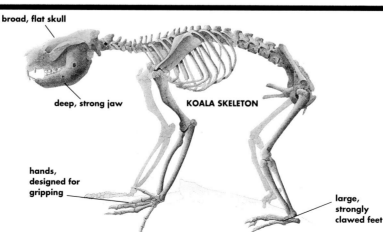

broad, flat skull

deep, strong jaw   KOALA SKELETON

hands, designed for gripping

large, strongly clawed feet

INCISOR TEETH

The koala, like the kangaroo and wallaby, is a diprotodont—a marsupial with only two incisor teeth in the lower jaw. These teeth grow forward from the jawbone to meet the upper incisors, forming a precision tool for cropping leaves or nibbling grass.

DIGESTIVE SYSTEM

The koala feeds on the leaves of various species of gum tree, or Eucalyptus. Eucalypt foliage is a poor-quality, unpalatable, and occasionally poisonous food. The koala has therefore developed a digestive system capable of neutralizing the less virulent toxins and converting the extremely tough plant fiber into useful nutrients.

enlarged cecum contains microflora to break down tough cellulose fiber

THE FUR

is dense and woolly, and for many decades the koala was hunted relentlessly for its pelt.

THE TAIL

has been reduced to little more than a stump, and is barely visible.

KOALA

CLASSIFICATION

GENUS: *PHASCOLARCTOS*

SPECIES: *CINEREUS*

SIZE

HEAD–BODY LENGTH: UP TO 33 IN (83 CM)

TAIL LENGTH: VESTIGIAL

AVERAGE WEIGHT/MALE: 26 LB (11.8 KG)

AVERAGE WEIGHT/FEMALE: 17.4 LB (7.9 KG)

WEIGHT AT BIRTH: 0.02 OZ (0.5 G)

IN THE NORTHERN PART OF THEIR RANGE KOALAS AVERAGE SOME 40 PERCENT LIGHTER THAN SOUTHERN INDIVIDUALS

COLORATION

GRAY TO TAWNY BROWN ABOVE, WITH WHITE FUR ON THE CHEST, CHIN, AND INNER SIDES OF THE FORELIMBS. THE EARS ARE ALSO FRINGED WITH WHITE. THE FUR OF NORTHERN KOALAS IS SHORTER AND PALER

FEATURES

TUBBY, BEARLIKE BUILD

BIG EARS AND LEATHERY NOSE

TWO "THUMBS" ON EACH BROAD, STRONGLY CLAWED HAND, AND PAIRED SECOND AND THIRD DIGITS ON EACH FOOT

VESTIGIAL TAIL

THE THIGH MUSCLES

are big and powerful, and anchored low down on the shin for maximum leverage. This reduces the koala's agility but makes it an excellent climber.

KOALA SKULL

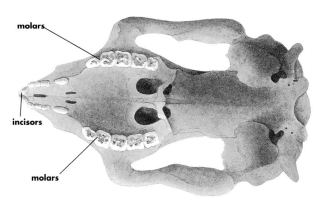

molars

incisors

molars

MOLAR TEETH
The molars or cheek teeth have broad, grinding surfaces with crescent-shaped ridges for reducing tough, fibrous eucalypt foliage to a pulp.

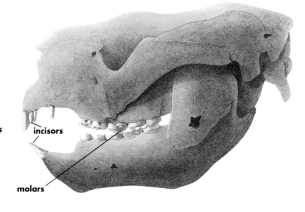

incisors

molars

Main illustration Kim Thompson

LEMMING

Most species have a head-and-body length of 4–4.5 in (10–11 cm), with a tail around 1.2–1.6 in (3–4 cm) long. These are typified by the Norway lemming (far left) and bank vole (left). Largest of the subfamily is the muskrat, which grows to the size of a small rabbit.

THE EARS

are barely visible among the thick fur, yet, are extremely sensitive to sound.

BODY SHAPE

is crucial to a lemming's survival. The stocky, compact, blunt-headed build of the Norway lemming minimizes the animal's surface area, helping it retain body heat in the cold tundra climate.

Collared lemmings have specialized forefeet for burrowing in snow. The claws on the third and fourth toes are enlarged and become double-pointed in winter as an adaptation to breaking through hard snow— a feature unique among rodents.

NORMAL CLAWS

WINTER CLAWS

THE FOREFEET

are used for burrowing through snow. The claw on the first digit is broad and flattened to aid digging.

SKELETON
The skeleton of the Norway lemming reveals the animal's compact, stocky body shape, along with the shortness of the limb bones. Short legs make crawling through tight burrows easier, as well as further reducing the animal's surface area to improve heat retention.

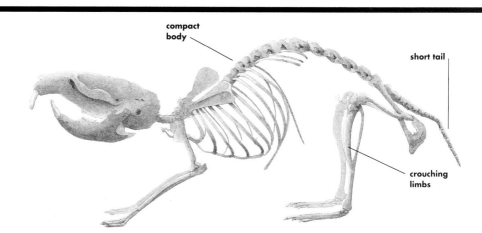

compact body

short tail

crouching limbs

X-ray illustrations Elisabeth Smith

NORWAY LEMMING

LOCATION: SCANDINAVIA & LAPLAND TUNDRA

CLASSIFICATION

GENUS: *LEMMUS*

SPECIES: *LEMMUS*

SIZE

HEAD–BODY LENGTH: 5–6 IN (130–150 MM)

TAIL LENGTH: 0.5–0.8 IN (15–20 MM)

WEIGHT: 2–4 OZ (50–115 G)

WEIGHT AT BIRTH: 0.1–0.12 OZ (3–3.5 G)

COLORATION

VARIEGATED BLACK, YELLOWISH BROWN, AND BUFF ON THE UPPER BODY, MUCH PALER (OFTEN WHITE) ON THE UNDERSIDE

FEATURES

STOCKY, COMPACT SHAPE

BROAD, ROUNDED HEAD

EARS ALMOST HIDDEN BY FUR

MEDIUM-LENGTH WHISKERS

VERY SHORT TAIL

SHORT LEGS

THE FUR

of the Norway lemming is dense and long, providing excellent insulation. It is also waterproof, keeping moisture away from the skin even when the animal is burrowing in thick snow.

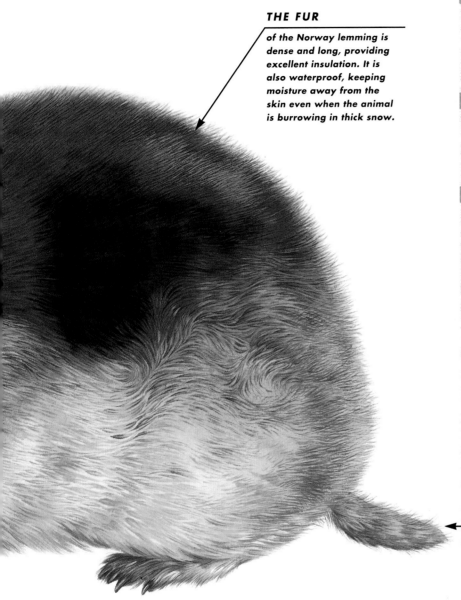

THE TAIL

is short and typical of burrowing animals. Like the ears and limbs, its small size helps reduce heat loss in cold climates.

SKULL

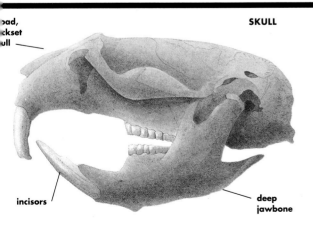

oad, ckset ull

incisors

deep jawbone

The Norway lemming has a short, thickset skull. The strong jawbones have large muscles to help the animal process tough plant matter.

TEETH
Lemmings and voles have twelve molar teeth, with flattened crowns for grinding food. The four incisors are used for cutting. Some voles have continuously growing molars that counteract the wear induced by eating coarse grasses.

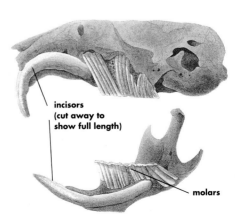

incisors (cut away to show full length)

molars

LEOPARD

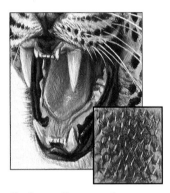

The snow leopard (above, center) is smaller than the leopard, measuring 39–51 in (100–130 cm), but its long fur makes it look the same size. The clouded leopard is the smallest, measuring 29–41 in (75–105 cm).

THE BACKS

of a leopard's ears are black around the edge with a white marking in the middle. According to some zoologists, this makes them easy for leopard cubs to focus on, enabling the cubs to follow their mother.

The leopard's tongue is covered with thousands of tiny, sharply pointed hairs, giving it a rough texture. The leopard uses its tongue not only to groom its fur but also to strip the fur off its kill before feeding.

RELATIVELY SHORT

but powerful legs end in feet with padded paws, which are very helpful for cushioning when the leopard leaps from tree branches.

Illustrations Mathew Hillier/Wildlife Art Agency

X RAY

The structure of the skeleton shows that a leopard relies on power to spring quickly. Its long, curved back and the position of its back leg joints allow it to leap and pounce.

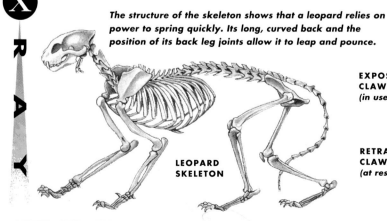

LEOPARD SKELETON

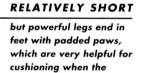

stretched ligament

EXPOSED CLAWS (in use)

contracted ligament

RETRACTED CLAWS (at rest)

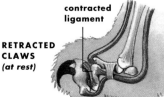
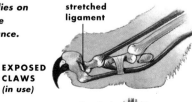

Leopards have very sharp claws, used for climbing trees and for slashing prey. If they were always exposed they would quickly wear down and lose their sharpness, so, when they are not in use, the leopard pulls them into its paws or "retracts" them by contracting a ligament. Then the claws lie hidden.

X-ray illustrations Sean Milne

LEOPARD

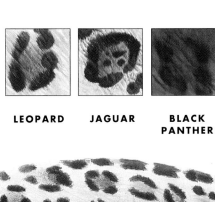

LEOPARD   JAGUAR   BLACK PANTHER

How to tell a leopard by its spots: Both the leopard and the jaguar have black spots or rosettes on lighter backgrounds, but the jaguar's rosettes often encircle one or more black spots, and its coat tends to be a rustier color. The black panther's fur, on the other hand, has black markings on a black background.

CLASSIFICATION

GENUS: *PANTHERA*

SPECIES: *PARDUS*

SIZE

HEAD–BODY LENGTH/MALE: **39-75** IN (100-190 CM)

SHOULDER HEIGHT/MALE: **18-31** IN (45–80 CM)

TAIL LENGTH/MALE: **28-39** IN (70-100 CM)

WEIGHT/MALE: **66-187** LB (30-85 KG)

WEIGHT AT BIRTH: **15-20** OZ (430-570 G)

ADULT MALES ARE ABOUT **30** PERCENT LARGER THAN FEMALES

COLORATION

BACKGROUND COLOR: HIGHLY VARIABLE, FROM SANDY YELLOW TO RUSTY ORANGE

SPOTS: BLACK, SOMETIMES CLUSTERED IN ROSETTES

CUBS: DARK WITH CLOSE-SET, INDISTINCT SPOTS

FEATURES

BLUE, GREEN, OR GOLDEN EYES

LONG, PALE WHISKERS

ROUND, HAIRY EARS

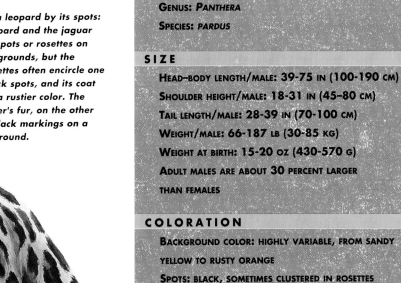

THE BELLY

and inside legs of a leopard are whitish or creamy yellow with some random spotting. Its stomach is able to expand to a huge degree to accommodate large amounts of food for when the leopard has just made a kill.

THE UPCURLED TAIL

is long and thick; it is used as a counterbalance when climbing. It has black rings along its length and a white tip, which acts as a "follow me" signal to cubs.

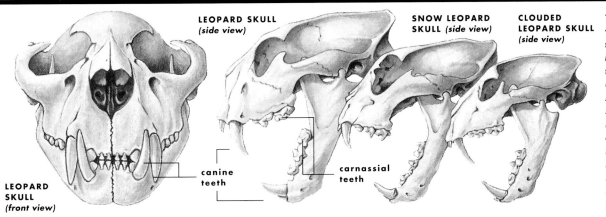

LEOPARD SKULL (side view)

SNOW LEOPARD SKULL (side view)

CLOUDED LEOPARD SKULL (side view)

LEOPARD SKULL (front view)

canine teeth

carnassial teeth

The skull of the leopard (front view) shows the forward-facing eyes, essential for binocular vision. The long front teeth, or canines, are used for stabbing prey. The snow leopard's skull is smaller than the leopard's, so its gape, or how wide its jaws open, is smaller; the clouded leopard's skull and gape are smaller still. Relative to the size of its skull, the clouded leopard has longer canines than any other cat.

LESSER GALAGO

The slow loris (below left) reaches 12 in (30 cm) from head to rump, with a 2 in (5 cm) tail. The Phillipine tarsier (below right) has a head-and-body length of 5 in (13 cm), with a tail up to 10 in (25 cm) long. The dwarf galago (below center) has similar proportions, but is a little smaller all around.

THE NOSE

is moist—tarsiers have a dry nose—and provides a keen sense of smell.

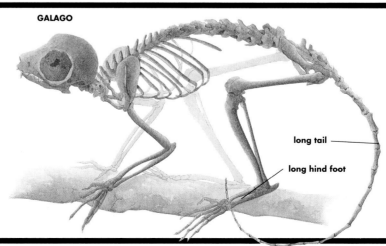

THE EARS

are large and batlike. The galago can retract these out of harm's way when subduing large, flapping insects. Folds within the ear improve sound orientation, making the ears exceptionally sensitive organs for tracking insects moving in the dark.

THE EYES

are huge, letting in plenty of light when necessary. They face forward, giving an excellent sense of distance. This helps galagos and tarsiers to judge leaps and bounds accurately, even in near-complete darkness.

GALAGO

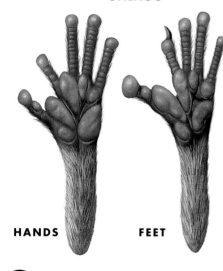

HANDS   **FEET**

Galagos, pottos, and lorises have large, opposable thumbs enabling them to grasp objects. Each digit of the hand and foot has a nail, except for the second toe which has a "toilet" claw used for grooming the head, neck, and ears—where the tooth-comb cannot reach. Flattened pads on the ends of the digits provide the animals with a delicate sense of touch.

SKELETON

The galago's skeleton clearly shows the longer length of the hind limbs, especially of the foot segment, giving the animal strong propulsion when leaping. The long tail is also important during leaps when it acts as a balancing device.

GALAGO

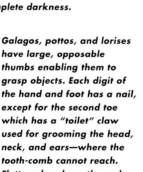

long tail

long hind foot

SKULLS

The skull of the galago has a fairly short snout and rounded braincase. The large eye sockets are ringed with a prominent ridge. The tarsier also has a short snout, and its eye sockets are extremely large, with pronounced rims and only a narrow ridge separating the two. Each enormous eye is similar in weight to the animal's brain.

X-ray illustrations Elisabeth Smith

HANDS   **FEET**

POTTO

The hands and feet of pottos and lorises can exert a firm grip on tree trunks, enabling them to creep slowly about the branches, or to remain stock-still in a posture for hours on end. Tarsiers differ from the lorisids in having two sets of grooming claws on their feet. They have long, slender fingers, which they can move independently.

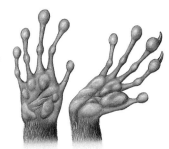

HANDS   **FEET**

TARSIER

LESSER GALAGO

LOCATION: WEST, CENTRAL & EAST AFRICA

CLASSIFICATION

GENUS: *GALAGO*

SPECIES: *SENEGALENSIS*

SIZE

HEAD-BODY LENGTH: 6.3–6.7 IN (16–17 CM)

TAIL LENGTH: 9–10 IN (23–25 CM)

WEIGHT: 5–7 OZ (150–200 G)

WEIGHT AT BIRTH: 0.4–0.5 OZ (12–15 G)

COLORATION

PALE GRAY TO BLUISH GRAY FUR, OFTEN BROWN OR YELLOW ON ARMS AND THIGHS

UNDERSIDE GENERALLY PALER

DARK PATCHES AROUND EYES AND WHITE BRIDGE OF NOSE

FEATURES

LARGE, ROUND EYES, FACING FORWARD AND SET CLOSE TOGETHER

PROMINENT BATLIKE EARS

ROUNDED HEAD AND SHORT SNOUT

LONG HIND LIMBS

LONG, BUSHY TAIL

THE FUR

is soft and thick, even woolly, and generally paler on the underside. Scent glands lie beneath the fur on the head and neck and around the sexual organs.

THE TAIL

is long and luxuriantly furred. It serves as a balancing device during leaps, but is not capable of grasping.

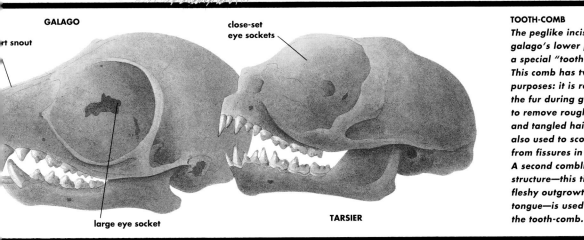

GALAGO

rt snout

close-set eye sockets

large eye socket

TARSIER

TOOTH-COMB
The peglike incisors in the galago's lower jaw form a special "tooth-comb." This comb has two purposes: it is raked over the fur during grooming to remove rough debris and tangled hair, and it is also used to scoop gum from fissures in tree bark. A second comblike structure—this time a fleshy outgrowth of the tongue—is used to clean the tooth-comb.

tooth-comb   canines

molars

Main illustration Steve Kingston

LION

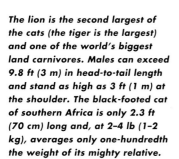

SHORT HEAD

The face is much shorter and rounder than that of a wolf, hyena, or other carnivore, a result of the reduction in the length of the nasal cavity and a shortening of the jaws.

MANE

The mane of the male lion serves a dual function. It makes the lion look bigger and more imposing to rival males, giving an illusion of great size without the drawback of an increase in weight. It also provides the throat with padding in the event of a fight.

The lion is the second largest of the cats (the tiger is the largest) and one of the world's biggest land carnivores. Males can exceed 9.8 ft (3 m) in head-to-tail length and stand as high as 3 ft (1 m) at the shoulder. The black-footed cat of southern Africa is only 2.3 ft (70 cm) long and, at 2–4 lb (1–2 kg), averages only one-hundredth the weight of its mighty relative.

SENSITIVE WHISKERS

help the lion find its way in dense cover or on moonless nights. Moving in for the kill, it spreads its whiskers like a living circular net, which helps it select the best spot to clamp its great jaws on its victim.

HEAD COMPARISON

In contrast to other cats—in which males and females, though differing in size, look very similar—adult male lions are easily distinguished from females because of their luxuriant manes.

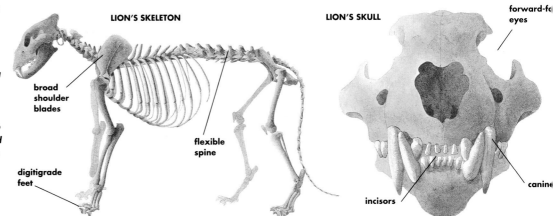

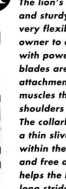

The lion's skeleton is strong and sturdy and its spine very flexible, enabling its owner to combine agility with power. The shoulder blades are broad, providing attachment for the great muscles that power the shoulders and forelimbs. The collarbone is reduced to a thin sliver of bone, lodged within the shoulder muscles and free at either end; this helps the lion achieve a long stride when running after its prey.

LION'S SKELETON

broad shoulder blades

digitigrade feet

flexible spine

LION'S SKULL

forward-fc eyes

incisors

canine

X-ray illustrations Elisabeth Smith

VIEW FROM OUTSIDE

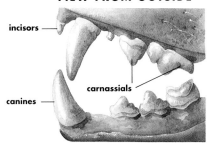

incisors

carnassials

canines

VIEW FROM INSIDE

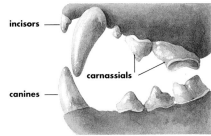

incisors

carnassials

canines

SCISSORLIKE TEETH

The lion uses its two pairs of greatly enlarged, cruelly pointed canine teeth to seize and throttle its prey. The small incisors, lying between the great canines, chop mouthfuls of flesh from the carcass. The molars and premolars are modified to form the carnassial teeth; their sharp cutting edges work against one another like shears to slice up prey.

LION

CLASSIFICATION

GENUS: *PANTHERA*

SPECIES: *LEO*

SIZE

HEAD–BODY LENGTH/MALE: 8–9 FT (2.4–3.3 M)

HEAD–BODY LENGTH/FEMALE: 7–8 FT (2.3–2.6 M)

SHOULDER HEIGHT/MALE: UP TO 4 FT (1.2 M)

SHOULDER HEIGHT/FEMALE: UP TO 3.6 FT (1.1 M)

WEIGHT/MALE: 330–550 LB (150–240 KG)

WEIGHT/FEMALE: 270–300 LB (120–180 KG)

WEIGHT AT BIRTH: 2–4 LB (1.1–2 KG)

COLORATION

TYPICALLY PALE SANDY OR TAWNY YELLOW, BUT VARYING FROM GRAYISH BUFF TO YELLOWISH RED AND DARK OCHER; WHITE AROUND MOUTH AND ON CHIN, UNDERPARTS, AND INNER SIDES OF LEGS MALE'S MANE DARK TAWNY, REDDISH BROWN, OR BLACK

FEATURES

TAIL, JUST OVER HALF THE LENGTH OF HEAD AND BODY, HAS LARGE TUFT OF LONG, BLACKISH HAIR AT TIP, WHICH CONCEALS A HORNY SPUR MANE OF HAIRS IN MALE ONLY, UP TO 6.3 IN (16 CM) LONG ON SIDES OF FACE AND TOP OF HEAD, EXTENDING ON TO SHOULDERS, AROUND NECK, AND SHORT WAY DOWN SPINE SHORT HAIR ON FACE, UPPER PARTS OF BODY, FLANKS, AND MOST OF TAIL; LONGER ON UNDERPARTS AND TAIL TIP LONG, WHITISH WHISKERS ARRANGED IN PARALLEL ROWS ON SIDES OF UPPER LIP. AMBER EYES AND BLACKISH NOSE; PROMINENT BLACK MARK AT BASE OF OUTSIDE OF ROUNDED EARS, USED IN VISUAL COMMUNICATION BETWEEN LIONS

HIND LIMBS

are sturdy and strongly muscled to provide power for the final sprint to catch prey and for leaping if necessary. A lion can run for short distances at about 40 mph (65 km/h) and leap up to 39 ft (12 m).

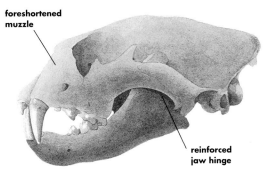

FORELIMBS

have powerfully developed muscles to enable the lion to knock down smaller prey with a single stroke and to seize and wrestle larger prey to the ground, where it can then give it a killing bite.

SKULL

The lion's skull is massive, thick, and heavy, weighing up to 6 lb (3 kg). There are deep ridges and hollows to provide attachment for the huge muscles that power the jaw. The temporal muscle, running from the lower jaw to a flange at the rear of the skull, enables the lion to exert tremendous force when clamping its jaws.

LION'S SKULL

foreshortened muzzle

reinforced jaw hinge

The outer bones of each toe, together with its claw, can be retracted into a fleshy sheath to create a padded paw for fast running (left). They are held in place by strong elastic ligaments. When the lion needs to extend its claws for attacking prey, in self-defense against a rival, or when climbing, flexor muscles straighten the outer toe bones so that the claws protrude (right).

MANATEE

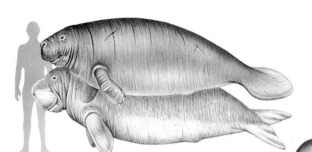

DUGONG

There is a dip in the forehead, and the upper lip is less deeply cleft than in the manatees.

THE SNOUT

varies in profile according to species; this owes much to their differing feeding habits. In the manatees the upper lip is deeply cleft.

At about 26 ft (8 m) long, the extinct Steller's sea cow would have dwarfed all other sirenians. The largest species today is the West Indian manatee (top), which grows to 15 ft (4.6 m) and weighs up to 3,500 lb (1,600 kg). The dugong (above) is smaller, reaching about 13 ft (4 m) in length and a maximum weight of 2,000 lb (900 kg).

THE TEETH

move forward from the back of the jaw as they grow, dropping out when they reach the front. The manatee may lose up to thirty teeth during its lifetime, and this unique method of tooth replacement means that the animal always has sharp chewing surfaces.

MANATEE TAIL

DUGONG TAIL

All manatee species have a rounded, paddle-shaped tail. The tail of the dugong, however, is fluke shaped. All sirenians move their tails up and down to swim.

THE FRONT FLIPPERS

of the West Indian manatee are fairly short. They are also very flexible and have four "fingernails," which are lacking in the Amazonian manatee. The flippers are used to push food into the mouth, to touch other manatees, and to help the animal move over the sea- or riverbed.

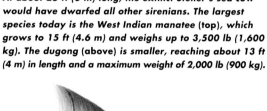

six neck vertebrae

MANATEE SKELETON

seven neck vertebrae

DUGONG SKELETON

barrel chest

five fingers

Manatee bones are extremely dense, and most lack marrow cavities. These dense bones act as ballast to offset the positive buoyancy caused by the large lungs and the intestinal gas generated during plant digestion. The sirenians' hand skeleton has five fingers.

X-ray illustrations Elisabeth Smith

WEST INDIAN MANATEE

LOCATION: SOUTHEASTERN USA & NORTHERN SOUTH AMERICA

AMAZONIAN MANATEE

The snout of the Amazonian manatee does not slope down as markedly as those of other manatees.

WEST INDIAN MANATEE

As in other manatees, the upper lip is deeply cleft and bears stiff but sensitive bristles.

AFRICAN MANATEE

The broad snout angles down slightly. Both upper and lower lips bear stiff bristles.

CLASSIFICATION

GENUS: *TRICHECHUS*

SPECIES: *MANATUS*

SIZE

HEAD–BODY LENGTH: 12–15 FT (3.7–4.6 M)

WEIGHT: 3,500 LB (1,600 KG)

WEIGHT AT BIRTH: 44 LB (20 KG)

LENGTH AT BIRTH: 3.3 FT (1 M)

COLORATION

GRAY OR BROWN SKIN, WITH SPARSE WHITE HAIRS SCATTERED ALL OVER BODY AT INTERVALS OF 0.5 IN (1.27 CM)

FEATURES

NAILS ON FLIPPERS

DOWN-SLOPING SNOUT

BROAD, PADDLE-SHAPED TAIL

WHISKERS ON UPPER LIP

THE SKIN

is generally gray or brown, but the color varies according to the type and amount of algae growing on it. It is rough and often covered by scars from injuries inflicted by propellers.

THE TAIL

is broad, paddle shaped, and huge in proportion to the body. Flipping it up and down, the manatee uses it like a paddle to move through the water.

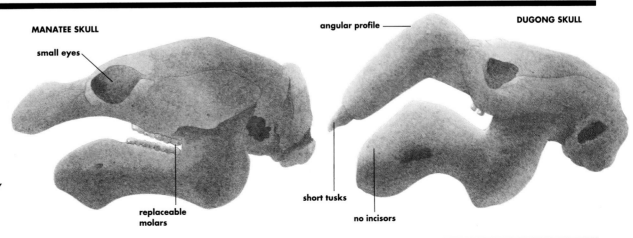

The skull of the dugong is about 24 in (61 cm) long. Its profile is more angular than that of the manatee, and it also has a pair of short tusks.

The manatee's skull is about 26 in (66 cm) long. It has only six neck vertebrae, whereas nearly all other mammals, including the dugong, have seven.

MANATEE SKULL

small eyes

replaceable molars

DUGONG SKULL

angular profile

short tusks

no incisors

Color illustrations Richard Tibbits

MANDRILL

The adult male mandrill is the biggest of the Old World monkeys, growing to a head-and-body length of some 31 in (80 cm). The smallest species is the talapoin monkey, one of the guenons, which grows to a head-and-body length of about 14 in (35 cm).

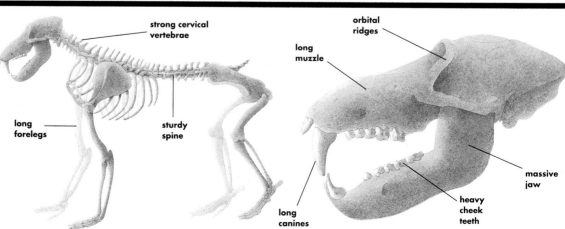

THE EYES

Monkeys are the only noncarnivorous mammals with forward-pointing eyes, giving binocular vision. Developed for judging distance in trees, this is also very useful for coordinating delicate actions during feeding and grooming.

LONG MUZZLE

A longer muzzle permits larger teeth, enhancing chewing power. The bulges are outgrowths of the nose bone. Set in a permanent snarl, the bright skin advertises the mandrill's maleness to rivals.

MACAQUE **BABOON** **GUENON**

BEARD, CREST, AND MANE

Best developed in adult males, the crest and mane serve as a signal of status within the group. When bristled up they also display states of excitement, limiting potentially damaging aggression when conflicts occur between males.

THE FORELEGS

are adapted for life on the ground, being longer than those of tree-dwelling monkeys to support the front of the body.

THE HANDS

have long fingers and well-developed thumbs; these enable the mandrill to sort and process edible material with great precision, allowing it to exploit a wide range of food sources.

HANDS AND FEET

The hands (upper row) and the feet (lower row) are very similar, with long digits for grasping branches, but macaques have stronger thumbs than guenons, and baboons are more suited to standing on the ground.

X R A Y

MANDRILL SKELETON
The mandrill is adapted for life on all fours, with relatively long forelegs that support the body in a "head-up" stance. The heavy skull is supported by strong cervical vertebrae with long dorsal spines to anchor powerful neck muscles, and the rest of the spine is equally sturdy. The tailbones are fused and reduced to a stump.

strong cervical vertebrae

long forelegs

sturdy spine

orbital ridges

long muzzle

massive jaw

heavy cheek teeth

long canines

X-ray illustrations Elisabeth Smith

PIG-TAILED MACAQUE FACE POUT

BARBARY MACAQUE LIP SMACKING

RHESUS MACAQUE AGGRESSIVE STARE

MANDRILL

LOCATION: WESTERN CENTRAL AFRICA

CLASSIFICATION

GENUS: *MANDRILLUS*

SPECIES: *SPHINX*

SIZE

HEAD–BODY LENGTH: UP TO 31 IN (80 CM)

TAIL LENGTH: 3 IN (7 CM)

HEIGHT AT SHOULDER: 20 IN (50 CM)

WEIGHT/MALE: UP TO 110 LB (50 KG)

WEIGHT/FEMALE: 60 LB (27 KG)

WEIGHT AT BIRTH: 18 OZ (500 G)

COLORATION

TAWNY GREEN FUR WITH YELLOWISH UNDERPARTS

MATURE MALE HAS BLUE CHEEKS SEPARATED BY A

SCARLET NASAL RIDGE, FEMALE HAS BLACK FACE

LILAC BUTTOCK SKIN, TINGED RED AT THE EDGES

FEATURES

DRAMATIC, COLORFUL FACE IN MALE

FORWARD-FACING, CLOSE-SET EYES

LONG MUZZLE

BRIGHT BUTTOCK SKIN

POWERFUL BUILD

LONG ARMS

FACIAL EXPRESSIONS

The faces of monkeys are highly expressive, although the meaning of each expression varies. An aggressive stare is clear, but a pouting face can precede an attack or an attempt to mate. Lip smacking in a male barbary macaque—but not in other species—signifies interest in an infant.

SHORT TAIL

Spending most of its life on the ground, the mandrill does not need a long tail for balance. A long tail could also obscure the display of the colorful buttocks.

COLORFUL BUTTOCKS

Mandrills live in deep, dense, dark rain forest. The colorful backside is thought to act as a flag, helping to keep the group together when moving through thick, dark vegetation. The colors penetrate particularly well through low light.

HEAVYSET BODY

The powerful, thickset body of the mandrill gives strength for defense against predators, for moving long distances in search of food, and for digging and overturning rocks while foraging.

THE FEET

have long toes for gripping branches, although the mandrill spends most of its time on the ground, but the soles are longer than those of most monkeys.

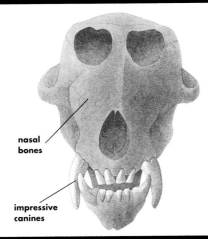

SKULL AND TEETH

Like other baboons, the mandrill has a long muzzle accommodating an impressive array of teeth. The large canines of the male are mainly symbolic, for threatening other males, though they can be used to attack predators if required. The heavy cheek teeth provide chewing power, backed up by the massive jaw. The forward-facing eyes are protected by strong ridges of bone.

nasal bones

impressive canines

The expanded nasal bones act as bases for a facial signaling device. The grooves, when covered in flesh, mimic the ridged muzzle of a snarling animal and give the male a permanent expression of aggression at minimal energy cost. When combined with the yawning display of the long canines, the effect is impressive, earning the mandrill an undeserved reputation for ferocity.

MANDRILL FACIAL MUSCLES

MANED WOLF

The maned wolf (above left) reaches a head-and-body length of some 41 in (105 cm) with an 18 in (45 cm) tail, and weighs, on average, 51 lb (23 kg). Males and females are the same size. The coyote (above right) has a head-and-body length of 27–38 in (70–97 cm), with a tail of 12–15 in (30–38 cm). The bush dog (above center) has a head-and-body length of 23–29 in (58–75 cm), with a tail 5–6 in (12.5–15 cm) long.

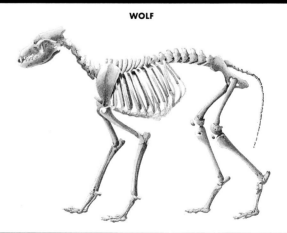

THE SOFT FUR

is always the same russet-red color, with a conspicuous black mane and black "stockings." There is no coat of woolly underfur, since the animal lives in hot climates and normally needs to lose heat rather than retain it.

THE FEET

are relatively broad, and the toes are capable of spreading to distribute the load more widely, enabling the maned wolf to travel over soft, marshy ground without sinking in.

THE TAIL

is moderately bushy, with long white hairs. It may not appear conspicuous, but this is due mainly to the length of the maned wolf's legs: The tail is a few inches longer than that of the coyote.

X

R A Y

MANED WOLF

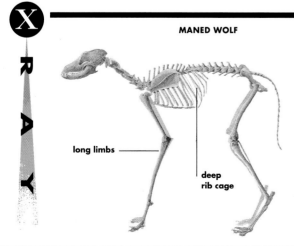

long limbs

deep rib cage

When looked at in skeleton, the maned wolf's legs seem immensely long even when compared to its rangy cousin the wolf. Visible also is the deep rib cage, which houses the capacious lungs. Although not particularly fast moving, the maned wolf needs plenty of strength and stamina to support its vertically extended frame.

WOLF

X-ray illustrations Elisabeth Smith

COYOTE

LOCATION: NORTHERN ALASKA TO COSTA RICA

CLASSIFICATION

GENUS: *CANIS*

SPECIES: *LATRANS*

SIZE

HEAD–BODY LENGTH: 27–38 IN (70–97 CM)

TAIL LENGTH: 12–15 IN (30–38 CM)

WEIGHT/MALE: 18–44 LB (8–20 KG)

AVERAGE WEIGHT/FEMALE: 15–40 LB (7–18 KG)

GREATEST RECORDED WEIGHT: 75 LB (34 KG)

COLORATION

BUFF, BROWN, OR GRAY, WITH GRIZZLED LOOK CREATED BY LONG, BLACK-TIPPED GUARD HAIRS. CREAM OR GRAY UNDERFUR. BLACK STRIPE DOWN MIDDLE OF BACK, AND BLACK TIP TO TAIL

FEATURES

LITHE, WOLFLIKE BUILD

LONG, SLIM LEGS

SLENDER, FOXLIKE MUZZLE

LARGE EARS

The coyote (above left) has a clearly wolflike head profile, whereas the bush dog (left) is closer in appearance to a small bear or a mongoose.

BIG, MOBILE EARS

give acute hearing, essential for locating prey amid long grass.

THE CHEST

is deep, allowing the lungs to draw in a lot of air. In many canids, such as the coyote, this gives the stamina necessary for pursuing prey over long distances, but the maned wolf generally uses stalking tactics.

COYOTE

BUSH DOG

THE LEGS

are extremely long, probably as an adaptation to living in tall grass. The lower leg bones are fused together for strength when running, as they are in all canids, but the maned wolf cannot run particularly fast.

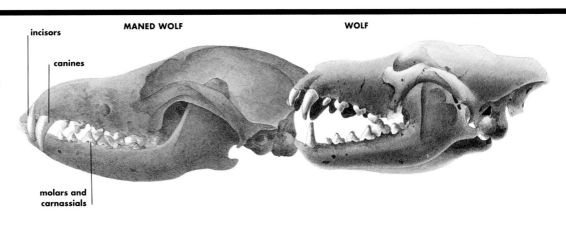

SKULL

The skull of the maned wolf is more elongated and tapered than that of the gray wolf, but otherwise there are few differences. The maned wolf's omnivorous diet is reflected in its simple, widely spaced molars, while the long, narrow canines are ideal for seizing and holding its small-mammal prey.

incisors

canines

MANED WOLF

WOLF

molars and carnassials

Main illustration Steve Kingston

MARMOSET

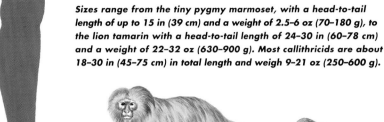

Sizes range from the tiny pygmy marmoset, with a head-to-tail length of up to 15 in (39 cm) and a weight of 2.5–6 oz (70–180 g), to the lion tamarin with a head-to-tail length of 24–30 in (60–78 cm) and a weight of 22–32 oz (630–900 g). Most callithricids are about 18–30 in (45–75 cm) in total length and weigh 9–21 oz (250–600 g).

VERVET MONKEY

GOELDI'S MONKEY

THE MARMOSET'S EYES

are large and round. They point forward to give binocular vision that is good for judging distance. However, the monkey has limited binocular cortex areas in the brain, so it cocks its head from side to side to give more than one view of an object and provide more clues for the brain to use.

DIFFERENT NOSES

The callithricids, together with the monkeys of the Cebidae family, are known as the platyrrhine (PLAT-i-rine)—meaning flat-nosed—monkeys.

The Goeldi's nose (above right), like all platyrrhine monkeys, is very flat and broad, and the nostrils point sideways.

The Old World monkeys, such as the vervet (above left), have a narrower nose with nostrils that point downward.

ALL FOUR LEGS

are covered in fur and are strong for tree climbing. The forelimbs are shorter than the hind limbs.

MARMOSET SKELETON

The skeleton clearly shows the relative length of the head, body, and tail, with the tail doubling the overall length. The body is small with fine bones, giving great agility in the trees.

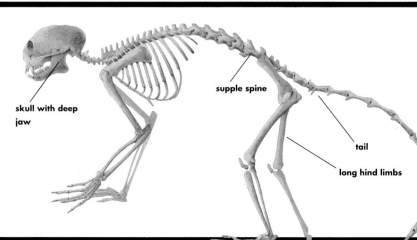

skull with deep jaw

supple spine

tail

long hind limbs

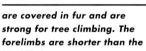

elbow joint

elongated fingers

long forearm

FOREARM/HAND

The fingers are very thin and elongated, clawed, and well adapted for probing tree-growing plants for insects. The thumb is not opposable (it cannot grasp).

FOREFOOT

FEET

The common marmoset's feet have toes that are all clawed except for the large toe on the hind foot, which bears a nail. The large toe is opposable.

large toe

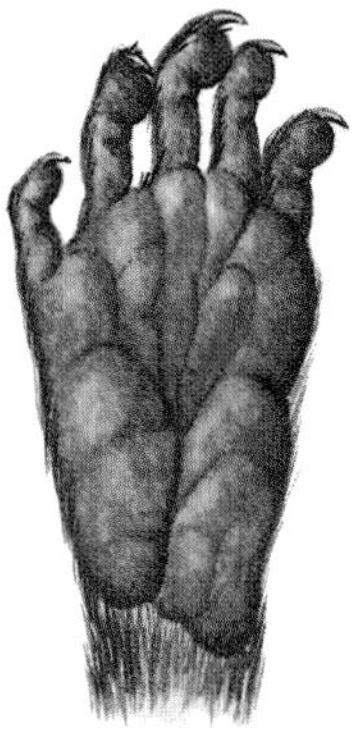

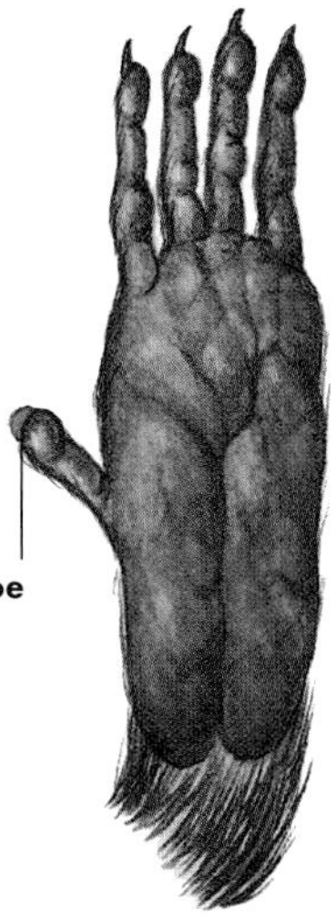

HIND FOOT

COMMON MARMOSET
LOCATION: NORTH-EAST BRAZIL

CLASSIFICATION

GENUS: *CALLITHRIX*

SPECIES: *JACCHUS*

SIZE

HEAD–BODY LENGTH: 8 IN (20 CM)

TAIL LENGTH: 10–12 IN (25–30 CM)

WEIGHT: 10.6–23 OZ (300–650 G)

COLORATION

MOTTLED BLACK-AND-GRAY BODY

BLACK HEAD, WITH A WHITE BLAZE ON FOREHEAD

TAIL RINGED WITH BROAD BLACK AND NARROW GRAY BANDS

FEATURES

LONG WHITE OR GRAY EAR TUFTS

RINGED TAIL

FUR

The marmoset coat is fine and silky and often very colorful. It is kept clean by individual and mutual grooming. Depending on the species, there may be manes, ruffs, ear tufts, or mustaches.

THE TAIL

is as long as the body but differs from those of other monkeys in that it cannot be used for grasping branches. So the marmoset scurries along, and leaps between, branches.

SKULL AND DENTITION *(RIGHT)*
In all monkeys, the eye sockets angle forward for binocular vision. The forehead bones fuse together early in life. The capacious braincase reflects the relatively large brain size. The two halves of the lower jaw are fused at the midline. The body of the jaw is fairly deep.

Callithricid molars have three cusps (there are four cusps in other anthropoids). In marmosets, the lower incisors are as long as the canines.

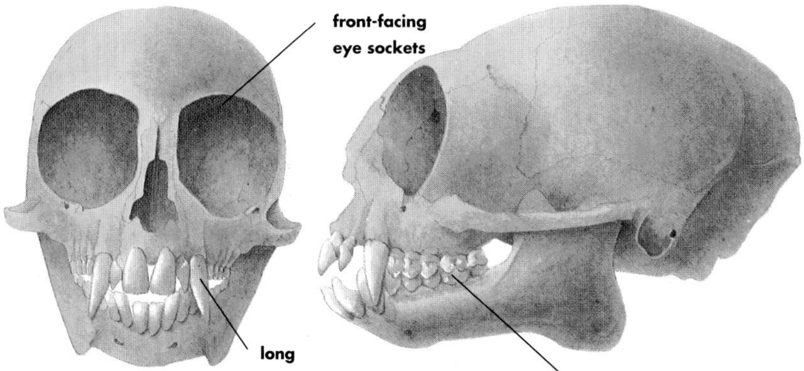

front-facing eye sockets

long canines

squared-off molars

MEERKAT

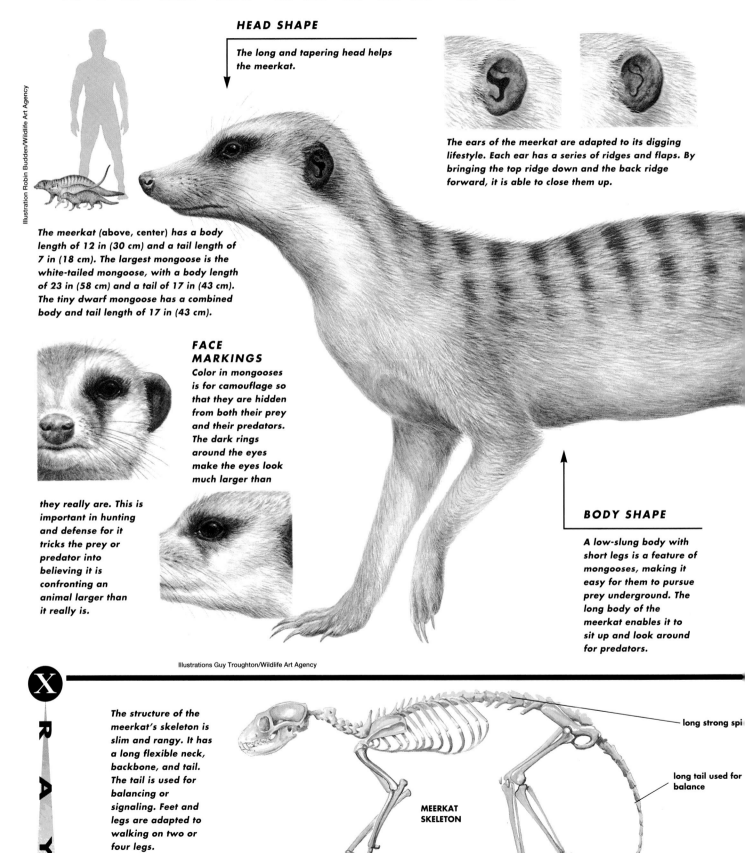

HEAD SHAPE

The long and tapering head helps the meerkat.

The ears of the meerkat are adapted to its digging lifestyle. Each ear has a series of ridges and flaps. By bringing the top ridge down and the back ridge forward, it is able to close them up.

The meerkat (above, center) has a body length of 12 in (30 cm) and a tail length of 7 in (18 cm). The largest mongoose is the white-tailed mongoose, with a body length of 23 in (58 cm) and a tail of 17 in (43 cm). The tiny dwarf mongoose has a combined body and tail length of 17 in (43 cm).

FACE MARKINGS

Color in mongooses is for camouflage so that they are hidden from both their prey and their predators. The dark rings around the eyes make the eyes look much larger than they really are. This is important in hunting and defense for it tricks the prey or predator into believing it is confronting an animal larger than it really is.

BODY SHAPE

A low-slung body with short legs is a feature of mongooses, making it easy for them to pursue prey underground. The long body of the meerkat enables it to sit up and look around for predators.

Illustration Robin Budden/Wildlife Art Agency

Illustrations Guy Troughton/Wildlife Art Agency

X-RAY

The structure of the meerkat's skeleton is slim and rangy. It has a long flexible neck, backbone, and tail. The tail is used for balancing or signaling. Feet and legs are adapted to walking on two or four legs.

MEERKAT SKELETON

long strong spi

long tail used for balance

X-ray illustrations Gary Martin/Wildlife Art Agency

MEERKAT

LOCATION: BOTSWANA, NAMIBIA & SOUTH AFRICA

HANDS AND FEET

The meerkat uses its hands, or forepaws, for eating and for activities like grooming its fellow pack members. They are also useful for cuffing a disobedient infant. The marsh mongoose has very sensitive hands with a highly developed sense of touch. It picks up stones with its hands as it searches for crabs and insects.

digital pads

planter pads

etacarpal/ metatarsal pads

BASIC ARRANGEMENT OF PAW PADS

Forepaw

Hind foot

CLASSIFICATION

GENUS: *SURICATA*

SPECIES: *SURICATTA*

SIZE

HEAD–BODY LENGTH/MALE: 12–13 IN (30–33 CM)

SHOULDER HEIGHT/MALE: 6 IN (15 CM)

TAIL LENGTH/MALE: 7–9 IN (18–23 CM)

WEIGHT/MALE: 22–34 OZ (623–964 G)

WEIGHT AT BIRTH: 1.16 OZ (33 G) [IN TWYCROSS ZOO, ENGLAND]

COLORATION

GROUND COLOR: GRAY COAT WITH REDDISH TINGE AND PALER UNDERPARTS

DARKER STRIPES ACROSS LOWER BACK AND TAIL

BLACK TIP TO TAIL

FEATURES

DARK PATCHES AROUND EYES

LONG CLAWS FOR DIGGING

UPRIGHT STANCE WHEN ON THE ALERT

NARROW BODY FOR BURROWING

LONG TAIL

The meerkat's long tail acts as a balance.

FEET AND CLAWS

The meerkat has claws 0.5 in (13 mm) long for digging. Hind feet are often elongated and adapted to life on the ground. Unlike other mongooses, meerkats have only four toes on their feet.

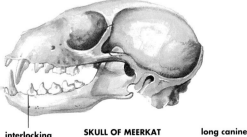

interlocking cusped teeth

SKULL OF MEERKAT
(side view)

This meerkat's skull shape is typical of the insect-eating mongooses.

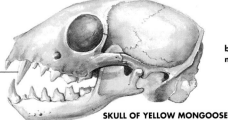

long canine teeth

SKULL OF YELLOW MONGOOSE
(side view)

The yellow mongoose is mainly a meat-eater, or carnivore. Because of this it has sharp canine teeth for tearing meat.

blunt molars

SKULL OF BLACK-LEGGED MONGOOSE
(side view)

Because it is an omnivore, the teeth of the black-legged mongoose are blunt to cope with a variety of foods.

NAKED MOLE RAT

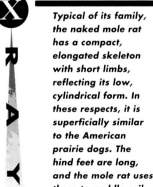

THE EYES

are tiny and almost useless. The mole rat usually closes its eyelids when their body is touched.

THE EARS

have no external pinnae (flaps), but they are otherwise normal and highly sensitive.

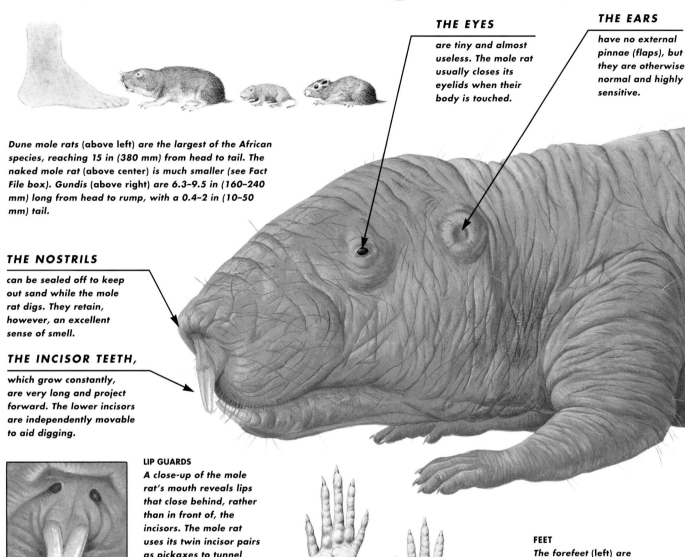

Dune mole rats (above left) are the largest of the African species, reaching 15 in (380 mm) from head to tail. The naked mole rat (above center) is much smaller (see Fact File box). Gundis (above right) are 6.3–9.5 in (160–240 mm) long from head to rump, with a 0.4–2 in (10–50 mm) tail.

THE NOSTRILS

can be sealed off to keep out sand while the mole rat digs. They retain, however, an excellent sense of smell.

THE INCISOR TEETH,

which grow constantly, are very long and project forward. The lower incisors are independently movable to aid digging.

LIP GUARDS

A close-up of the mole rat's mouth reveals lips that close behind, rather than in front of, the incisors. The mole rat uses its twin incisor pairs as pickaxes to tunnel huge distances through soil and sand, and the lip barrier helps to keep the excavated debris out of the animal's mouth.

FEET

The forefeet (left) are short, since they are used very little in digging. The hind feet (far left) are markedly longer, being used to move soil.

HIND FOOT   **FOREFOOT**

Typical of its family, the naked mole rat has a compact, elongated skeleton with short limbs, reflecting its low, cylindrical form. In these respects, it is superficially similar to the American prairie dogs. The hind feet are long, and the mole rat uses these to paddle soil backward as it tunnels.

X

RAY

NAKED MOLE RAT SKELETON

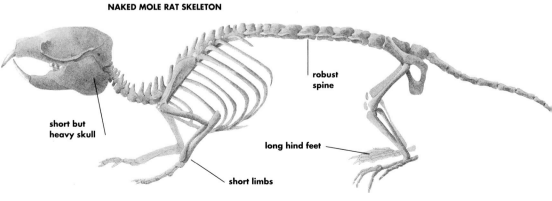

robust spine

short but heavy skull

long hind feet

short limbs

X-ray illustrations Elisabeth Smith

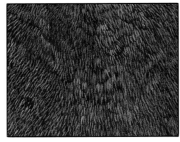

The naked mole rat's intricately wrinkled skin is scattered with a few fine hairs.

The common mole rat is more typical of its family in possessing thick, velvety fur.

NAKED MOLE RAT

LOCATION: ETHIOPIA, SOMALIA & KENYA

CLASSIFICATION

GENUS: *HETEROCEPHALUS*

SPECIES: *GLABER*

SIZE

HEAD–BODY LENGTH: 3-3.5 IN (8-9 CM)

TAIL LENGTH: 1-1.5 IN (3-4 CM)

WEIGHT: 1-3 OZ (28-85 G)

WEIGHT AT BIRTH: 0.07 OZ (2 G)

COLORATION

BLUISH-PINK TO YELLOW SKIN

PALE YELLOW HAIRS

FEATURES

ALMOST NAKED SKIN

LARGE HANDS AND FEET

PROMINENT INCISOR TEETH

SENSITIVE VIBRISSAE AROUND MOUTH

VERY SMALL EYES

NO EXTERNAL EARS

NO SWEAT GLANDS

NO LAYER OF FAT BENEATH

THE SKIN

THE SKIN

is loose, allowing the mole rat to move around a little inside it. The sparse hairs are touch-sensitive.

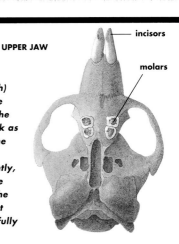

THE BODY

is low and barrel shaped to improve streamlining.

THE LEGS

are squat but powerful, although the naked mole rat uses them little in actual digging.

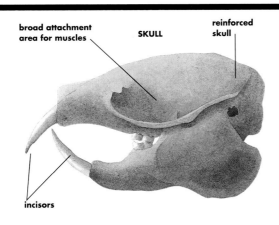

A mole rat possesses a typically short but solidly built skull, which is heavily reinforced in order to support the huge incisors. The eye sockets are much reduced, since the animal has little need for sharp vision. In fact, the eye sockets are largely occupied by the highly developed cheek muscles, which give immense power to the mole rat's jaw-closing mechanism.

broad attachment area for muscles

SKULL

reinforced skull

incisors

UPPER JAW

incisors

molars

The high-crowned molars (cheek teeth) are dwarfed by the massive incisors. The upper incisors work as a fixed pair, but the lower pair can be moved independently, since, in all but one mole rat species, the lower left and right jawbones are not fully fused at the front.

Main illustration Barry Croucher/Wildlife Art Agency

OPOSSUM

HEARING

is the opossum's most acute sense, and the thin, hairless ears are usually moving. Many Virginia opossums at the northern extremes of their range lose their ear flaps to frostbite.

Opossums range in size from the mouse opossum (above left), with a head-and-body length of 2.7 in (6.8 cm), to the Virginia opossum (above right), which has a head-and-body length of 13–22 in (33–54 cm).

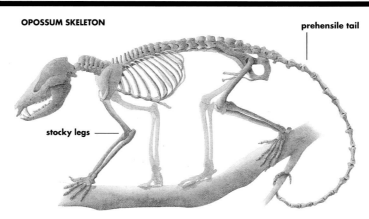

THE EYES

protrude and are specially adapted to help the opossum see better during its twilight and nighttime hours of activity.

VIRGINIA OPOSSUM POUCH

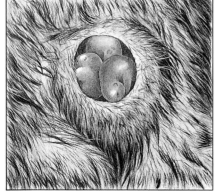

YAPOK POUCH

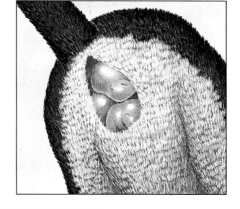

POUCHES

There is a great deal of variety in pouch shape among species, and some simply have lateral skin folds or no pouch at all. The Virginia opossum pouch (far left) is fully formed and faces forward. The backward-facing yapok pouch (left) can be shut tight with the sphincter muscle.

X RAY

SKELETON

The long, prehensile tail and clawed, five-digit feet enable the Virginia opossum and other arboreal relatives to climb easily and to remain secure on branches. The Virginia opossum has a cat-sized body but is heavier and has shorter legs.

OPOSSUM SKELETON

prehensile tail

stocky legs

SKULL

The facial part of the opossum's skull, which is long and pointed, coupled with a narrow cranial part give an overall effect of elongation. There is a pronounced ridge—the sagittal crest—along the top of the cranium. The jaws are flexible enough to remain open at right angles for up to fifteen minutes.

X-ray illustrations Elisabeth Smith

OPOSSUM TRACKS

There are five fully developed toes on all four feet, although tracks made by the hind feet are easily recognizable because of the opposable "big toe."

HIND FOOT

FOREFOOT

VIRGINIA OPOSSUM

LOCATION: SOUTHERN USA & CENTRAL AMERICA

CLASSIFICATION

GENUS: *DIDELPHIS*

SPECIES: *VIRGINIANA*

SIZE

HEAD–BODY LENGTH: 13–22 IN (33–54 CM)

TAIL LENGTH: 10–22 IN (25–54 CM)

HEIGHT: 7–10 IN (16–25 CM)

WEIGHT: 4.4–13.2 LB (2–6 KG)

WEIGHT AT BIRTH: 0.007 OZ (0.2 G)

COLORATION

VARIES FROM ALMOST BLACK THROUGH MOTTLED TO CREAMY YELLOW. FACE AND SNOUT ALWAYS WHITE, REGARDLESS OF BODY COLOR

FEATURES

DISTINCT, REAR-FACING POUCH

LONG PREHENSILE TAIL

LONG, NARROW MUZZLE

SHORT LIMBS, WITH HIND LIMBS LONGER THAN FORELIMBS

OPPOSABLE LARGE TOE

THE FUR

varies among species, from smooth in mouse opossums to woolly in woolly opossums. Some genera, such as the Virginia opossum, have long, projecting guard hairs.

THE TAIL

of an opossum is frequently longer than the body, and the base is enlarged to store fat in some species. The tail, often prehensile, is either naked or only partially covered in fur.

THE HIND LEGS

are longer than the forelegs in adults, although newborn opossums have well-developed forelegs to pull them to the mother's pouch.

THE CLAWS

are sharp to help in grasping or climbing. They grow on all digits except the opposable large toe on each hind foot.

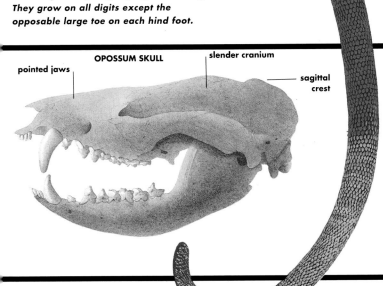

OPOSSUM SKULL

pointed jaws

slender cranium

sagittal crest

TEETH

Opossums have fifty teeth, more than any other marsupial. They have many incisors in both the upper and lower jaws, as well as long canines and sharp molars. This arrangement favors an omnivorous diet.

several incisors

long canines

sharp molars

Main illustrations Barry Croucher/Wildlife Art Agency

ORANGUTAN

There is a vast difference in size between the sexes, with males weighing in at about 165 lb (75 kg) and females at about 88 lb (40 kg). Adult males stand 5 ft (1.5 m) tall; females 3 ft (1 m) tall. A tall human male stands about 6 ft (2 m) tall.

EYES, BRAIN, AND FACE
Forward-facing eyes allow orangutans to judge distances well, and relatively large brains allow excellent coordination, vital requirements for a tree-dwelling creature. Males (above left) grow beards or mustaches, and face flaps develop between the ages of twelve and fourteen. The female face (above right) is relatively hairless.

HANDS
Orangutans show greater mechanical aptitude and manual dexterity than chimpanzees do (in captivity), being able to undo nuts and bolts that would fool a chimpanzee.

EARS
Orangutans have the flat ears that are typical of primates. Hearing is all-important as adult males (male ear—near left) keep each other informed of their whereabouts through screeches and barking.

LONG ARMS
Long arms are a necessity if you spend your life swinging through the trees. An orangutan has an arm span of 5–8 ft (1.5–2.5 m). It uses its long, powerful arms to swing its large body through the trees, underneath the branches, and to reach fruit.

Illustrations Guy Troughton

The orangutan has a skeleton adapted for vertical posture. Features include a short back, broad rib cage, and sturdy pelvis. The orangutan's arms are considerably longer than its legs to make it easier to swing through the forest trees. You can tell apes from monkeys by their lack of a tail.

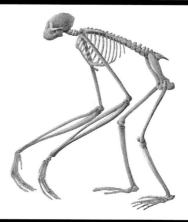

Orangutans have broad, powerful feet and hands for gripping and grasping. They have long, strong, hook-shaped fingers and toes, with shorter, opposable thumbs and big toes for greater mobility. The nails are flat and blunt.

HAND   FOOT

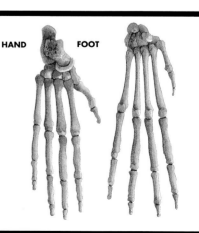

X-ray illustrations Elisabeth Smith

ORANGUTAN

LOCATION: NORTHERN SUMATRA
& LOWLAND BORNEO

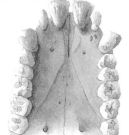

SKIN
In younger orangutans, the skin on the muzzle and around the eyes is pinkish. In adults, the facial skin is bare and completely black.

CLASSIFICATION

FAMILY: PONGIDAE

GENUS AND SPECIES: *PONGO PYGMAEUS*

SUBSPECIES: *PONGO PYGMAEUS PYGMAEUS* (BORNEO)

***PONGO PYGMAEUS ABELII* (SUMATRA)**

SIZE

HEIGHT/MALE: 5 FT (1.5 M)

HEIGHT/FEMALE: 3 FT (1 M)

WEIGHT/MALE: 165 LB (75 KG)

WEIGHT/FEMALE: 88 LB (40 KG)

WEIGHT AT BIRTH: 3 LB (1.5 KG)

ON AVERAGE, MALES ARE TWICE THE SIZE OF FEMALES

COLORATION

REDDISH BROWN COATS BUT RANGES FROM BRIGHT ORANGE IN YOUNG TO DARK BROWN IN SOME ADULTS; LIGHTER IN SUMATRAN ORANGS; DARKER IN ZOO-BRED ORANGS. ADULTS HAVE BLACK FACES; YOUNG HAVE PINK MUZZLES AND PINK SKIN AROUND THEIR EYES

FEATURES

AS THEY GET OLDER, MALES DEVELOP LARGE, FATTY CHEEK PADS (WHICH ENHANCE THEIR AGGRESSIVE DISPLAYS) AND INFLATABLE THROAT POUCHES

VERY LONG ARM SPAN—5–8 FT (1.5–2.5 M) FROM FINGERTIP TO FINGERTIP (FOR ARBOREAL LOCOMOTION)

LARGE BRAINS FOR THEIR SIZE; HIGHLY INTELLIGENT

THE HEAVIEST TREE-LIVING ANIMAL

LIFE SPAN: 30–40 YEARS

COAT
Orangutans are famous for their striking appearance, thanks mainly to their long, shaggy coats of reddish brown hair. Sumatran orangutans have longer, lighter hair than their Bornean cousins, and males tend to have longer hair than females. Sumatran males also have conspicuous mustaches and beards.

LOWER MANDIBLE

The orangutan's large jaws and molars are adapted for grinding tough plants, nuts, and bark.

**MALE SKULL
(SIDE VIEW)**

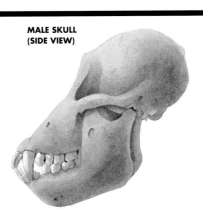

SKULLS
Orangutans' skulls have a relatively large brain capacity, being up to 27 c in (450 cc) in volume. Their brains are about as large as those of chimpanzees.

**FEMALE SKULL
(SIDE VIEW)**

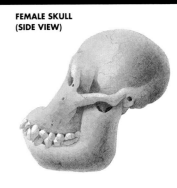

OTTER

THE GLOSSY FUR

varies in its coloring from individual to individual, while the thickness of the pelt on the whole depends on its habitat: The colder the climate, the denser the otter's coat.

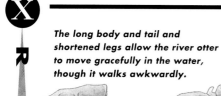

Otters range in size from the Asian small-clawed otter, which usually measures less than 35 in (90 cm) from head to tail, to the slightly larger Eurasian otter, to the giant otter, which can attain a length of 6 ft (1.8 m).

THE MUZZLE

is broad, with whiskers or vibrissae (vie-BRISS-eye) on each side of the nose. These are used to detect prey in conditions of poor visibility.

AMERICAN RIVER OTTER   **EURASIAN OTTER**

SEA CAT   **GIANT OTTER**

The hairiness of an otter's nose pad varies, becoming hairier as the otter's habitat moves nearer the equator. Nose pads range from the hairless American river otter to the very hairy giant otter.

RIVER OTTER   **ASIAN SMALL-CLAWED OTTER**   **SEA OTTER**

Three forepaws (left): River otters have curved claws and a large amount of webbing, while Asian small-clawed otters have narrow paws with little webbing and small claws. Sea otters have fingers that are almost fused.

X RAY

The long body and tail and shortened legs allow the river otter to move gracefully in the water, though it walks awkwardly.

hind legs longer than front legs

baculum

torpedo-shaped body

OTTER SKELETON

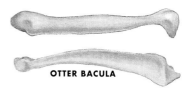

OTTER BACULA

The three tribes have differently shaped bacula or penis bones. The baculum of the Lutrini tribe (top) is shaped like a hockey stick, while that of the Aonychini and Hydrictini (bottom) looks more like a baseball bat.

EURASIAN OTTER

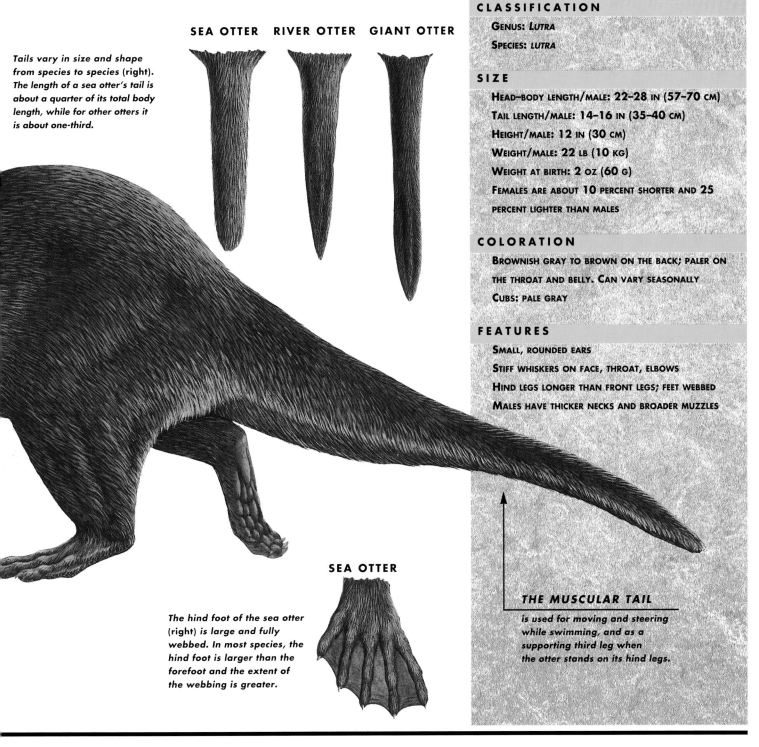

LOCATION: EUROPE, ASIA & NORTH AFRICA

SEA OTTER   RIVER OTTER   GIANT OTTER

Tails vary in size and shape from species to species (right). The length of a sea otter's tail is about a quarter of its total body length, while for other otters it is about one-third.

CLASSIFICATION

GENUS: *LUTRA*

SPECIES: *LUTRA*

SIZE

HEAD–BODY LENGTH/MALE: **22–28 IN (57–70 CM)**

TAIL LENGTH/MALE: **14–16 IN (35–40 CM)**

HEIGHT/MALE: **12 IN (30 CM)**

WEIGHT/MALE: **22 LB (10 KG)**

WEIGHT AT BIRTH: **2 OZ (60 G)**

FEMALES ARE ABOUT **10** PERCENT SHORTER AND **25** PERCENT LIGHTER THAN MALES

COLORATION

BROWNISH GRAY TO BROWN ON THE BACK; PALER ON THE THROAT AND BELLY. CAN VARY SEASONALLY

CUBS: PALE GRAY

FEATURES

SMALL, ROUNDED EARS

STIFF WHISKERS ON FACE, THROAT, ELBOWS

HIND LEGS LONGER THAN FRONT LEGS; FEET WEBBED

MALES HAVE THICKER NECKS AND BROADER MUZZLES

SEA OTTER

The hind foot of the sea otter (right) is large and fully webbed. In most species, the hind foot is larger than the forefoot and the extent of the webbing is greater.

THE MUSCULAR TAIL is used for moving and steering while swimming, and as a supporting third leg when the otter stands on its hind legs.

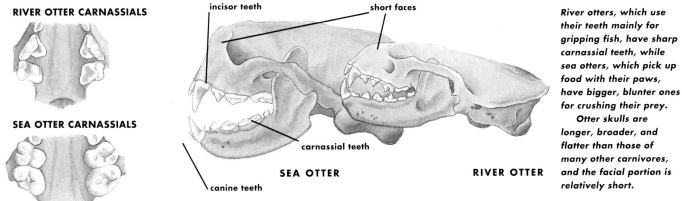

RIVER OTTER CARNASSIALS

SEA OTTER CARNASSIALS

incisor teeth

short faces

carnassial teeth

SEA OTTER

canine teeth

RIVER OTTER

River otters, which use their teeth mainly for gripping fish, have sharp carnassial teeth, while sea otters, which pick up food with their paws, have bigger, blunter ones for crushing their prey.
    Otter skulls are longer, broader, and flatter than those of many other carnivores, and the facial portion is relatively short.

PINE MARTEN

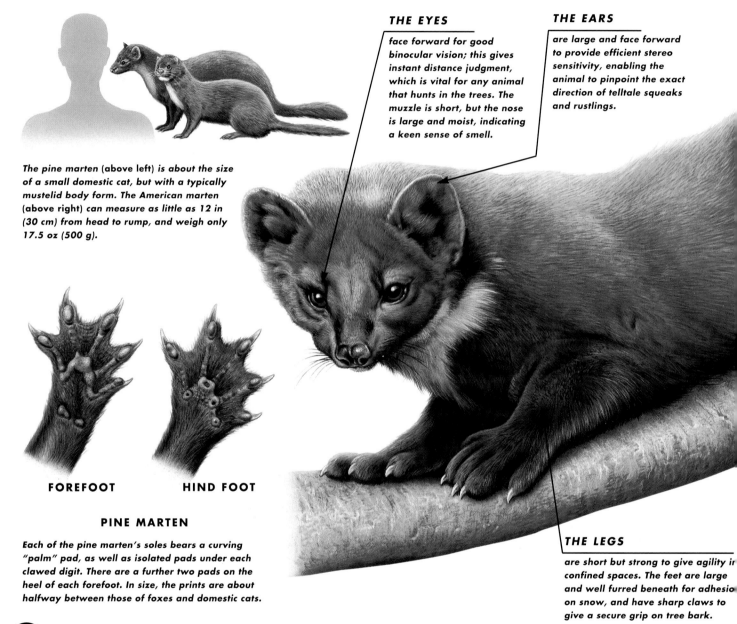

The pine marten (above left) is about the size of a small domestic cat, but with a typically mustelid body form. The American marten (above right) can measure as little as 12 in (30 cm) from head to rump, and weigh only 17.5 oz (500 g).

THE EYES

face forward for good binocular vision; this gives instant distance judgment, which is vital for any animal that hunts in the trees. The muzzle is short, but the nose is large and moist, indicating a keen sense of smell.

THE EARS

are large and face forward to provide efficient stereo sensitivity, enabling the animal to pinpoint the exact direction of telltale squeaks and rustlings.

FOREFOOT **HIND FOOT**

PINE MARTEN

Each of the pine marten's soles bears a curving "palm" pad, as well as isolated pads under each clawed digit. There are a further two pads on the heel of each forefoot. In size, the prints are about halfway between those of foxes and domestic cats.

THE LEGS

are short but strong to give agility in confined spaces. The feet are large and well furred beneath for adhesion on snow, and have sharp claws to give a secure grip on tree bark.

The loosely articulated vertebrae of the marten's spine allow it to turn around in a confined space, or gallop at speed by arching and extending its back to provide a long stride. With the exception of the skull, the other bones are lightly built. The legs are short in relation to the cat-sized body, but the marten is not so "low-slung" as the stoat or weasel.

PINE MARTEN SKELETON

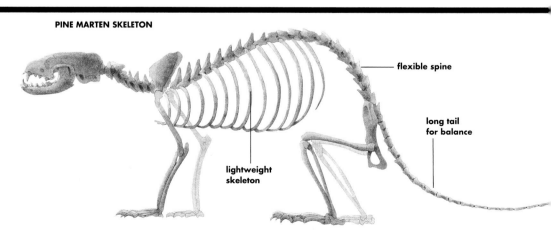

flexible spine

long tail for balance

lightweight skeleton

X-ray illustrations Elisabeth Smith

AMERICAN MINK

The mink's feet are slightly smaller than those of the pine marten. The five toes are widely splayed, and are partly webbed. The mink leaves copious tracks on muddy riverbanks, and the fine, star-shaped prints are the best proof of its identity.

FOREFOOT   **HIND FOOT**

PINE MARTEN

LOCATION: CENTRAL & NORTHERN EUROPE, WESTERN ASIA

CLASSIFICATION

GENUS: *Martes*

SPECIES: *MARTES*

SIZE

HEAD-BODY LENGTH: 16-23 IN (41-58 CM)

TAIL LENGTH: 8-11 IN (20-28 CM)

WEIGHT: 1.8-4.4 LB (0.8-2 KG)

WEIGHT AT BIRTH: 1 OZ (28 G)

COLORATION

CHOCOLATE-BROWN FUR WITH A WHITE, YELLOW-TINGED CHEST PATCH

FEATURES

LUXURIANT FUR

ELONGATED, SINUOUS BODY

SHORT LEGS

BUSHY TAIL

THE TAIL

is long and bushy, and acts as a rudder when the pine marten is leaping from branch to branch.

THE BODY

is long and sinuous, but more thickset than that of a weasel or polecat—although the bulky impression is largely due to the long, luxuriant fur for warmth in the northern winters. The pelt of the sable, the pine marten's closest relative, has always been considered the finest of all furs.

AMERICAN MARTEN SKULL

short lower jaw

The skull of a pine marten (right) is elongated, with a short lower jaw hinged well forward. This increases the leverage on the teeth, both for slicing meat with the scissorlike carnassial cheek teeth, and for delivering the fatal neck bite with the long, stabbing canines. Flattened molar teeth behind the carnassials enable the pine marten to chew fruit when it is seasonally abundant. The skull of the smaller American marten (left) has less prominent lower canines.

PINE MARTEN SKULL

carnassial teeth

canines

Main illustration Steve Kingston

PIPISTRELLE BAT

THE FUR

is dense and long, making the bat look much plumper than it really is. The bat grooms its fur regularly and thoroughly with its hind feet, keeping it meticulously clean, and it is molted and replaced every year.

The pipistrelle is tiny, much smaller than a mouse, with a head-and-body length of less than 2 in (50 mm), but its wingspan extends to 10 in (250 mm).

THE EARS

are smaller than those of many bats, yet highly sensitive to high-pitched sounds and the ultrasonic sonar echoes reflected from obstacles and flying insects.

THE EYES

work perfectly well, but they cannot distinguish color because they are adapted for high sensitivity in low light levels rather than color reception.

B/W illustration Ruth Grewcock

VESPER BAT'S FACE

The faces of vesper bats are more appealing than those of many insectivorous bats. Typical species like the mouse-eared bat (left) have simple muzzles like hedgehogs.

X
R
A
Y

SKELETON

A bat has slender bones and small hind legs to minimize weight. All the strength of its skeleton is concentrated in its shoulders and the inner parts of its wings. The outer wing is supported by the elongated finger bones. It has movable collarbones and shoulder blades for greater maneuverability.

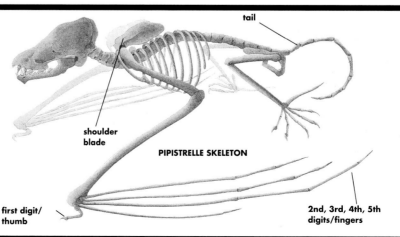

tail

shoulder blade

PIPISTRELLE SKELETON

first digit/ thumb

2nd, 3rd, 4th, 5th digits/fingers

SKULL

The shape of the skull of the different vesper bat species varies depending on their diet. Those bats that eat hard-shelled insects, such as beetles, have a shorter, broader muzzle and may have a more domed head. The skulls of species, such as the pipistrelle, that feed on moths and flies, are flatter and more elongated, with a longer, narrower muzzle.

X-ray illustrations Elisabeth Smith

EAR SHAPES

Most vesper bats have big ears that are equipped with an extra lobe called the tragus. The massive ears of the barbastelle (right) dominate its broad, puglike face, and those of the long-eared bat (far right) are longer than its body.

**BARBASTELLE
BAT**

**COMMON
LONG-EARED BAT**

COMMON PIPISTRELLE

LOCATION: NORTHERN & EASTERN EUROPE,
NORTH AFRICA

CLASSIFICATION

GENUS: *PIPISTRELLUS*

SPECIES: *PIPISTRELLUS*

SIZE

HEAD-BODY LENGTH: 1.25-1.75 IN (35-45 MM)

WINGSPAN: 7.5-10 IN (190-250 MM)

WEIGHT: 0.1-0.3 OZ (3-8 G)

WEIGHT AT BIRTH: 0.03-0.06 OZ (1-2 G)

COLORATION

DARK BROWN ABOVE, PALER BELOW;
BROWN-BLACK WING MEMBRANES, EARS, AND
FEET. YOUNG ARE PINK.

FEATURES

TINY BODY WITH THICK, BROWN FUR

RELATIVELY SHORT, BROAD EARS

SMALL, BROWN EYES

"NORMAL" NOSE

WELL-DEVELOPED TAIL MEMBRANE WITH
PROTRUDING TAIL

THE TAIL

is roughly half as long as the bat's body and supports a membrane stretched between the two hind legs. The last joint of the tail is free and prehensile, and the bat uses it as a support as it crawls around.

THE HIND FEET

have sharp claws capable of gripping the slightest irregularity in a wall or timber beam. As the bat hangs upside down, its weight pulls down on a special arrangement of tendons that tighten the grip, ensuring it does not fall off as it sleeps.

E WINGS

*formed from two
ts of skin
dwiching a layer of
tic tissue and muscle
rs. They are
orted by the
gated arm and
er bones.*

THE HIND LEGS

are short and slender and, as with all bats, they are turned "back to front," so they bend forward below the knee.

PIPISTRELLE SKULL

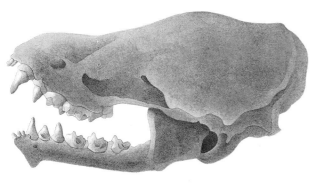

TEETH

Many vesper bats have powerful jaws and strong, pointed teeth for catching and killing well-armored insects and even small vertebrates, such as lizards and fish. The front incisors are often missing, leaving a gap in the center of the jaw. The hard, zigzag cusps on the cheek teeth make short work of crunching up the bat's victims.

SKULL OF *EPTESICUS*
(top section looking up)

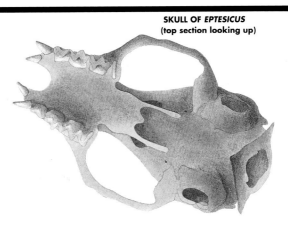

Main illustration Guy Troughton/Wildlife Art Agency

PLAINS ZEBRA

THE EARS
are mobile and tapering, but small in comparison to the other zebras.

Grevy's zebra (above left) is the largest of the zebras and of all wild equids: It reaches a maximum shoulder height of 63 in (160 cm), a head-and-body length of 118 in (300 cm) and weight of 992 lb (450 kg). The Brazilian tapir (above right) has a head-and-body length of 71–99 in (180–250 cm), a shoulder height of 30–47 in (75–120 cm) and a weight of 500–660 lb (225–300 kg).

STRIPE PATTERNS

The torso and head stripes are narrow over a buff or white base, while the neck stripes tend to be broad. Stripes take on a concentric pattern on the rump. The belly is white and there are two white stripes along the spine.

The forequarter stripes are narrow. A set of stripes form a "gridiron" pattern over the rump and tail. Hindquarter and flank stripes are broader. The legs are striped and the belly is white, except for a black stripe on the chest.

The broad body stripes extend under the belly; they usually continue down the legs, either to the hooves or to the fetlocks (ankles). Southerly animals are less boldly striped with fewer stripes on the belly, hindquarters, and legs.

GREVY'S ZEBRA

MOUNTAIN ZEBRA

PLAINS ZEBRA

X
R
A
Y

ZEBRA SKULL
The skull is greatly elongated with long, narrow nasal bones. The eye socket is set behind the teeth so as to avoid any pressure on the eyes by the long molars. The lower jawbone is particularly big to accommodate the large cheek teeth and to serve as a broad anchorage for the chewing muscles.

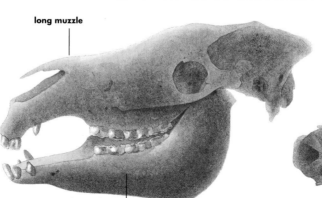

long muzzle

deep jawbone

TEETH
The zebra is well equipped to deal with its diet of tough, fibrous grass. The strong incisors are used to crop the sward, and the high-crowned molars grind it efficiently.

incisors

large molars

X-ray illustrations Elisabeth Smith

PLAINS ZEBRA
LOCATION: EAST AFRICA

THE MANE
is a scrubby, erect crest of hairs extending from between the ears to the withers (base of the neck). Stripes continue into the mane, but the core hairs are black.

THE BODY
is rather dumpy in appearance, and plains zebras tend to appear overweight.

CLASSIFICATION
GENUS: *EQUUS*

SPECIES: *BURCHELLI*

SIZE
HEIGHT TO SHOULDER: 49–53 IN (125–135 CM)

HEAD–BODY LENGTH: 83–102 IN (210–260 CM)

TAIL LENGTH: 16–22 IN (40–55 CM)

COLORATION
BROAD, VERTICAL BLACK AND WHITE STRIPES ON BODY AND DOWN CENTER OF FACE, BECOMING ALMOST HORIZONTAL ON THE SIDES OF THE FACE, HAUNCHES, AND LEGS

FEATURES
FAIRLY SMALL, NEAT HEAD

COMPACT, WELL-PROPORTIONED BODY CHARACTERIZED BY SLEEK ROUNDNESS ON BELLY AND HINDQUARTERS

LEGS SHORTER THAN IN GREVY'S ZEBRA, GIVING A DUMPIER APPEARANCE

THE FEET
have a single toe, in which the nail has developed into a horny, protective outer wall, known as the hoof.

THE TAIL
is long, with horizontal black and white stripes ending in a tuft of long dark and pale intermingling hairs. There is a black line down the center.

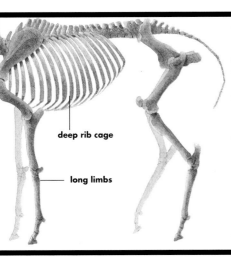

SKELETON
The long spine is almost straight compared with the markedly more arched, convex spine of primitive species, such as the tapirs. Combined with the deep rib cage, which gives plenty of room for lungs, and the long limbs, this gives speed and stamina for sustained galloping.

deep rib cage

long limbs

TAPIR SKULL
This is relatively short and narrow. The nasal bones are short and arched, the long "trunk" solely comprising tissue and muscle, not elongated bone. Tapirs have the same number of teeth as equids but they are relatively smaller, and the cheek teeth are particularly low-crowned.

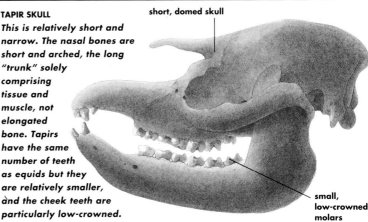

short, domed skull

small, low-crowned molars

Main illustrations Kim Thompson

PLATYPUS

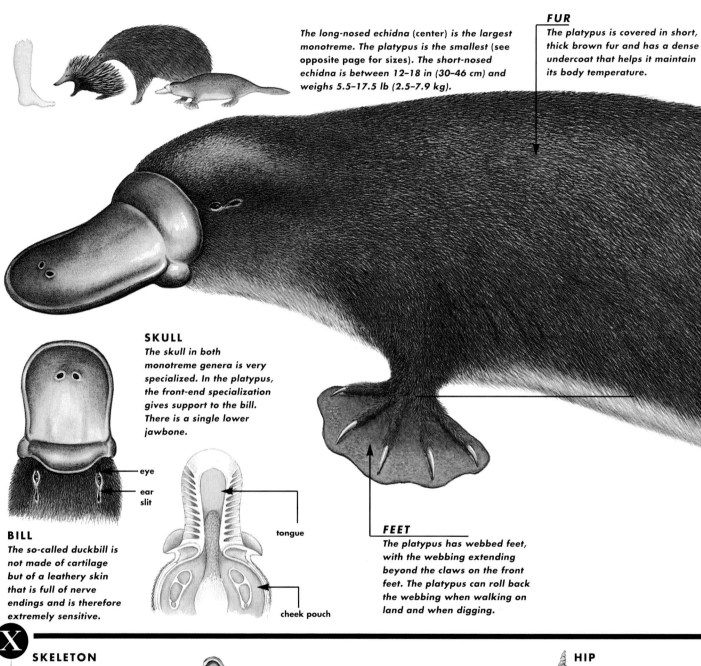

The long-nosed echidna (center) is the largest monotreme. The platypus is the smallest (see opposite page for sizes). The short-nosed echidna is between 12–18 in (30–46 cm) and weighs 5.5–17.5 lb (2.5–7.9 kg).

FUR
The platypus is covered in short, thick brown fur and has a dense undercoat that helps it maintain its body temperature.

SKULL
The skull in both monotreme genera is very specialized. In the platypus, the front-end specialization gives support to the bill. There is a single lower jawbone.

eye

ear slit

BILL
The so-called duckbill is not made of cartilage but of a leathery skin that is full of nerve endings and is therefore extremely sensitive.

tongue

cheek pouch

FEET
The platypus has webbed feet, with the webbing extending beyond the claws on the front feet. The platypus can roll back the webbing when walking on land and when digging.

SKELETON
The hip and leg structure of the platypus is like that of lizards and crocodiles, not like other mammals. The legs splay out from the sides instead of supporting the creature from underneath. The same is true for the echidna.

PLATYPUS HIPBONE

epipubic bone

PLATYPUS SKELETON

HIP
Another reptilian characteristic is the structure of the skeleton at the shoulder girdle and the presence of epipubic bones attached to the pelvic girdle (far left), which are bony extensions that presumably are partly for the support of the female's pouch.

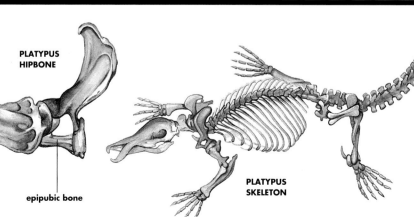

X-ray illustrations Gary Martin/Wildlife Art Agency

PLATYPUS

LOCATION: EASTERN AUSTRALIA & TASMANIA

CLASSIFICATION

GENUS: *ORNITHORHYNCHUS*

SPECIES: *ANATINUS*

SIZE

HEAD–BODY LENGTH: MALE UP TO **24** IN (**60** CM)
FEMALE UP TO **20** IN (**50** CM)

TAIL LENGTH: **6–7.5** IN (**15–19** CM)

WEIGHT/DIET: **2.2–4.8** LB (**1–2** KG)/EATS INSECT
LARVAE, WORMS, CRUSTACEANS, TADPOLES

LIFESPAN: **10** TO **15** YEARS

COLORATION

DARK BROWN BACK, SILVER TO LIGHT BROWN
(SOMETIMES TINGED WITH PINK OR YELLOW)
UNDERSIDE WITH RUSTY BROWN MIDLINE,
ESPECIALLY IN YOUNG ANIMALS, WHICH HAVE
LIGHTEST FUR. FEMALES CAN BE IDENTIFIED BY A
MORE PRONOUNCED REDDISH TINT TO THEIR FUR

THE LONG-NOSED ECHIDNA

CLASSIFICATION

GENUS: *ZAGLOSSUS*

SPECIES: *BRUIJNI*

SIZE

HEAD–BODY LENGTH: **18–35** IN (**46–89** CM)

TAIL LENGTH: VESTIGIAL TAIL

WEIGHT/DIET: UP TO **22** LB (**10** KG)/EATS MAINLY
EARTHWORMS

LIFESPAN: ABOUT **15** YEARS IN THE WILD
(UP TO **30** YEARS IN CAPTIVITY)

muscle

gland

exposed poison spur

reservoir

spur

foot

SPUR

The male platypus has horny spurs on the ankles of its hind legs that can deliver poison secreted by specialized poison glands. Only monotreme mammals have these spurs.

TAIL

The tail is used for storing fat, steering while swimming, and incubating eggs.

Illustrations Wayne Ford/Wildlife Art Agency

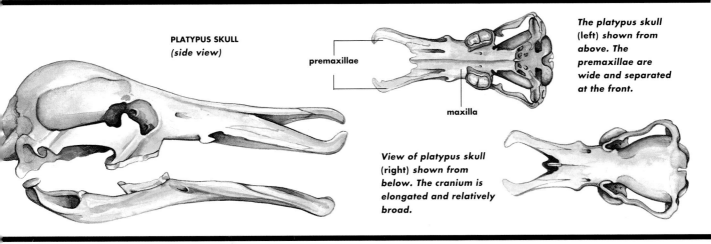

PLATYPUS SKULL
(side view)

premaxillae

maxilla

The platypus skull (left) shown from above. The premaxillae are wide and separated at the front.

View of platypus skull (right) shown from below. The cranium is elongated and relatively broad.

POLAR BEAR

LONG NECK

Polar bears have longer necks than other bears, making them streamlined for swimming.

The polar bear is the largest living land carnivore. Males reach up to 5 ft (1.6 m) at the shoulder. In comparison, the sun bear of Southeast Asia, which is the smallest member of the bear family, reaches a maximum height of only 2.3 ft (70 cm), about the length of a polar bear's legs.

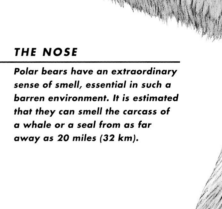

BROWN BEAR

Compared to the polar bear, the brown or grizzly bear has a much larger head, with a broader face and prominent muzzle.

BLACK BEAR

Otherwise similar in appearance to the brown bear, the American black bear has a narrower head and face and a shorter, sleeker coat.

THE NOSE

Polar bears have an extraordinary sense of smell, essential in such a barren environment. It is estimated that they can smell the carcass of a whale or a seal from as far away as 20 miles (32 km).

POLAR BEAR   **BROWN BEAR**

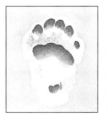 

The polar bear's claws are protected by thick fur padding, which provides traction as it walks, while the brown bear's longer claws dig in the ground.

X R A Y

short tail

The bones that make up the polar bear's skeleton are very heavy in order to support its muscular bulk.

long legs

large, strong feet

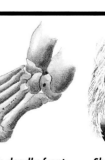

The bear's deadly front paws act like a 25-lb (11-kg) sledgehammer on its unsuspecting prey.

Short but extremely sharp claws are perfect for holding on to a slippery seal.

POLAR BEAR

LOCATION: CIRCUMPOLAR IN NORTHERN HEMISPHERE

CLASSIFICATION

GENUS: *URSUS*

SPECIES: *MARITIMUS*

SIZE

HEAD–BODY LENGTH/MALE: 8–10 FT (2.5–3 M)

HEAD–BODY LENGTH/FEMALE: 6.5–8 FT (2–2.5 M)

SHOULDER HEIGHT/MALE: 5 FT (1.6 M)

WEIGHT/MALE: 770–1,540 LB (350–700 KG)

WEIGHT/FEMALE: 330–1,000 LB (150–450 KG)

WEIGHT AT BIRTH: 1–1.5 LB (500–700 G)

COLORATION

VARIES FROM PURE WHITE IN CUBS TO BLUISH WHITE, CREAMY WHITE, OR YELLOWISH IN ADULTS (THE YELLOW COLOR MAY BE CAUSED BY THE OXIDATION OF SEA OIL)

FEATURES

HUGE PAWS UP TO **12** IN **(30 CM)** ACROSS

POWERFUL, STREAMLINED BODY

BLACK SKIN BENEATH FUR

DARK EYES AND A BLACK NOSE

EXTREMELY SHARP CLAWS

Despite appearances, a polar bear's skin is, in fact, black. The bear looks white because its fur is made up of hollow hairs that reflect the sun. Beneath its skin lies a layer of fat that keeps the bear warm in the coldest Arctic winters.

hollow hairs

black skin

fat

CROSS SECTION OF SKIN AND HAIR

STRONG LEGS

The polar bear's long, square legs need to be very strong to support such bulk. They enable the bear to cover huge distances (up to 700 miles/1,200 km a year) in its endless search for prey.

HUGE STOMACH

Because of the scarcity of prey in the Arctic, the polar bear must make the most of every meal. The stomach of an adult male can expand to take up to 220 lb (90 kg) of meat and blubber in one sitting.

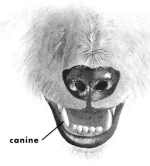

canine

The polar bear's long canine teeth show it to be a true carnivore, the only bear almost wholly dependent on meat. Most bears tend to be largely omnivorous, but the polar bear's diet of seal meat has resulted in the evolution of carnassial, or flesh-shearing, teeth, a feature undeveloped in the other bears.

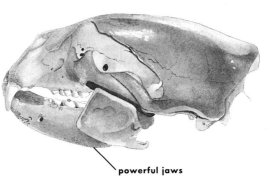

powerful jaws

Although the polar bear's powerful jaws are typical of a hunter, they are not actually used to kill prey; this duty is performed by a heavy blow from the bear's awesome paws. The jaws are used to pull victims from the water. In the case of such prey as beluga whales, this is quite some task.

P O R C U P I N E

The North American porcupine (below center) is the largest of the New World porcupines, up to 47 in (120 cm) long including the tail. The crested porcupine (below left) has a head-and-body length of about 33 in (85 cm). Smallest of all is the long-tailed porcupine (below right), which measures a maximum of 19 in (48 cm) and weighs up to 5 lb (2.2 kg).

THE HEAD

is small but thickset. Although the small ears are mainly lost in the fur, hearing is one of the best developed of the senses.

THE EYES

are small and round; this animal tends to be very nearsighted and often fails to notice the approach of other animals when on the ground.

THE LEGS

are short and stocky, giving a short stride and a waddling gait. This animal moves at a faster, but still clumsy, trot or gallop when alarmed.

THE FEET

are broad and heavy. The naked soles have small, fleshy ridges that improve grip. Four toes on the forefeet and five on the hind feet all have long claws.

X RAY

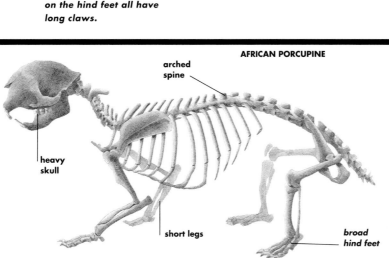

AFRICAN PORCUPINE

arched spine

heavy skull

short legs

broad hind feet

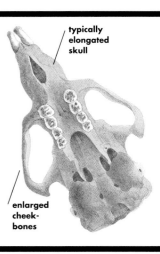

typically elongated skull

enlarged cheek-bones

The African porcupine (left) is stoutly built, with short, stocky legs and a sturdy neck. It walks on the soles of its broad, five-toed feet. Like the North American species, it has a noticeably arched spine. The tail is shorter than in the other Old World porcupines.

X-ray illustrations Elisabeth Smith

NORTH AMERICAN PORCUPINE

LOCATION: CANADA & THE USA, NORTH MEXICO

THE QUILLS

grow most densely on the back and rump, giving the animal an almost impregnable defense.

EACH QUILL

is sharply pointed and armed with barbs. Once a quill is fixed in an animal's skin, the victim's muscular action works upon the barbs to draw the quill in deeper.

THE BODY

is large and robust, with an arching back. The quills on the upper parts are intermingled with long, stiff guard hairs. Beneath these lies a softer underfur. The belly lacks quills but has a thick coat of stiff hairs.

CLASSIFICATION

GENUS: *ERETHIZON*

SPECIES: *DORSATUM*

SIZE

HEAD-BODY LENGTH: 25–35 IN (64–89 CM)

TAIL: 6–12 IN (15–30 CM)

LENGTH OF QUILLS: UP TO 3 IN (7.6 CM)

WEIGHT AT BIRTH: 12–22 OZ (340–624 G)

WEIGHT: 8–40 LBS (3.6–18 KG)

COLORATION

UPPER PARTS OF BODY ARE USUALLY BLACK OR BROWN IN EASTERN PART OF RANGE, BUT MORE YELLOW IN WESTERN AREAS. QUILLS HAVE A CREAM-COLORED BASE, DARKENING TOWARD THE TIP. THE OVERALL EFFECT IS QUITE PALE ON TOP, DUE TO LIGHT GUARD HAIRS, AND MUCH DARKER UNDERNEATH

FEATURES

SMALL, ROUNDED, DARK EYES. SMALL EARS ARE ALMOST HIDDEN IN THE FUR

QUILLS CAN BE ERECTED AS A DEFENSE MECHANISM, AND THE TAIL IS SWUNG VIOLENTLY FROM SIDE TO SIDE AT THE SAME TIME

BROAD, HAIRLESS, AND SLIGHTLY RIDGED SOLES OF THE FEET GIVE GOOD GRIP ON BRANCHES

FAIRLY POOR EYESIGHT, BUT GOOD SENSES OF SMELL, TOUCH, AND HEARING

THE TAIL

is short and thick, heavily armored with quills on the upper surface and stiff hairs below.

NORTH AMERICAN PORCUPINE

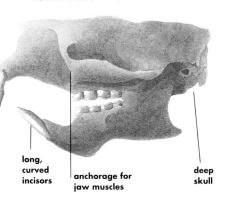

long, curved incisors

anchorage for jaw muscles

deep skull

The differences between porcupines' skulls are highly important, as they enable zoologists to classify the various species. The African porcupine has a heavy skull (right); the back of the head supports powerful neck muscles. The North American porcupine (left) has an elongated skull, with lighter bone and a flatter top.

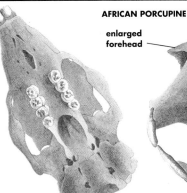

AFRICAN PORCUPINE

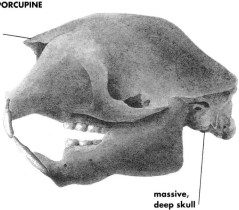

enlarged forehead

massive, deep skull

Main illustration Rachel Lockwood/Wildlife Art Agency

PRAIRIE DOG

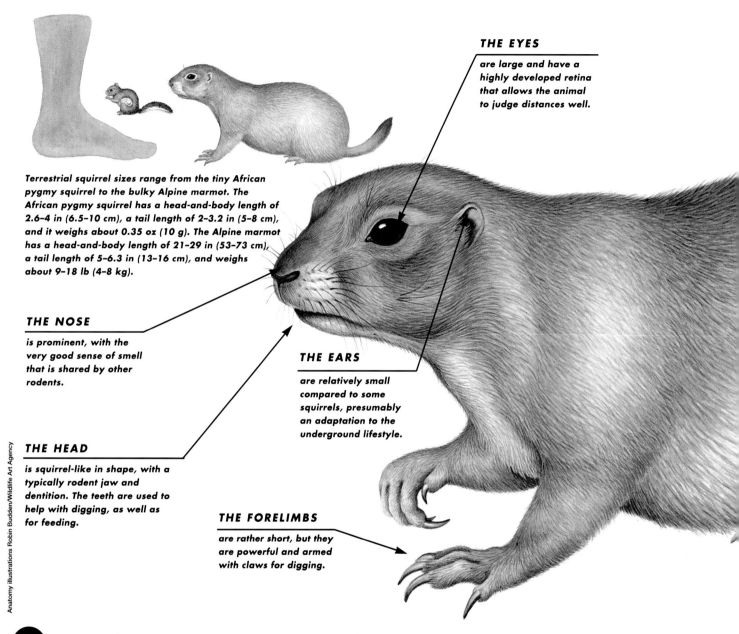

THE EYES

are large and have a highly developed retina that allows the animal to judge distances well.

Terrestrial squirrel sizes range from the tiny African pygmy squirrel to the bulky Alpine marmot. The African pygmy squirrel has a head-and-body length of 2.6–4 in (6.5–10 cm), a tail length of 2–3.2 in (5–8 cm), and it weighs about 0.35 oz (10 g). The Alpine marmot has a head-and-body length of 21–29 in (53–73 cm), a tail length of 5–6.3 in (13–16 cm), and weighs about 9–18 lb (4–8 kg).

THE NOSE

is prominent, with the very good sense of smell that is shared by other rodents.

THE EARS

are relatively small compared to some squirrels, presumably an adaptation to the underground lifestyle.

THE HEAD

is squirrel-like in shape, with a typically rodent jaw and dentition. The teeth are used to help with digging, as well as for feeding.

THE FORELIMBS

are rather short, but they are powerful and armed with claws for digging.

The sciurid skeleton shows that the hind legs are not more than twice the length of the forelegs, and there are four digits on each forefoot and five on each hind foot. The tail can be any length, but is usually well covered with hair and bushy. Claws are common to the ground-living squirrels and squirrel-like rodents, but the long-clawed ground squirrel has thick, powerful claws that are often more than 0.4 in (1 cm) long. No other genus except Hyosciurus has such large claws.

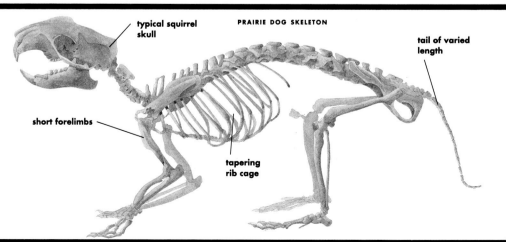

typical squirrel skull

PRAIRIE DOG SKELETON

tail of varied length

short forelimbs

tapering rib cage

BLACK-TAILED PRAIRIE DOG

LOCATION: SOUTHERN CANADA & THE USA, NORTHERN MEXICO

CLASSIFICATION
GENUS: *CYNOMYS*

SPECIES: *LUDOVICIANUS*

SIZE
HEAD–BODY LENGTH: 11–13 IN (28–33 CM)

TAIL LENGTH: 1.2–4.7 IN (3–12 CM)

WEIGHT: 24.5–49 OZ (700–1,400 G)

COLORATION
GRIZZLED YELLOW-GRAY OR BUFF BACK, WITH PALER UNDERPARTS, AND A BLACK-TIPPED, SLIGHTLY FLATTENED TAIL

FEATURES
THE DISPLAY HABIT CALLED THE JUMP-YIP, COMBINING A SPECIAL LEAP INTO THE AIR AND A LOUD BARK. THIS IS USED AS A PRELUDE TO TERRITORIAL DEFENSE

13-LINED GROUND SQUIRREL

CLASSIFICATION
GENUS: *SPERMOPHILUS*

SPECIES: *TRIDECEMLINEATUS*

SIZE
HEAD–BODY LENGTH: 5–16 IN (13–41 CM)

TAIL LENGTH: 1.6–9.9 IN (4–25 CM)

WEIGHT: 3–35 OZ (85–1,000 G)

COLORATION
A SERIES OF ALTERNATING PALE AND DARK STRIPES ALONG THE BODY

FEATURES
A ROW OF PALE SPOTS IN EACH OF THE DARK BODY STRIPES

NEARLY DOUBLES IN WEIGHT BEFORE A DORMANCY THAT LASTS UP TO SEVEN MONTHS

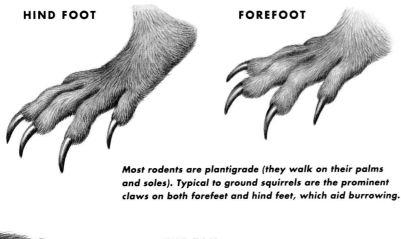

HIND FOOT   **FOREFOOT**

Most rodents are plantigrade (they walk on their palms and soles). Typical to ground squirrels are the prominent claws on both forefeet and hind feet, which aid burrowing.

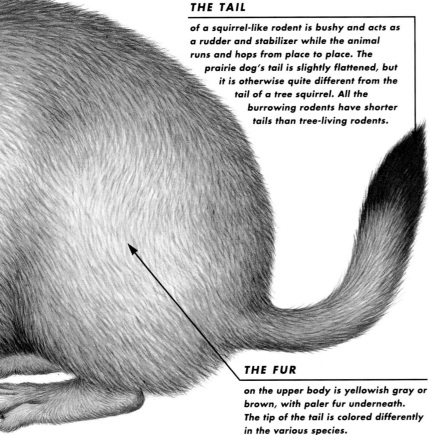

THE TAIL

of a squirrel-like rodent is bushy and acts as a rudder and stabilizer while the animal runs and hops from place to place. The prairie dog's tail is slightly flattened, but it is otherwise quite different from the tail of a tree squirrel. All the burrowing rodents have shorter tails than tree-living rodents.

THE FUR

on the upper body is yellowish gray or brown, with paler fur underneath. The tip of the tail is colored differently in the various species.

SKULL
The sciurid skull has widely spaced eye sockets and thick, bony areas around each socket. It also has the typical rodent jaw, with just one pair of incisors on each jaw.

DENTITION
Squirrels have a small upper premolar. In some species this is lost before maturity. There are twenty or twenty-two teeth in total. The molars have roots, are low-crowned, and have enameled cusps on the lower teeth and ridges and cusps on the upper teeth.

long incisors

PRONGHORN

THE RUMP

bears a patch of pure-white hairs. When disturbed, the pronghorn raises these hairs to flash an alarm signal and also releases a scent from rump glands.

Male pronghorns measure 3.3–5 ft (1–1.5 m) from head to rump, with a tail of 3–4 in (7.5–10 cm). The shoulder height is 31.5–41 in (80–104 cm). Females are smaller.

The water chevrotain is the largest of its family. It has a head-and-body length of 23.6–33.5 in (60–85 cm), with a shoulder height of 12–16 in (30–40 cm). The lesser Malay chevrotain has a head-and-body length of only 17.3–19 in (44–48 cm), and stands just 8 in (20 cm) high at the shoulder.

THE LIMBS

are slender, but they give the pronghorn astonishing agility: It can cover 27 ft (8 m) of ground in a single leap.

THE HOOVES

are long and pointed. Springy pads of gristle act as shock absorbers when the animal is leaping and running at full tilt.

THE COAT

comprises an outer layer of long, protective guard hairs over an undercoat of dense, woolly fur that retains warmth. The pronghorn flexes special muscles to erect or relax the guard hairs in order to regulate its body temperature.

Anatomy illustrations Wayne Ford/Wildlife Art Agency

The pronghorn's bone structure is fine and lightweight, offering a profile not unlike the true antelopes. The limbs, however, are highly resilient, easily capable of sustaining the shocks induced by the animal's rapid pace. The forefeet take the brunt of the pressure when the pronghorn runs fast.

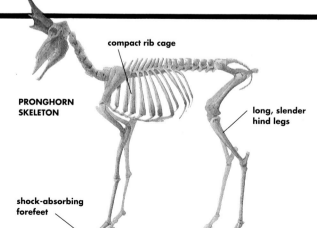

compact rib cage

PRONGHORN SKELETON

long, slender hind legs

shock-absorbing forefeet

TEETH

The pronghorn has a row of sharp incisors and canines in the lower jaw; these bite onto a hard pad in the upper jaw. Behind these teeth is a space, behind which lie the flat, high-crowned premolars and molars for grinding up vegetation.

X-ray illustrations Elisabeth Smith

PRONGHORN

LOCATION: WESTERN NORTH AMERICA

CLASSIFICATION

GENUS: *ANTILOCAPRA*

SPECIES: *AMERICANA*

SIZE

HEAD–BODY LENGTH: 3.3–5 FT (1–1.5 M)

TAIL LENGTH: 3–4 IN (7.5–10 CM)

SHOULDER HEIGHT: 31.5–41 IN (80–104 CM)

COLORATION

LIGHT BROWN TO TAN

THE UNDERSIDE HAS A RECTANGULAR WHITE PATCH BETWEEN THE SHOULDERS AND THE HIND LEGS

THERE ARE TWO WHITE PATCHES ON THE FRONT OF THE NECK AND WHITE PATCHES ON THE RUMP

THE MALE HAS A BLACK MANE

FEATURES

SLENDER LEGS, LONG BACK, AND SHORT TAIL

MUZZLE IS HAIRLESS ONLY AROUND THE NOSTRILS

A PAIR OF FORKED HORNS THAT GROW ON LARGE, BONY KNOBS. THE LATTER ARE PERMANENT BUT THE HORNS ARE SHED EACH YEAR

THE EYES

are protected from the sun by long, black lashes. Surprisingly large and prominent, they are set well back in the skull to give 360° vision. The pronghorn can reputedly detect objects up to 4 miles (6.5 km) away.

THE NOSE

is sensitive, particularly to the sexual, territorial, and alarm scents given off by other pronghorns.

THE FOREFEET

are used by the pronghorn to dig latrine holes in the soil, and to scrape away snow to expose food.

HORN

The pronghorn sheds only the sheath of its horns each year. The sheath is formed from skin covered in bristlelike hairs, which gradually turns into true horn. Central to the horn is a laterally flattened, bony core: This is not shed.

sheath

horn core

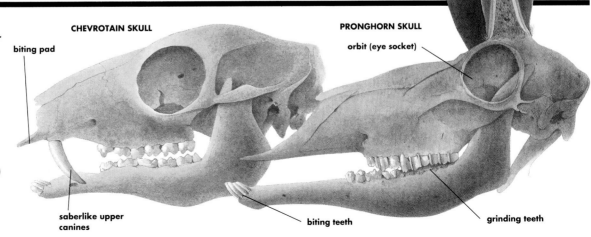

The chevrotain has a similar dentition to that of the pronghorn, except that it possesses a pair of canines in the upper jaw. In the male these are elongated into the form of saberlike tusks, while in the female they are mere studs.

Clearly visible on the pronghorn's skull (far right) is the placement of the eye orbits far back in the cranium.

CHEVROTAIN SKULL

biting pad

saberlike upper canines

biting teeth

PRONGHORN SKULL

orbit (eye socket)

grinding teeth

PRZHEVALSKI'S HORSE

Przhevalski's horse (right) is medium-sized, standing 47–55 in (120–142 cm) at the withers (shoulder). The smallest horse breed in existence, the Falabella (center), stands 28 in (72 cm) high at the shoulder, while the largest, the Shire (left), averages 67 in (170 cm) at the shoulder.

THE COAT

is a sandy yellow color that merges with its arid background. It may be slightly paler on the underbelly. Usually there is a dark dorsal stripe that extends from the base of the neck along the length of the spine to the tail. Together with the color of the coat, this is a characteristic of a primitive and old type of equid.

VOMERONASAL POUCH

The vomeronasal (voe-mer-o-NAY-zal) pouch lies within the horse's nose and is used to analyze pheromones. In an act known as the flehmen response, a stallion sniffs at a mare's urine, drawing the air into the pouch, to see if she is ready to mate.

THE MANE

runs the length of the neck and is a dark brown or black. Coarse, scrubby hairs stand upright and there is no forelock (hair falling over the face between the ears).

THE FEET

comprise a single toe on each limb, in which the nail has developed into a horny outer wall, known as the hoof. The horse therefore walks on four toes; the added length this gives to each limb increases its ability to move at high speed.

Anatomy illustrations Barry Croucher/Wildlife Art Agency

 X-RAY

THE SPINE
Long and almost straight, rather than arched as in more primitive equids, the spine allows for speed over a distance rather than a quick, springy start-up movement. There are five sections of vertebral bones. From neck to tail, these are the cervical, dorsal, lumbar, sacral, and caudal vertebrae.

PRZHEVALSKI'S HORSE SKELETON

near-horizontal spine

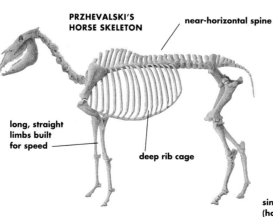

long, straight limbs built for speed

deep rib cage

LEG

In the forelimbs the ulna and radius bones are fused, with the ulna reduced in size. In the hind limbs the tibia and fibula are fused, with the tibia being enlarged. This allows for twisting and turning at high speed with less risk of injury to the ankle and wrist joints. There are strong ligaments in all legs.

wrist joint

single toe (hoof)

X-ray illustrations Elisabeth Smith

PRZHEVALSKI'S HORSE

LOCATION: NONE IN THE WILD; FORMERLY
MONGOLIA

Main illustration Rachel Lockwood/Wildlife Art Agency

CLASSIFICATION

GENUS: *EQUUS*

SPECIES: *PRZEWALSKII*

SIZE

HEIGHT TO SHOULDER: 47–60 IN (120–142 CM)

HEAD–BODY LENGTH: 85-110 IN (220–280 CM)

TAIL LENGTH: 36–43 IN (92–110 CM)

WEIGHT AT BIRTH: 55–66 LB (25–30 KG)

ADULT WEIGHT: 550–660 LB (250–300 KG)

COLORATION

DUN (SAND-COLORED) COAT WITH PALER
UNDERSIDES AND MUZZLE

DARK BROWN OR BLACK MANE, TAIL, AND LEGS

DARK STRIPE DOWN THE CENTER OF THE BACK

FEATURES

LARGE, HEAVY HEAD, USUALLY CONVEX IN PROFILE

COMPARATIVELY LONG, POINTED EARS

LONG, THICKLY HAIRED TAIL, OFTEN SCRUBBY AT
THE TOP

THE EARS

are comparatively long and pointed
and extremely expressive of a horse's
mood. Pricked forward, the animal is
alert and attentive. If they are pressed
backward, this indicates anger, fear,
or aggression.

THE NECK

is thick and comparatively
short, with well-developed
muscles.

THE MUZZLE

is generally paler than
the rest of the coat. The
nostrils are large and
the upper lip is soft and
remarkably mobile.

LIMBS

The Przhevalski's
limbs are usually
dark brown or
black, but
sometimes they
have bar markings
around them.

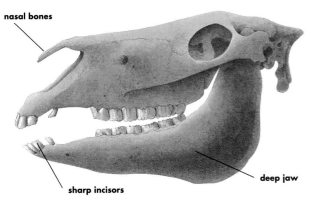

nasal bones

sharp incisors

deep jaw

SKULL

The face is elongated,
with the eye socket set
high and wide behind the
teeth to ensure that there
is no pressure on the
eyes from the molars. The
skull lengthened during
the course of evolution to
accommodate the large
cheek teeth and
jawbones. The nasal
bones are long and
narrow.

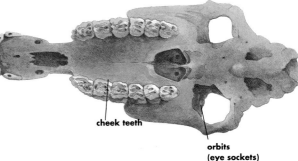

cheek teeth

orbits
(eye sockets)

P U M A

RED-BROWN FUR

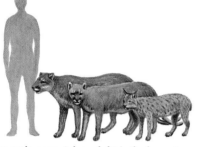

The male puma (above left) is the largest of the New World cats and, in spite of being classed as a small cat, is as large as the jaguar (see Fact File). Females (above center) are slightly smaller. The lynx (above right) has a head-and-body length of 26–43 in (67–110 cm). The little spotted cat and kodkod are the smallest at about 20 in (52 cm).

EARS
These are relatively small. However, the refined muscular control of the ears, possessed by all cats, increases both the sensitivity of hearing and ear mobility.

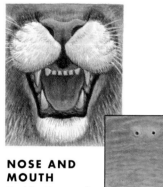

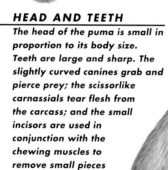

NOSE AND MOUTH
Besides the nasal olfactory sensors possessed by most animals, cats have a vomeronasal organ (above right)—two auxiliary olfactory membranes located in canals that lead from the roof of the mouth on each side. Their function is not known.

HEAD AND TEETH
The head of the puma is small in proportion to its body size. Teeth are large and sharp. The slightly curved canines grab and pierce prey; the scissorlike carnassials tear flesh from the carcass; and the small incisors are used in conjunction with the chewing muscles to remove small pieces of meat from bones.

LEGS
The legs seem longer than they are because cats are digitigrade —that is, they walk on their toes. In the puma, a cat with remarkable leaping ability, the hind legs are considerably longer than the front ones.

Illustrations Simon Turvey/Wildlife Art Agency

X
R
A
Y

The puma's skeleton shows a vertebral column that is curved like a taut bow. This shape supports the body but allows great flexibility of movement.

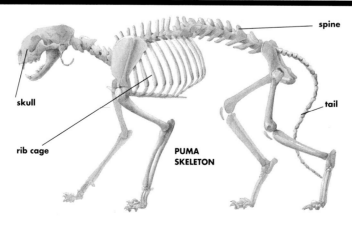

spine

skull

tail

rib cage

PUMA SKELETON

Pumas have retractile claws, which are contained in sheaths in the feet when not in use. This means they are elevated above the ground and are not subject to constant wear that would quickly make them dull. The claws are controlled by ligaments and extensor and flexor muscles.

X-ray illustrations Elisabeth Smith

PUMA

LOCATION: SOUTHERN CANADA TO SOUTH AMERICA

COAT COLORS

The puma's varying coat colors are associated with different locations. Reds are more common in the tropics, and blue-gray is found in northern areas. Black is very rare anywhere.

BLUE-GRAY FUR   **BLACK FUR**

CLASSIFICATION

GENUS: *FELIS*

SPECIES: *CONCOLOR*

SIZE

HEAD–BODY LENGTH: 41–79 IN (105–200 CM)

TAIL LENGTH: 26–31 IN (67–78 CM)

WEIGHT: 79–231 LB (36–105 KG)

SIZE VARIES GREATLY ACROSS THE RANGE; MALES ARE A LITTLE LARGER THAN FEMALES

WEIGHT AT BIRTH: 8–16 OZ (226–453 G)

COLORATION

SOLID COAT COLOR, USUALLY A TAWNY YELLOW ABOVE AND PALER UNDERNEATH

CUBS ARE BORN SPOTTED WITH RINGED TAILS; THESE MARKINGS FADE AFTER A FEW MONTHS

FEATURES

EYE COLOR IS AMBER

EARS ARE SMALL, SHORT, AND ROUNDED; BACKS ARE DARKER

TAIL IS LONG WITH A BLACK TIP

HIND LEGS ARE CONSIDERABLY LONGER THAN FRONT

FEET ARE LARGE

BODY SHAPE

Fairly long and streamlined with powerful limbs, the body is designed for bursts of speed.

FEET AND TRACKS

The puma's large feet leave rounded tracks, usually with all four lower toes imprinted, although there are generally no claw marks. The fore prints are slightly larger than the hind prints.

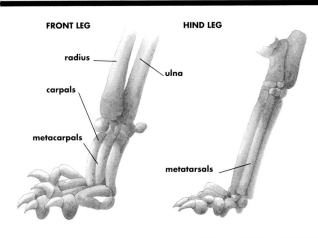

FRONT LEG   **HIND LEG**

radius

ulna

carpals

metacarpals

metatarsals

Like other cats, the puma has a relatively small skull. However, its eyes are unusually large for the skull size. Large eyes have better light-gathering abilities for vision in poor light.

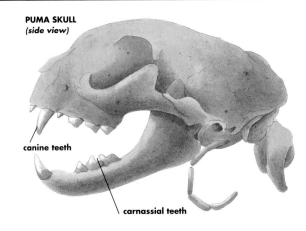

PUMA SKULL
(side view)

canine teeth

carnassial teeth

RABBIT

The rabbit (above center) ranges in size from 10 to 11.5 in (25–29 cm) in the pygmy rabbit to 17–20 in (43–51 cm) in the Amami rabbit. Hares are larger (top left) and have bigger ears. Pikas (top right) are much smaller. The largest pika measures about 8 in (20 cm).

RABBIT'S TRACKS

When hopping or running, the hind feet fall almost level with the forefeet to give a uniform track pattern. When running, the European rabbit can reach speeds of 24 mph (39 km/h), which is about half the speed of a brown hare.

HOPPING **RUNNING**

Simon Turvey/ Wildlife Art Agency

X
R
A
Y

The structure of the skeleton shows how the curving spine and long hind feet enable the rabbit to propel its body forward, often using the two feet together.

RABBIT SKELETON

The rabbit's hind legs are made for bounding. The long, flat feet give it a good grip on hard ground. On snow the feet act like snowshoes.

HARE'S HIND LEG

long metatarsals

RABBIT'S HIND LEG

X-ray illustrations Elisabeth Smith

EUROPEAN RABBIT

LOCATION: WESTERN EUROPE, AUSTRALIA
& SOUTH AMERICA

CLASSIFICATION

GENUS: *ORYCTOLAGUS*

SPECIES: *CUNICULUS*

SIZE

LENGTH/MALE: UP TO 20 IN (51 CM)

WEIGHT/MALE: UP TO 6.6 LB (3 KG)

WEIGHT AT BIRTH: 1.4 OZ (40 G)

FEMALES ARE SMALLER THAN MALES,
WITH NARROWER HEADS

COLORATION

GRAYISH WITH A BROWN TINGE ABOVE,
PARTICULARLY AT NAPE; LIGHT GRAY BELOW

TAIL: BLACK ABOVE, WHITE BENEATH

DARK PATCHES AROUND EYES

LONG CLAWS FOR DIGGING

FEATURES

LONG, MOBILE EARS

HIGH-SET EYES ON SIDE OF HEAD

LONG HIND LEGS AND HOPPING GAIT

"POWDER-PUFF" TAIL FLASHES WHITE DURING FLIGHT

THE EARS

The rabbit's hearing is its most important sense. Its ears are fairly mobile and can turn toward sounds or lie back for running.

THE FUR

density varies between species and climate. The European rabbit has a dense winter coat.

HINDQUARTERS

are powerful and enable the rabbit to change direction rapidly when it is being chased by predators.

THE TAIL

is short, leaving nothing for a chasing, outstretched predator to grab while pursuing the rabbit.

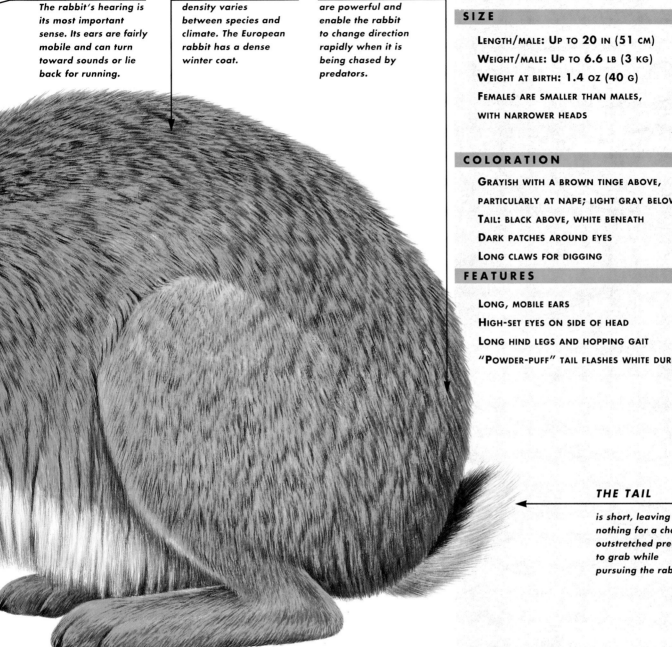

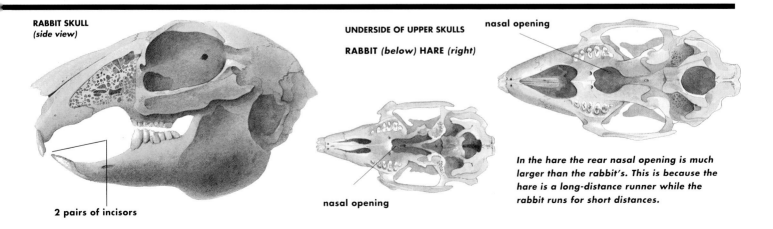

RABBIT SKULL
(side view)

2 pairs of incisors

UNDERSIDE OF UPPER SKULLS

RABBIT (below) **HARE** (right)

nasal opening

nasal opening

In the hare the rear nasal opening is much larger than the rabbit's. This is because the hare is a long-distance runner while the rabbit runs for short distances.

RACCOON

THE FUR

on the body is longer and more dense than on the face. It consists of a soft, woolly undercoat, with a top coat of longer, coarser hairs. Its denseness gives the raccoon an impression of robustness.

THE EARS

are comparatively small and rounded. They are usually tipped with white hairs. The inner surface of the ears is covered with longer but less dense, hair than on the outside.

The common raccoon (above left) is as big as a medium-sized dog, although there is a marked size variation among individuals (see Fact File). The ring-tailed coati (above center) has a head-to-tail length of 32–50 in (81–127 cm), somewhat more than half being tail. The kinkajou (above right) has a head-and-body length of 16.5–22.5 in (42–57 cm); its prehensile tail measures 15.7–22 in (40–56 cm).

FOREFOOT

HIND FOOT

RACCOON FOOT FACTS

The common raccoon has highly dexterous forepaws, comparable to some of the primates. There are five toes on each foot; those on the forefeet are relatively long and can be spread widely. The soles are naked and planted on the ground as the animal walks, in the same way as bears and humans.

THE EYES

are framed by the raccoon's most distinctive feature—the mask. Patches of black around each eye extend across the cheeks and are accentuated by a white line of fur above and below.

THE FACE

is somewhat foxlike in appearance; quite broad at the forehead, it tapers to a pointed muzzle. The nose is black and round.

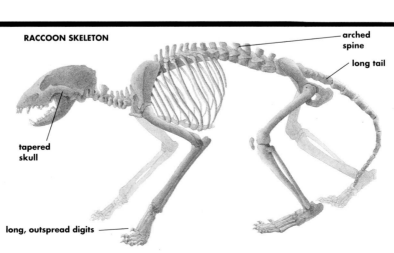

SKELETON

Likened in size to a small to medium dog and in build to a stout cat, the common raccoon has a distinctly arched back. It also has a foxlike head, which is broad at the base but tapers to a pointed muzzle. The hind feet can grow up to 3 in (7.5 cm) long.

RACCOON SKELETON

arched spine

long tail

tapered skull

long, outspread digits

SKULLS

All procyonids have fairly robust, elongate skulls. The raccoon has forty teeth; this number varies slightly in the different species. In keeping with the omnivorous diet, the carnassials are adapted for cutting, rather than tearing, flesh.

X-ray illustrations Elisabeth Smith

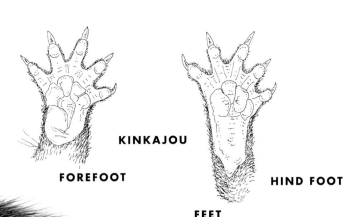

KINKAJOU

FOREFOOT

HIND FOOT

FEET
The forefeet of most members of this family are considerably shorter than the hind feet— with the exception of the ringtail, which has more catlike paws. The kinkajou, however, is unusual in having hairy soles on its feet. The toes of each foot are also joined by a weblike membrane that extends about a third of the way down.

COMMON RACCOON
LOCATION: SOUTHERN CANADA, USA & CENTRAL AMERICA

CLASSIFICATION

GENUS: *PROCYON*

SPECIES: *LOTOR*

SIZE

HEAD-BODY LENGTH: 16–37 IN (41–94 CM)

TAIL LENGTH: 7.5–16 IN (19–41 CM)

WEIGHT: 11–46 LB (5–21 KG); MALES ARE LARGER THAN FEMALES

WEIGHT AT BIRTH: 2 OZ (56 G)

COLORATION

GENERALLY A GRIZZLED GRAY, VARYING FROM PALE TO QUITE DARK. OCCASIONALLY MORE REDDISH AND OFTEN WITH YELLOW-BROWN FUR AROUND NAPE OF NECK

FEATURES

THE FACE HAS A CHARACTERISTIC BLACK EYE MASK EDGED WITH WHITE, AND LONGER TUFTS OF HAIR BEHIND THE CHEEKS. THE EYES THEMSELVES ARE BLACK, ROUND, AND MEDIUM SIZED

THE TAIL IS BUSHY AND DISTINCTIVELY RINGED IN DARK AND PALE BANDS

FIVE TOES ON EACH FOOT, WITH PARTICULARLY LONG AND MANIPULATIVE DIGITS ON THE FOREPAWS. THE CLAWS ARE SHARP BUT CANNOT BE RETRACTED

ARCHED BACK

THE LEGS
are fairly long, but tend not to look so because they are quite heavily furred at the top. The feet are characterized by long toes.

THE TAIL
is very bushy, with five to ten black or dark brown rings around it; the tip is always dark.

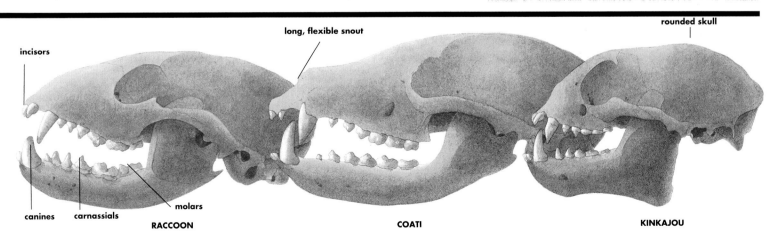

rounded skull

long, flexible snout

incisors

canines   carnassials

molars

RACCOON

COATI

KINKAJOU

Illustrations Steve Kingston/B/W illustrations Ruth Grewcock

RAT KANGAROO

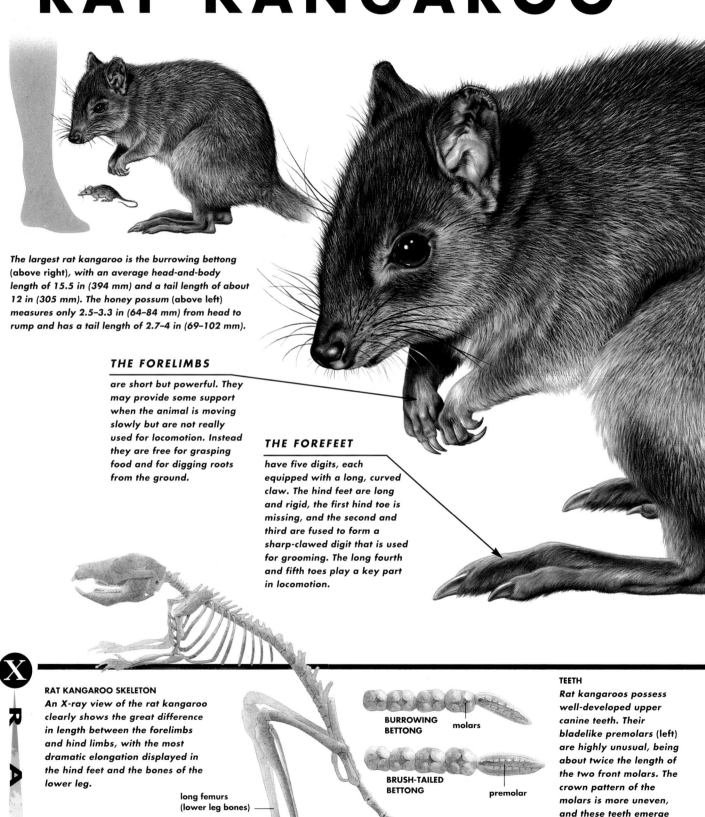

The largest rat kangaroo is the burrowing bettong (above right), with an average head-and-body length of 15.5 in (394 mm) and a tail length of about 12 in (305 mm). The honey possum (above left) measures only 2.5–3.3 in (64–84 mm) from head to rump and has a tail length of 2.7–4 in (69–102 mm).

THE FORELIMBS

are short but powerful. They may provide some support when the animal is moving slowly but are not really used for locomotion. Instead they are free for grasping food and for digging roots from the ground.

THE FOREFEET

have five digits, each equipped with a long, curved claw. The hind feet are long and rigid, the first hind toe is missing, and the second and third are fused to form a sharp-clawed digit that is used for grooming. The long fourth and fifth toes play a key part in locomotion.

X-RAY

RAT KANGAROO SKELETON
An X-ray view of the rat kangaroo clearly shows the great difference in length between the forelimbs and hind limbs, with the most dramatic elongation displayed in the hind feet and the bones of the lower leg.

long femurs (lower leg bones)

very long toe bones

supportive tail

BURROWING BETTONG

molars

BRUSH-TAILED BETTONG

premolar

TEETH
Rat kangaroos possess well-developed upper canine teeth. Their bladelike premolars (left) are highly unusual, being about twice the length of the two front molars. The crown pattern of the molars is more uneven, and these teeth emerge simultaneously rather than in a sequence over time.

X-ray illustrations Elisabeth Smith

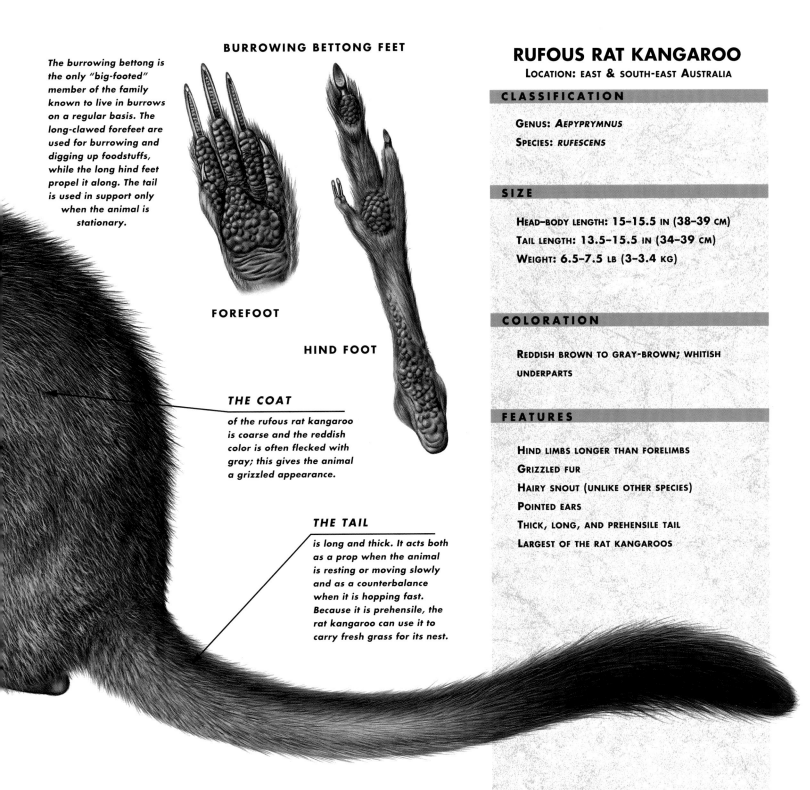

BURROWING BETTONG FEET

The burrowing bettong is the only "big-footed" member of the family known to live in burrows on a regular basis. The long-clawed forefeet are used for burrowing and digging up foodstuffs, while the long hind feet propel it along. The tail is used in support only when the animal is stationary.

FOREFOOT

HIND FOOT

THE COAT

of the rufous rat kangaroo is coarse and the reddish color is often flecked with gray; this gives the animal a grizzled appearance.

THE TAIL

is long and thick. It acts both as a prop when the animal is resting or moving slowly and as a counterbalance when it is hopping fast. Because it is prehensile, the rat kangaroo can use it to carry fresh grass for its nest.

RUFOUS RAT KANGAROO
LOCATION: EAST & SOUTH-EAST AUSTRALIA

CLASSIFICATION

GENUS: *AEPYPRYMNUS*

SPECIES: *RUFESCENS*

SIZE

HEAD–BODY LENGTH: 15–15.5 IN (38–39 CM)

TAIL LENGTH: 13.5–15.5 IN (34–39 CM)

WEIGHT: 6.5–7.5 LB (3–3.4 KG)

COLORATION

REDDISH BROWN TO GRAY-BROWN; WHITISH UNDERPARTS

FEATURES

HIND LIMBS LONGER THAN FORELIMBS

GRIZZLED FUR

HAIRY SNOUT (UNLIKE OTHER SPECIES)

POINTED EARS

THICK, LONG, AND PREHENSILE TAIL

LARGEST OF THE RAT KANGAROOS

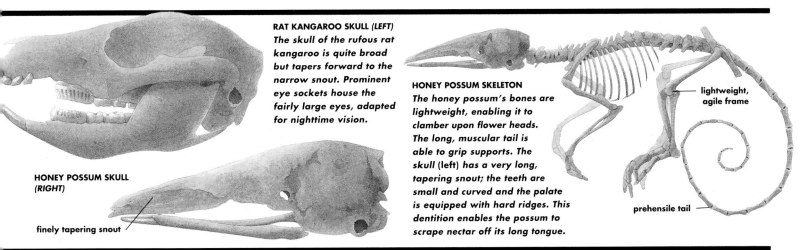

RAT KANGAROO SKULL (LEFT)
The skull of the rufous rat kangaroo is quite broad but tapers forward to the narrow snout. Prominent eye sockets house the fairly large eyes, adapted for nighttime vision.

HONEY POSSUM SKULL (RIGHT)

finely tapering snout

HONEY POSSUM SKELETON
The honey possum's bones are lightweight, enabling it to clamber upon flower heads. The long, muscular tail is able to grip supports. The skull (left) has a very long, tapering snout; the teeth are small and curved and the palate is equipped with hard ridges. This dentition enables the possum to scrape nectar off its long tongue.

lightweight, agile frame

prehensile tail

Main illustration Steve Kingston

RED COLOBUS

The Hanuman langur (above left) measures 16–31 in (41–78 cm) from head to rump, and has a tail length of 27–42.5 in (69–108 cm). The olive colobus (above right) has a head-and-body length of 17–19.5 in (43–49 cm) and a tail length of 22.5–25 in (57–64 cm).

THE FACE

bears the downward-pointing nostrils that are typical of the Old World monkeys, and there is a pronounced ridge framing the eyes. It is near naked, to enable full facial expression of moods and emotions.

PROBOSCIS MONKEY

GOLDEN LEAF MONKEY

HANUMAN MONKEY

Collectively, the colobines can boast a sumptuous array of finery in the form of coats, colors, and hairstyles. One of them alone has a face that suggests one of nature's practical jokes: the proboscis monkey.

THE LIMBS

are lean, but powerful muscles on the hind legs enable long leaps across gaps in the trees. Nevertheless, although the red colobus can stand erect, it travels on all fours and is a surprisingly clumsy climber.

SKELETON

The colobus's long muscle fibers and elastic ligaments are stretched over a light, long-boned and loose-jointed frame. Hands and feet are fine-boned for added dexterity, and, like most primates, the colobus can rotate the two forearm bones (the radius and ulna) about each other to aid hand-over-hand movement through the branches.

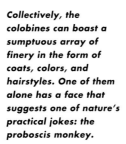

compact skull

flexible, slender frame

forelimbs are only slightly shorter than hind limbs

long, fine-boned hands

long tail

COLOBUS HAND

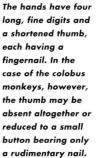

The hands have four long, fine digits and a shortened thumb, each having a fingernail. In the case of the colobus monkeys, however, the thumb may be absent altogether or reduced to a small button bearing only a rudimentary nail.

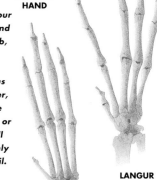

LANGUR HAND

X-ray illustrations Elisabeth Smith

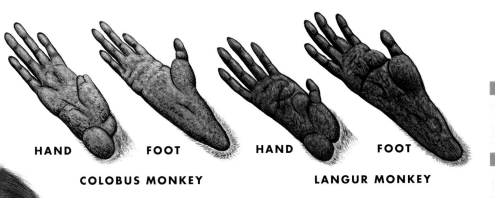

HAND | FOOT
COLOBUS MONKEY

HAND | FOOT
LANGUR MONKEY

Like all primates, colobines have long dexterous digits on both their hands and their feet, but what sets them apart from their other relatives is their shortened thumbs. The length of the thumb varies between the colobine species. In the case of the colobus monkeys the thumb is practically nonexistent—their leafy diet and arboreal lifestyle does not require too much dexterity.

RED COLOBUS
LOCATION: EQUATORIAL AFRICA

CLASSIFICATION

GENUS: *PILIOCOLOBUS*

SPECIES: *BADIUS*

SIZE

HEAD–BODY LENGTH: 18.5–25 IN (47–63 CM)

TAIL LENGTH: 20.5–29.5 IN (52–75 CM)

WEIGHT: 12–22 LB (5.5–10 KG). BLACK COLOBUSES ARE ABOUT 10 PERCENT LARGER THAN REDS

COLORATION

VERY VARIABLE ACCORDING TO THE RACE

THE RED CONTENT VARIES FROM A FULL, RICH CHESTNUT BROWN BACK IN ONE RACE TO LITTLE MORE THAN A RUSTY BROWN CROWN IN ANOTHER

UNDERPARTS WHITE WITH A TINGE OF ORANGE, YELLOW, ORANGE-RED, OR CHESTNUT

UPPER PARTS GRAY, CHARCOAL, MOTTLED GRAY AND CREAM, CHESTNUT, OR GRAYISH BLACK

TAIL REDDISH BLACK OR GRAY

FEATURES

ARMS SLIGHTLY SHORTER THAN LEGS

GENITAL SWELLINGS VISIBLE IN ADULT FEMALE AND YOUNG MALE

FACIAL WHISKERS ARE USUALLY GRAY

MALE HAS A LARGER HEAD THAN FEMALE, COMPLETE WITH LARGER CANINE TEETH AND BEARD

ALMOST ALWAYS SEEN UP IN THE TREES, RARELY DESCENDING TO THE GROUND

MALE'S BUTTOCK CALLUSES ARE SEPARATED BY FURRED SKIN, UNLIKE MOST OTHER MALE COLOBINE SPECIES

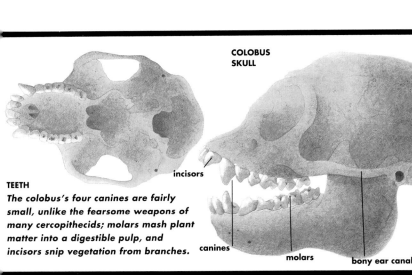

THE STOMACH
often appears rather potbellied. This is simply because it is huge and contains many separate chambers. Special "waiting rooms" for the monkey's food contain bacteria that attack vegetation, fermenting and softening it before stomach acids get to work in the main chamber.

THE TAIL
is long and fine, unlike the flamboyant "brushes" of some pied colobus races. It is often held aloft in a social gesture to other troop members.

COLOBUS SKULL

The typical colobine skull (left and right) has a compact form, unlike the elongated, more doglike muzzle of cercopithecids such as drills and baboons. The male's head is larger, being equipped with more formidable jaw muscles. On the underside of the braincase can be seen the bony ear canals, features that are absent in New World monkeys and marmosets.

incisors

TEETH
The colobus's four canines are fairly small, unlike the fearsome weapons of many cercopithecids; molars mash plant matter into a digestible pulp, and incisors snip vegetation from branches.

canines

molars

bony ear canal

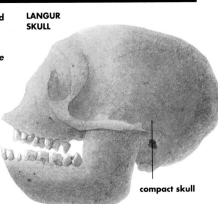

LANGUR SKULL

compact skull

Main illustration Craig Greenwood/Wildlife Art Agency. Detail artworks Simon Turvey/Wildlife Art Agency

RED DEER

THE ANTLERS
are used in trials of
strength as stags fight to
establish their place in
the hierarchy during the
rutting season.

*A human being is
dwarfed by the moose,
the largest living deer,
with a shoulder height
of 55-92.5 in (140-235
cm). At the other end of
the scale, a pudu is only
about the size of a
domestic dog.*

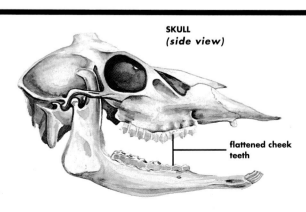

THE RUMP
often has a white patch,
used for signaling
danger to other deer.

THE CLOVEN HOOVES
are slightly concave
underneath and help to
provide a good grip
when running.

3rd YEAR

4th YEAR

2nd YEAR

1st YEAR

5th YEAR

6th YEAR

*Antlers grow
progressively larger as
a stag gets older. In its
first year a red deer is
known as a
"knobber." In its
second year it is a
"pricket." In the sixth
year, when there is a
total of twelve points
on the antlers, the
head and antlers is
known as "royal."*

Illustrations William Oliver/Wildlife Art Agency

*Deer have powerful legs for
swift running and a long neck
for grazing or browsing. Like all
artiodactyls, a deer walks on
the tips of its toes. And because
these are on the ends of very
long foot bones, the effective
length of the leg is greatly
increased, thus enabling the
animal to run very swiftly.*

DEER SKELETON

**LONG
FOOT
BONES**

**SKULL
(side view)**

**flattened cheek
teeth**

RED DEER

LOCATION: EUROPE, NORTH AFRICA
& WESTERN ASIA

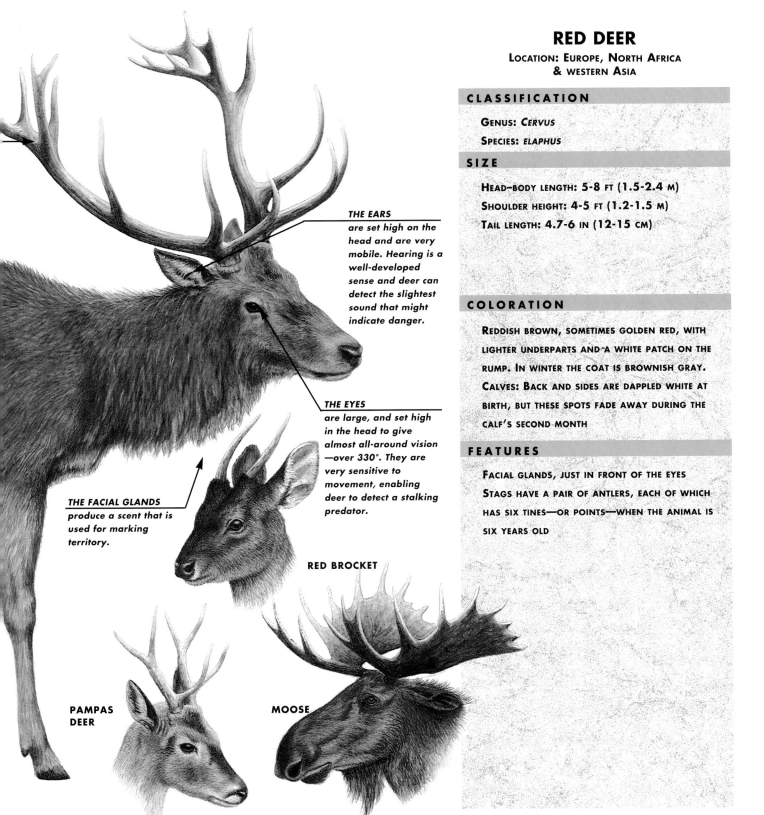

CLASSIFICATION

GENUS: *CERVUS*

SPECIES: *ELAPHUS*

SIZE

HEAD–BODY LENGTH: 5-8 FT (1.5-2.4 M)

SHOULDER HEIGHT: 4-5 FT (1.2-1.5 M)

TAIL LENGTH: 4.7-6 IN (12-15 CM)

COLORATION

REDDISH BROWN, SOMETIMES GOLDEN RED, WITH LIGHTER UNDERPARTS AND A WHITE PATCH ON THE RUMP. IN WINTER THE COAT IS BROWNISH GRAY. CALVES: BACK AND SIDES ARE DAPPLED WHITE AT BIRTH, BUT THESE SPOTS FADE AWAY DURING THE CALF'S SECOND MONTH

FEATURES

FACIAL GLANDS, JUST IN FRONT OF THE EYES
STAGS HAVE A PAIR OF ANTLERS, EACH OF WHICH HAS SIX TINES—OR POINTS—WHEN THE ANIMAL IS SIX YEARS OLD

THE EARS
are set high on the head and are very mobile. Hearing is a well-developed sense and deer can detect the slightest sound that might indicate danger.

THE EYES
are large, and set high in the head to give almost all-around vision —over 330°. They are very sensitive to movement, enabling deer to detect a stalking predator.

THE FACIAL GLANDS
produce a scent that is used for marking territory.

RED BROCKET

PAMPAS DEER

MOOSE

The upper jaw of a typical ruminant has no incisors—the lower incisors bite against a tough pad. Behind the incisors there is a gap, followed by the six premolars (three on each side) and six molars.

The premolars and molars are used for chewing tough plant food. Thus they are equipped with ridges suitable for grinding, rather than with pointed cusps.

Members of the cattle family have permanent horns. A horn consists of a horny sheath (made of keratin—the same material that forms nails and claws) inside which there is a core of bone. Once the velvet on a deer's antlers has been discarded, they consist only of bone; however, unlike horns they are shed each year.

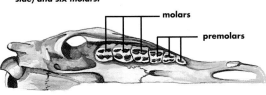

molars

premolars

**UPPER JAW
(cutaway)**

HORN

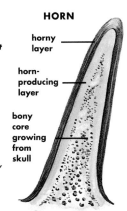

horny layer

horn-producing layer

bony core growing from skull

ANTLER

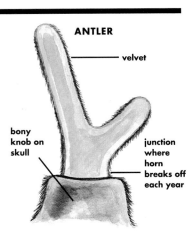

velvet

bony knob on skull

junction where horn breaks off each year

RED FOX

THE EARS

are large, mobile, and forward-facing for picking up and locating the sound of moving prey. A fox's ears can even detect the whisper of an earthworm stretching in the grass.

The largest of the vulpine foxes is the red fox (above left), which typically grows to a head-and-body length of 26 in (66 cm) and a weight of 13 lb (6 kg). Occasionally the red fox may grow to twice this weight. The smallest fox in the genus Vulpes is the fennec fox (above right), which grows to a head-and-body length of up to 15.5 in (39 cm) and may weigh as little as 1.8 lb (0.8 kg).

FOREFOOT   **HIND FOOT**

FEET AND TRACKS

The fox's tracks can easily be confused with those of a small dog. However, the fox leaves a more oval, less broad print, with the central two toes placed some way ahead of the other two. When walking or trotting, its tracks form a straight line. The hind prints are placed upon the foreprints, and, as a result, each footprint may misleadingly show five toes.

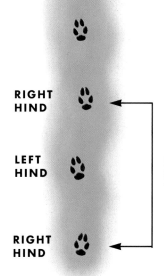

THE MUZZLE

is long and slender, adapted for probing crevices and gripping prey rather than strength and killing power.

RIGHT HIND

LEFT HIND

RIGHT HIND

WALKING STRIDE: 10-14 IN

RED FOX SKELETON

The leaping method employed by foxes to hunt small prey has favored a lightweight build, and a fox's slender leg bones are far lighter than those of other canids. The vertebrae in the shoulder region have long dorsal processes that act as anchors for strong muscles, enabling the fox to carry heavy prey in its teeth as it trots back to the den.

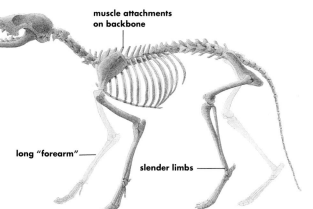

muscle attachments on backbone

long "forearm"

slender limbs

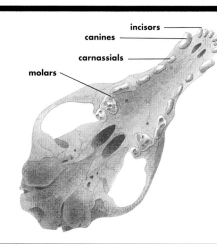

incisors
canines
carnassials
molars

X-ray illustrations Elisabeth Smith

RED FOX

LOCATION: EUROPE, NORTH AFRICA, CENTRAL
AMERICA & NORTHERN ASIA

CLASSIFICATION

GENUS: *VULPES*

SPECIES: *VULPES*

SIZE

HEAD–BODY LENGTH: 22–30 IN (56–76 CM)

TAIL LENGTH: 11–19 IN (28–48 CM)

AVERAGE WEIGHT/MALE: 14 LB (6.4 KG)

AVERAGE WEIGHT/FEMALE: 12 LB (5.5 KG)

COLORATION

VARIABLE, BUT TYPICALLY PALE YELLOW RED TO
DEEP RED BROWN ON THE UPPER PARTS AND
WHITE OR GRAY WHITE BENEATH. THE FEET AND
LOWER LEGS ARE USUALLY BLACK, THE EAR TIPS
ARE OFTEN BLACK, AND THE TAIL TIP IS
USUALLY WHITE. ALL-BLACK FOXES
OCCUR, WHILE THE SILVER FOX HAS
BLACKISH FUR WITH WHITE TIPS

FEATURES

LITHE, SLENDER BUILD
LONG, SLIM LEGS
SLENDER MUZZLE
LARGE EARS

THE EYES

are amber with vertically slit pupils. A reflective tapetum behind the retina increases their sensitivity in the dark. They face forward to provide the binocular, distance-judging vision essential for a hunter.

THE BODY

is lightly built compared to most canids, saving weight and giving the fox great agility on its feet. The light build also reduces the fox's energy needs, enabling it to thrive on small game and scraps.

THE HIND LEGS

are proportionately longer than those of most canids to provide the springing power for the fox's characteristic "mouse leap" hunting technique.

THE FEET

are small and delicate, with semiretractile claws. Dark fur clothing the feet and lower legs can create the impression that the fox is wearing boots.

THE TAIL

or "brush" is bushy and luxuriant. It acts as a rudder when the fox leaps to pounce on its victims. A large scent gland on the upper surface is marked by a dark patch.

RED FOX SKULL *(left and right)*

The fox has a long jaw with limited movement from side to side. This scissors action ensures the shearing efficiency of the carnassials, but it means that the fox cannot chew its food. The jaw is closed by heavy muscles attached to the crest at the back of the cranium, enabling the molar teeth at the back of the jaw to exert considerable pressure.

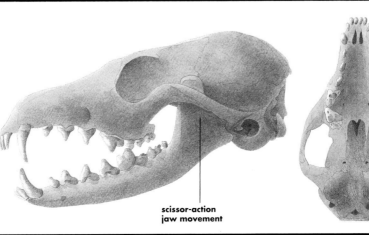

scissor-action
jaw movement

SWIFT FOX SKULL

Another vulpine, the swift fox differs from the red fox in the nature of its skull—along with being smaller. A denizen of semiarid and prairie regions, it relies on its full range of teeth to dispatch a wide variety of prey.

RED SQUIRREL

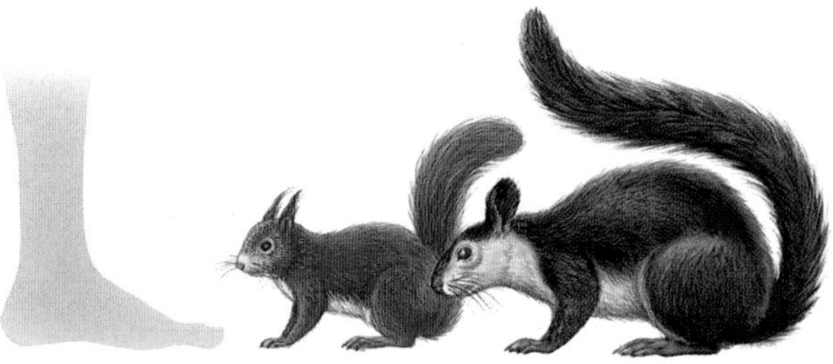

SIZE COMPARISON
The red squirrel (above left) can reach 8.7 in (22 cm) from nose to rump, with a tail up to 7 in (18 cm) long and a maximum weight of 11.3 oz (320 g). The black giant squirrel (above right) of Southeast Asia may grow to 18 in (45.7 cm) from nose to rump, with a tail as long as its body or even longer. This giant can weigh up to 6.5 lb (3 kg).

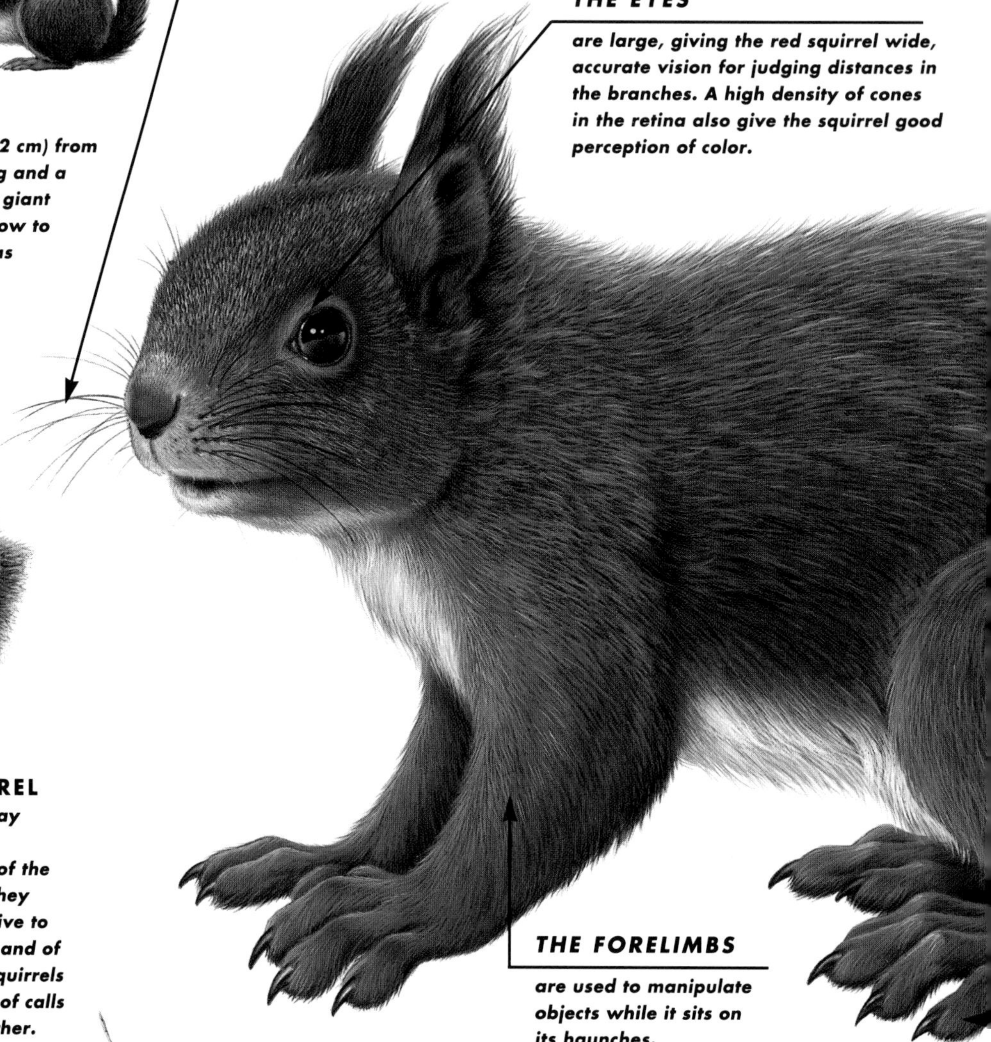

THE LONG WHISKERS

enhance the sense of touch around the head. Further touch-sensitive bristles grow from the feet, the outside of the forelegs, and the underside.

THE EYES

are large, giving the red squirrel wide, accurate vision for judging distances in the branches. A high density of cones in the retina also give the squirrel good perception of color.

THE FORELIMBS

are used to manipulate objects while it sits on its haunches.

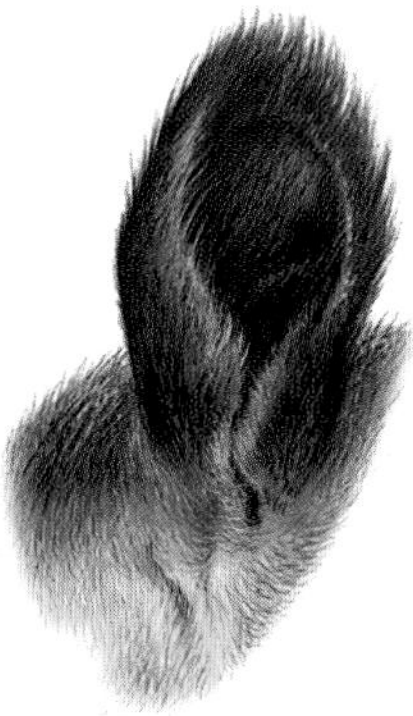

GIANT FLYING SQUIRREL

Hearing is a vital sense for flying squirrels, since they are active in the inky darkness of the forest at night and need to detect the approach of any nocturnal predators as soon as possible.

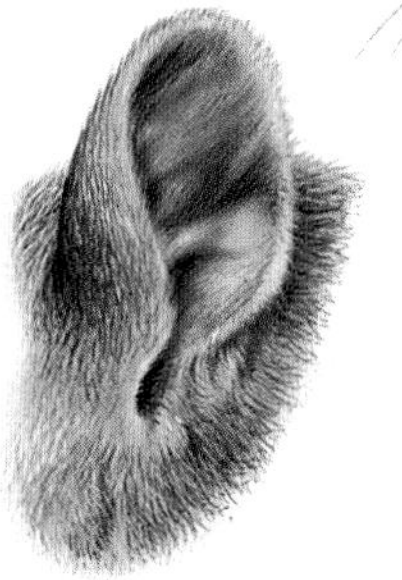

GRAY SQUIRREL

The ears of the gray squirrel lack the conspicuous tufts of the red squirrel, but they are equally sensitive to sounds of danger and of communication. Squirrels use a wide range of calls to signal one another.

X-RAY

The skeleton of the red squirrel reveals the light, flexible frame that enables the animal to move so easily in the trees. The hind limbs, which are larger than the forelimbs, give the animal most of the propulsion required when running or climbing. The long tail is an excellent balancing aid.

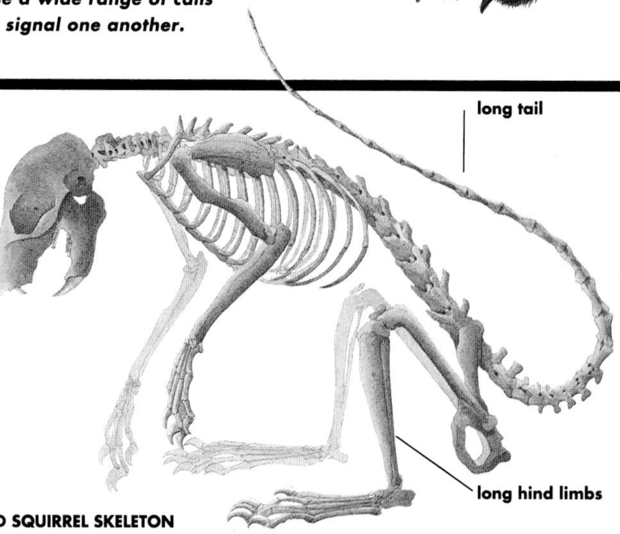

RED SQUIRREL SKELETON

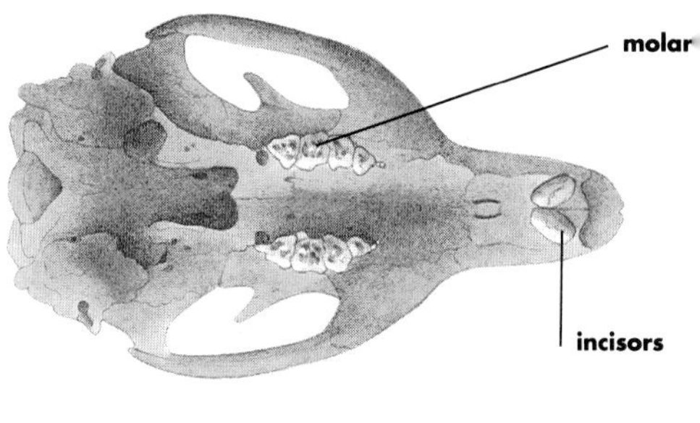

RED SQUIRREL'S SKULL
As with all rodents, the rootless incisors grow continually and must be worn down to prevent excessive length. The molars possess roots.

X-ray illustrations Elisabeth Smith

RED SQUIRREL

LOCATION: EUROPE & CENTRAL ASIA

CLASSIFICATION

GENUS: *SCIURUS*

SPECIES: *VULGARIS*

SIZE

HEAD–BODY LENGTH: 8–8.7 IN (205–220 MM)

TAIL LENGTH: 6.7–7 IN (170–180 MM)

WEIGHT: 9–11.3 OZ (250–320 G)

WEIGHT AT BIRTH: 0.3–0.4 OZ (8–12 G)

COLORATION

VARIES FROM BRIGHT, REDDISH BROWN TO DARK, GRAYISH BROWN OR ALMOST BLACK. IN WINTER, THE REDDISH FORM BECOMES DARKER AND GRAYER. UNDERSIDE IS PALE

FEATURES

LARGE, DARK EYES

PROMINENT EAR TUFTS

ROUNDED HEAD

THICK, BUSHY TAIL HELD UPRIGHT WHEN SITTING

LONG FACIAL WHISKERS

THE TAIL

is more than extravagant decoration. It can serve as a balancing rod when the animal is leaping or perching on a thin branch. It is also used like a flag to make complex signals to other squirrels, and it can function alternatively as a muffler or a sunshade in uncomfortable weather.

THE FUR

is soft and particularly dense in winter. The coat is deep reddish-brown above, with a creamy-white underbelly. The thin tail is chestnut to creamy white. The body fur is molted twice each year, in spring and autumn. The ear tufts and tail molt only once each year.

SHARP CLAWS

on the squirrel's feet allow it to hold fast to precariously sloping surfaces. The ankle joints are so flexible that the animal can rotate its hind feet backward to provide better support when descending a tree trunk.

SKULL

The squirrel has a fairly generalized skull for a rodent, with a rounded shape and simple teeth. When the animal is gnawing, the lower jaw is pulled forward by a muscle called the later masseter anchored in front of the eye. The scaly-tailed squirrel has a deeper, shorter skull, with much smaller projections of bone behind the eye socket.

RED SQUIRREL

anchorage for masseter muscle

rounded braincase

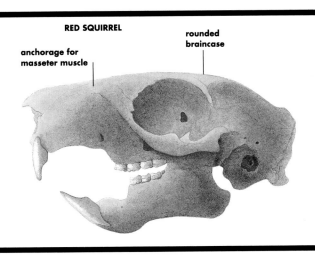

SCALY-TAILED SQUIRREL

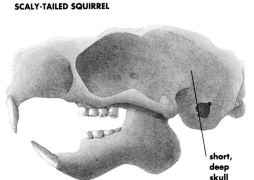

short, deep skull

Main illustration Steve Kingston

RHINO

INDIAN RHINO

SUMATRAN RHINO

THE HUMP

Long, bony spines stick up from the backbone on the back of the white rhino's neck. The massive muscles that lift the head are attached here, creating a hump.

The smallest rhino, the Sumatran, weighs in at a mere 2,200 lb (1,000 kg), while the heaviest is the white rhino (below), with an adult male tipping the scales at an average of 6,600 lb (3,000 kg)—the equivalent of over forty men!

INDIAN RHINO

THE EARS

can be moved independently, so when the rhino is in a vulnerable position—head down drinking, for example— it is common to see one ear pointing forward and one pointing backward.

The Indian rhino (above) has only one blunt horn, while the Sumatran rhino (below) has two; these are shorter and rounder than those of the white rhino (right).

SUMATRAN RHINO

THE HORNS

are anchored onto the head over a large bump on the front of the skull.

Illustrations Mathew Hillier/Wildlife Art Agency

X

R A Y

head carried low

long rib cage

WHITE RHINO SKELETON

front feet slightly larger than hind feet

short legs

The rhinoceros has an extremely robust and strong skeleton, which has evolved to take the enormous weight of its muscles and organs. Its long head is counterbalanced by the rest of its body. The white rhino has a longer head and shorter neck than the black rhino.

Rhinos walk on points, like ballet dancers. The rhino foot has three hooves and leaves a track that looks similar to the club in a deck of cards. The middle hoof carries more weight than the other two.

X-ray illustrations Elisabeth Smith

INDIAN RHINO

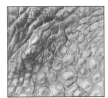

JAVAN RHINO

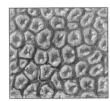

Both Indian and Javan rhinos have bumpy, hairless skin. The hide of the Javan rhino (left) looks scaly and has a mosaic pattern all over, while that of the Indian rhino (far left) is unevenly patterned. Its shoulder and upper leg areas are covered with wartlike bumps, while the rest is comparatively smooth.

WHITE RHINO

LOCATION: SOUTH & NORTH-EAST AFRICA

CLASSIFICATION

GENUS: *CERATOTHERIUM*

SPECIES: *SIMUM*

SIZE

HEAD–BODY LENGTH/MALE: 12–14 FT (3.7–4.3 M)

TAIL LENGTH/MALE: 25 IN (65 CM)

HEIGHT/MALE: 5–6 FT (1.5–1.8 M)

WEIGHT/MALE: 5,000–8,000 LB (2,300–3,600 KG)

FRONT HORN LENGTH/MALE: ABOUT 28 IN (71 CM)

REAR HORN LENGTH/MALE: 9 IN (23 CM)

FEMALES ARE SMALLER AND LIGHTER THAN MALES

COLORATION

GRAY, TEXTURED SKIN, BUT USUALLY COVERED WITH MUD OR DUST

BLACK HAIR (EYELASHES, EAR FRINGES, AND TAIL)

FEATURES

LONG HEAD

POINTED EARS

BROAD, SQUARED-OFF MUZZLE

LARGE HUMP ON BACK OF NECK

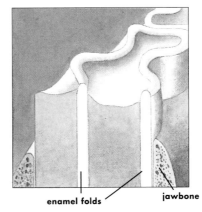

THE TAIL

serves as a fly whisk and is equipped with a row of thick, black, wiry hairs that grow in a line along the underside and the top of the tip. Sometimes rhinos lose part or all of their tails if they are attacked by predators such as hyenas.

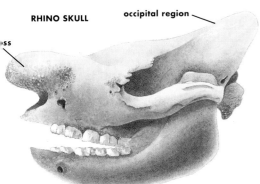

THE LEGS

are built like pillars to support its bulk. The long bones tend to rest in a straight line, enabling the rhino to stand without exerting too much energy.

RHINO SKULL

occipital region

boss

Perhaps the most interesting feature of a rhino skull is the big bony mound, or boss, on which the horn grows. The occipital region at the back of the skull is long and deep, providing a firm attachment for the huge muscles, which are necessary to hold up the heavy head.

A rhino's cheek teeth are designed for grinding up vegetation. Its molars and premolars in both upper and lower jaws have folds in the enamel surface. As they get worn down they form ridges (left), which shred food under the great pressure exerted by the jaws.

enamel folds

jawbone

SERVAL

THE EARS

are very large, oval, and erect. The serval has especially good hearing because the ears work as "antennae" to pick up the slightest rustle of small animals in the grass. The backs of the ears are black with a striking white or yellowish patch.

The serval (above left) is the tallest of the African small cats, reaching 25.6 in (65 cm) at the shoulder. However, it is often lighter in build than the caracal. Both have a top weight of about 40 lb (18 kg), but the serval may weigh only 15.4 lb (7 kg). The smallest of these cats is the black–footed cat (above right), which has a shoulder height of about 10 in (25 cm) and a head-and-body length of 13.5–19.7 in (34–50 cm). It may weigh as little as 3.3 lb (1.5 kg).

PUGS

Pawprints, often referred to as pugs, are not always a secure guide to a cat's size. The tiny print of the black-footed cat reflects its small stature, but that of the serval is dwarfed by the caracal's print—although the serval is usually larger. This is because the serval is adapted to catching small rodents, while the caracal may tackle young deer.

BLACK-FOOTED CAT

SERVAL

CARACAL

EYES

All cats have superb vision. The maximum amount of light is reflected into each retina, giving good vision in low light. Cats can see at least six times better than humans in poor light. To protect the eyes in bright light, the iris contracts to a narrow slit. The eyes are positioned on the front of the head, giving good binocular vision for judging distances.

X-RAY

SERVAL SKELETON

The serval's basic skeleton is similar to that of other cats. The highly flexible spine gives the cat extra speed when pursuing prey by increasing the length of its stride. It also accounts for why cats can twist in midair and land on their feet when jumping or falling.

flexible spine

long legs

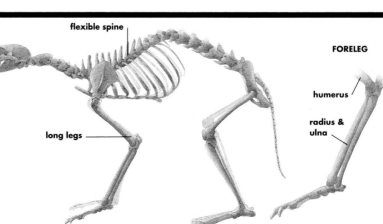

FORELEG

humerus

radius & ulna

SERVAL LEGS

In the foreleg, the humerus makes an acute angle at the elbow to improve leaping power. The radius and ulna are greatly elongated, giving the cat extra height and extending its stride. The hind legs bend sharply at the hock, increasing their leaping power.

hock

HIND LEG

CARACAL

The caracal's short coat is usually a rusty brown, with pale belly, inner flanks, and throat. There are no markings.

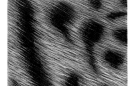

BLACK-FOOTED CAT

In addition to its distinct smoky-black paws, this species has a rich, tawny coat covered with black spots, bands, or rings.

GOLDEN CAT

This coat can in fact be almost any color from gray to orange or even black, and it may bear any form of marking.

SERVAL

LOCATION: AFRICA

CLASSIFICATION

GENUS: *FELIS*

SPECIES: *SERVAL*

SIZE

HEAD–BODY LENGTH: 27.6–39.4 IN (70–100 CM)

HEIGHT TO SHOULDER: 21–25.6 IN (54–65 CM)

TAIL LENGTH: 9.5–17.7 IN (24–45 CM)

WEIGHT: 30–39.6 LB (13.6–18 KG)

WEIGHT AT BIRTH: 8–9 OZ (230–260 G)

COLORATION

BASIC COAT COLOR VARIES FROM PALE FAWN TO A REDDISH GOLD. FOUR BLACK LINES EXTEND FROM BEHIND NECK TO SHOULDERS. BACK AND CHEST COVERED IN BLACK SPOTS THAT MERGE INTO LINES OR BARS DOWN THE SIDES. LOWER AREA OF LEGS COVERED IN SMALL SPOTS UNDERSIDE PALER THAN THE PREDOMINANT COAT COLOR

FEATURES

VERY LARGE, ERECT, AND OVAL EARS; BACKS ARE BLACK WITH A STRIKING WHITE OR YELLOW SPOT IN THE MIDDLE

SLENDER, WHITE MUZZLE

VERY LONG LEGS; FORELEGS ARE SIGNIFICANTLY LONGER THAN THE HIND LEGS

SMALL FEET FOR ITS BODY SIZE

COMPARATIVELY SHORT TAIL WITH DARK RINGS AND A BLACK TIP

LONG AND SLENDER NECK

THE COAT

is always spotted and barred, but the markings vary among individuals. The base color varies from a pale tawny to a russet-gold; four black stripes run down over the shoulders; and the back, chest, and flanks are covered in spots. Generally, the markings are boldest in the driest parts of the range.

THE LEGS

are markedly longer, proportionally, than those of other cats. The serval's high profile gives it an advantage in the long grasses of the savanna.

THE TAIL

is fairly short, reaching only to the level of the hocks. Dark blotches at the base change to rings toward the bushy, black tip.

THE PAWS

are small and neat, reflecting the size of the serval's fairly small prey. The soles are naked. In common with all other cats except the cheetah, the hooked claws can be extended at will; they are normally retracted into the toes to protect the pin-sharp tips.

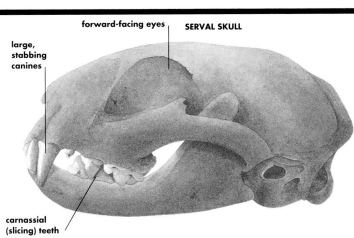

SKULL

Cats' skulls are shorter and more rounded than those of many other carnivores, but there is plenty of bone to support the large jaw muscles; these muscles achieve an immense biting force for inflicting fatal wounds. The jaws are hinged to give movement in one plane only; this restricts the ability to chew, but ensures effective use of the carnassials.

forward-facing eyes

SERVAL SKULL

large, stabbing canines

carnassial (slicing) teeth

BLACK-FOOTED CAT SKULL

The skull of this species and of the African wildcat resemble that of a domestic cat—small, neat, rounded, and equipped with typical feline teeth for meat shearing.

Color illustrations Steve Kingston

SHREW

The smallest shrew, Savi's pymgy shrew (above left), has a head-and-body length of 1.4–2 in (36–51 mm), with a tail 1–1.2 in (25–30 mm) long. The largest shrew, the African forest shrew (above center), has a head-and-body length of 6 in (152 mm). The Hispaniolan solenodon (above right) is 11–13 in (280–330 mm) long from snout to rump, with a tail length of 8.5–10 in (216–254 mm).

THE EYES

are small, largely hidden by fur, and provide poor eyesight. Shrews also have small ears, although their hearing is excellent.

THE COAT

is short and thick. In most shrews, the fur is brown or gray. Shrews that live in colder climates have longer, thicker fur than those found in warmer regions.

WHISKERS

on the head and snout help the animal navigate and find its prey. They are also used in confrontations between strangers.

GROUND-DWELLING SHREW   **CLIMBING SHREW**

SEMIAQUATIC SHREW

FEET

Insectivores have five toes and claws on each foot. Solenodons use their huge claws to dig and tear open rotten branches for food. Climbing shrews have dexterous toes for gripping branches. Water shrews have larger, broader feet than land-based shrews, with toes fringed with hairs to give their feet a greater surface area for paddling and pushing through the water. The feet of the Tibetan water shrew have evolved even further: This is the only species of shrew with truly webbed feet.

X-RAY

TEETH
The Soricidae family of shrews is divided into two groups based on their teeth. Red-toothed shrews, such as the European common shrew, have red tips to their teeth. White-toothed shrews have pure white teeth. Solenodons have grooves in their lower incisor teeth, down which their venom flows as they bite into prey.

incisor   molars and premolars

COMMON SHREW SKULL

pincer-action incisors

The primitive skull shape is typical of insectivores, with a small braincase and long jaws. The incisors are prominent: In the shrew they project to

SOLENODON SKULL

venom teeth   sharp-cusped molars

form a beak, while in the solenodon the massive upper incisor is angled backward. The crowns of the molars have sharp cusps for crunching insects.

X-ray illustrations Elisabeth Smith

WATER SHREW

COMMON SHREW

WHITE-TOOTHED SHREW

TAIL SHAPES
The shrew's tail is covered with short bristles. Shrews' tails lose their hair with age. Some species have naked tails; others store fat in their tails for times when food is scarce.

THE BODY
is typically cylindrical. The shrew's compact, tubular form enables it to push efficiently through undergrowth and to squeeze into narrow tunnels to escape predators.

EUROPEAN COMMON SHREW

LOCATION: NORTHERN & EASTERN EUROPE

CLASSIFICATION

GENUS: *SOREX*

SPECIES: *ARANEUS*

SIZE

HEAD–BODY LENGTH: 2–3 IN (51–76 MM)

TAIL LENGTH: 1–1.7 IN (25–43 MM)

WEIGHT: 0.2–0.5 OZ (5.7–14 G)

WEIGHT AT BIRTH: 0.02 OZ (0.57 G)

HEAD–BODY LENGTH AT BIRTH: 0.6 IN (15 MM)

COLORATION

ADULT HAS A TRICOLORED COAT WITH DARK BROWN FUR ON THE BACK, LIGHT BROWN ON THE SIDES, AND A PALE BELLY. YOUNG SHREWS ARE PALE BROWN UNTIL THEIR FIRST MOLT AT THE AGE OF THREE MONTHS

FEATURES

LONG, POINTED SNOUT

CYLINDRICAL BODY

TINY EYES

VERY ACTIVE NIGHT AND DAY

NESTS UNDER LOGS OR AMONG GRASSY CLUMPS

SEVERAL LITTERS OF 5–7 YOUNG IN THE SUMMER BREEDING SEASON

SHRILL, TWITTERING CALL

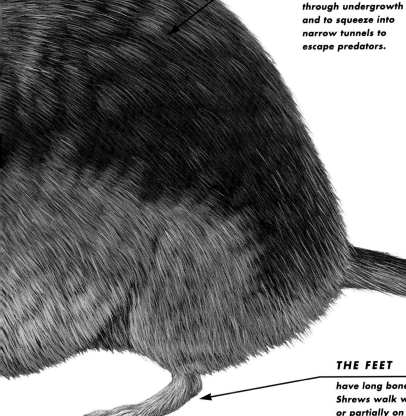

THE FEET
have long bones. Shrews walk wholly or partially on their soles; solenodons, however, use only their toes when in motion.

COMMON SHREW AND ARMORED SHREW SKELETONS
The common shrew (below) has the fine bone structure typical of most shrews. The armored shrew (right), however, has interlocking spines on the vertebrae, providing a superbly strong backbone.

typically lightweight bones

reinforced vertebrae

Main illustration Barry Croucher/Wildlife Art Agency

SPECTACLED BEAR

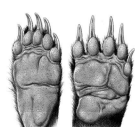

The sun bear (below right) is about the size of a large dog. The spectacled and sloth bears (below center) are a little larger. The Asian black bear (below left) is probably the heaviest, with a top weight of 330 lb (150 kg), but this is still far short of the polar bear, which can tip the scales at more than half a ton (500 kg).

CLAWS

The sun bear and sloth bear both have long, curved claws. These are black and pointed on the sun bear, while those of the sloth bear are ivory in color and quite blunt. The soles of the sun bear's large feet are completely naked, to help it climb trees. The claws on the hind feet of the Asian black bear are much shorter than those on its forefeet.

HIND   FORE

BLACK BEAR

FORE   HIND

SUN BEAR

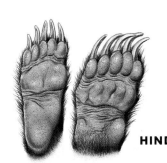

HIND

FORE   SLOTH BEAR

THE FACE

has distinctive pale markings around the eyes; these extend over the chest. The markings around the eyes often form rings that resemble spectacles, but sometimes look more like eyebrows. The markings are never exactly the same in any two bears and occasionally may be lacking altogether.

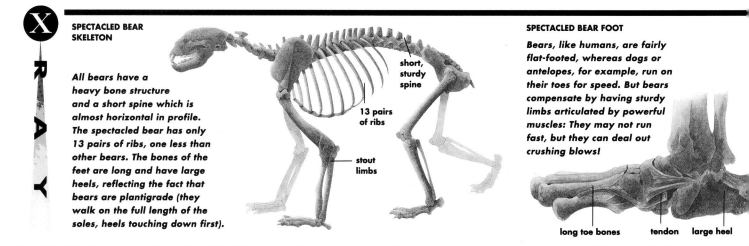

SPECTACLED BEAR SKELETON

All bears have a heavy bone structure and a short spine which is almost horizontal in profile. The spectacled bear has only 13 pairs of ribs, one less than other bears. The bones of the feet are long and have large heels, reflecting the fact that bears are plantigrade (they walk on the full length of the soles, heels touching down first).

short, sturdy spine

13 pairs of ribs

stout limbs

SPECTACLED BEAR FOOT

Bears, like humans, are fairly flat-footed, whereas dogs or antelopes, for example, run on their toes for speed. But bears compensate by having sturdy limbs articulated by powerful muscles: They may not run fast, but they can deal out crushing blows!

long toe bones   tendon   large heel

X-ray illustrations Elisabeth Smith

The Asian black bear is also known as the moon bear, owing to the crescent-shaped "necklace" on its chest. The blunt head tapers to a pointed snout and has large, rounded ears.

ASIAN BLACK BEAR

SLOTH BEAR

The sloth bear has a long, almost tubular muzzle with only a sparse covering of pale hair. The lips are extremely mobile and completely naked, and the nostrils can be closed at will.

SUN BEAR

The sun bear has a large, rather flat-crowned head. The pale muzzle is quite short. The ears are small and round, and the tongue is long.

SPECTACLED BEAR
LOCATION: THE ANDES OF SOUTH AMERICA

CLASSIFICATION

GENUS: *TREMARCTOS*

SPECIES: *ORNATUS*

SIZE

HEAD–BODY LENGTH: 3.9–5.9 FT (1.2–1.8 M)

SHOULDER HEIGHT: 27.5–32 IN (70–81 CM)

TAIL LENGTH: 2.7 IN (70 MM)

WEIGHT/MALE: UP TO 308 LB (140 KG)

WEIGHT/FEMALE: 132–136 LB (60–62 KG)

COLORATION

UNIFORMLY BLACK OR DARK BROWN, EXCEPT FOR WHITE OR YELLOWISH MARKINGS ON FACE AND CHEST

FEATURES

MOST NOTICEABLE FEATURES ARE FACIAL MARKINGS
SIMILAR IN SIZE TO SLOTH AND ASIAN BLACK BEAR
VESTIGIAL TAIL

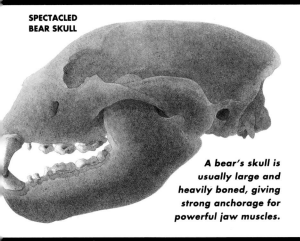

THE COAT

is uniformly black or dark brown, apart from the distinctive markings, and the fur is long and dense.

THE LEGS

are longer and more slender than in most other species. Each foot has five long, sharp claws.

SPECTACLED BEAR SKULL

A bear's skull is usually large and heavily boned, giving strong anchorage for powerful jaw muscles.

Although the teeth are strong, they have adapted from the slicing carnassials of a typical carnivore to long canines and grinding molars with broad flat crowns— more suited to a broad diet. The sloth bear lacks the inner pair of upper incisors, giving it a gap in the front teeth, an adaptation to its habit of eating termites.

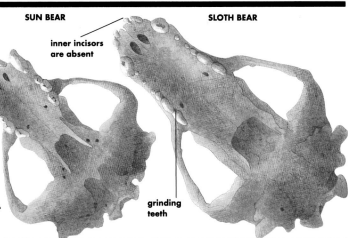

SUN BEAR

inner incisors are absent

SLOTH BEAR

grinding teeth

Main illustration Steve Kingston

SPERM WHALE

The male sperm whale may weigh as much as 1,800 ten-year-old children! It grows to a maximum of 65 ft (20 m), the equivalent of six cars placed end to end. The dwarf sperm whale (top) is only 8 ft (2.5 m) long and weighs 440–550 lbs (200–250 kg). Yet even this is one-and-a-half times longer and three times heavier than an adult human.

BRAIN

The sperm whale has the largest brain of any animal. The size and shape of a basketball, it weighs over 15 lb (7 kg). However, this is far smaller compared to its body size (0.02 percent) than a human brain compared to human body size (2 percent).

BLOWHOLE

The sperm whale's S-shaped blowhole (breathing nostril) is at the front left tip of the forehead, which is a unique position among whales. When it blows after a dive, the spout of spray emerges to the whale's left at an unmistakable 45-degree angle.

SKIN SCARS

The skin is smooth and hairless, as in most whales. The pale ridges and crescents of scar tissue that usually crisscross the head of old males are the result of fights with giant squid and other animals.

EYE

Relatively small compared with body size, the eye cannot swivel in its socket, so the whale can only see to the side. Eyesight is limited to the surface waters, down to about 650–1,000 ft (200–300 m). Below this it is too dark to see.

X-RAY

The bones of a whale are light and spongy because they do not have to support the animal's weight—the water does this. Their main function is as an anchor for muscles. The sperm whale's rear limbs have disappeared during evolution. There are not even tiny remnants like those found in the baleen (whalebone) whales.

backbone

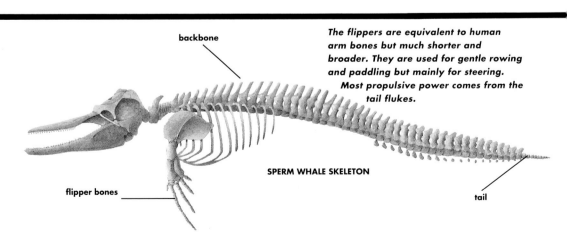

The flippers are equivalent to human arm bones but much shorter and broader. They are used for gentle rowing and paddling but mainly for steering. Most propulsive power comes from the tail flukes.

SPERM WHALE SKELETON

flipper bones

tail

SPERM WHALE

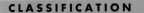

LOCATION: ALL WORLD'S OCEANS
& ADJOINING SEAS

The head diagram with labels:

- blowhole
- maxillonasalis muscle
- left nasal passage
- case
- nasofrontar sac
- vestibular sac
- right nasal passage
- spermaceti tissue of trunk
- lower jaw
- skull
- brain
- lung

THE HEAD SHOWING SPERMACETI ORGAN

The huge, squared-off, barrel-shaped forehead mainly houses the spermaceti organ. This is a tough, fibrous sheath, encased by muscle and blubber, which contains up to 2.9 tons (3 tonnes) of spermaceti—a milky-white, waxy liquid. It is probably a buoyancy and pressure adjuster for deep diving. On breathing, air passes from the blowhole, along the nasal passages, which go through the spermaceti organ, down and back to the whale's windpipe and lungs.

DORSAL HUMP

There is no proper dorsal fin but only a low hump. This generally has several more humps behind it, each one smaller in size, running down to the tail.

TAIL FLUKES

These are wide, roughly triangular, and extremely powerful. They have the central rear notch, characteristic of many other whales.

CLASSIFICATION

GENUS: *PHYSETER*

SPECIES: *CATODON*

SIZE

TOTAL LENGTH/MALE: AVERAGE 49 FT (15 M); HEAD IS ONE-QUARTER TO ONE-THIRD TOTAL LENGTH

WEIGHT/MALE: AVERAGE 33–43 TONS (30–40 TONNES)

SIZE AT BIRTH: 9.8–13 FT (3–4 M) LONG; 440–660 LB (200–300 KG) IN WEIGHT

THE SPERM WHALE IS ONE OF THE MOST SEXUALLY DIMORPHIC OF WHALE SPECIES—THAT IS, THERE IS A GREAT DIFFERENCE BETWEEN THE SEXES. FEMALES (COWS) ARE ABOUT ONE-HALF TO TWO-THIRDS THE SIZE OF MALES (BULLS)

COLORATION

USUALLY DARK GRAY, BLUE-GRAY OR BROWN-GRAY OVER MOST OF THE BODY. THE LIPS AND MIDDLE BELLY MAY BE PALER. THERE ARE CORRUGATIONS (RIPPLES OR WRINKLES) ALONG THE BODY

FEATURES

HUGE, PROMINENT, BLUNT, SQUARED-OFF HEAD

NO DISTINCT DORSAL FIN

RELATIVELY SMALL, LONG, THIN LOWER JAW

LOPSIDED AND ANGLED BLOWHOLE, ON THE EXTREME FRONT TOP OF HEAD, ON THE LEFT SIDE

SPERM WHALE SKULL LOCATION

The skull occupies only a small portion of the lower rear head, as the position of the eye shows. Most of the head is the spermaceti organ (see above).

SPERM WHALE UPPER JAW

About ten to twenty small teeth grow in the upper jaw, but in many sperm whales they never get large enough to show above the gum surface. There are also sockets in the upper jaw, into which the teeth of the lower jaw fit.

SPERM WHALE LOWER JAW AND TEETH

The lower mandible (jaw) is slim and almost cylindrical for much of its length. The lower jaw does not reach the end of the head. On each side is a row of twenty to twenty-five teeth, which are rounded, cone-shaped, and fairly blunt. They fit into sockets in the upper jaw.

SPRINGBOK

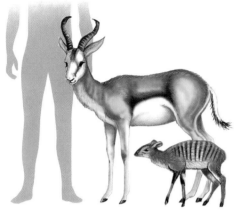

The largest of the gazelles, the dama gazelle, measures 57–68 in (145–172 cm) from head to rump, whereas the springbok (above left) is a medium-sized gazelle. The striped-back duiker (above right) is approximately 40 in (100 cm) long, while the royal antelope is the smallest antelope at about 22.5 in (575 mm) in length and about 4.5 lb (2 kg) in weight.

HORNS

The curving shape, outward spread, and ringed ridges of the springbok's horns are typical of gazelles. Those of males, which engage in sparring bouts especially at mating time, are thicker and more curved. The curves and rings help rivals lock horns, making fights more of a head wrestle than a stabbing match.

THE LIMBS

are fine and fragile in appearance, but they are structured so as to minimize weight and maximize anchorage for those muscles that provide speed and jumping power—like those of a human sprinter or hurdler.

THE COAT COLOR

of most duiker species is subdued, in a range of bluish grays and dull browns. Stripes add to the camouflaging effect and help to hide the animal in thickets of ground cover.

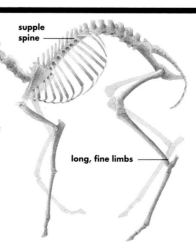

STRIPED-BACK DUIKER

A duiker, with its humped back, shorter neck, and shorter legs, has a much more compact, crouched build than the typical gazelle. A low profile and well-developed hind legs help the animal push its way rapidly through densely vegetated habitats.

X
RAY

supple spine

PYGMY ANTELOPE

The skeletal profile reveals the slightness of a pygmy antelope's build. The limb bones are long and fine, giving the animal a ballerina-like agility and grace of movement.

long, fine limbs

SKULL

The lightweight skull of a common duiker features large eye sockets placed well to the sides, showing the importance of keen peripheral vision for an animal that relies mainly on early warning and running speed to evade predators.

COMMON DUIKER

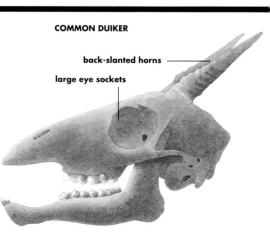

back-slanted horns

large eye sockets

X-ray illustrations Elisabeth Smith

The horns of a male salt dik-dik are tiny but lethally sharp; they are angled backward.

The klipspringer's horns, like those of the dik-dik, are short and sharp. They are used almost exclusively in defense.

The gerenuk's S-shaped horns are used both as stabbing rapiers and as battering rams. The thick bases also protect the skull. The ridges lock with an enemy's horns to prevent him from launching a stabbing attack.

SPRINGBOK

LOCATION: SOUTHERN AFRICA TO ANGOLA

CLASSIFICATION

GENUS: *ANTIDORCAS*

SPECIES: *MARSUPIALIS*

SIZE

HEAD–BODY LENGTH: 48–56 IN (120–140 CM)

SHOULDER HEIGHT: 27–34 IN (70–87 CM)

TAIL LENGTH: 8–11 IN (20–28 CM)

HORNS: 14–19 IN (35–48 CM)

WEIGHT: 55–100 LB (25–45 KG)

COLORATION

CINNAMON-BROWN UPPER PARTS

DARK BROWN BAND ACROSS FLANKS

WHITE TAIL, UNDERSIDE, AND RUMP

FEATURES

SLENDER BUILD

NARROW, ELONGATED MUZZLE

LONG LEGS

LONG NECK

CURVING, RINGED HORNS

RAISABLE PALE CREST ON RUMP

DARK STRIPES ALONG SIDES OF FACE

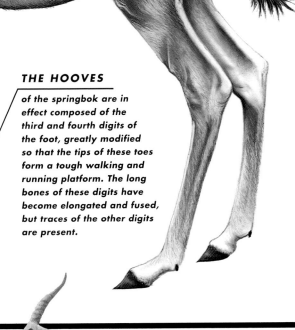

COAT

The springbok is one of several gazelles that possess a prominent dark stripe along the flank. The stripe may have the effect of helping to break up the animal's outline in a tight herd. Alternatively it may function in a short range as a prominent social signal to other members of the herd, and its movement in a bolting gazelle may instantly communicate alarm.

THE HOOVES

of the springbok are in effect composed of the third and fourth digits of the foot, greatly modified so that the tips of these toes form a tough walking and running platform. The long bones of these digits have become elongated and fused, but traces of the other digits are present.

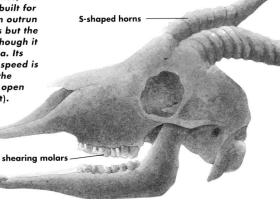

THOMSON'S GAZELLE

long limbs for high speed

Like all gazelles, the "tommy" is built for speed—it can outrun all predators but the cheetah—although it lacks stamina. Its capacity for speed is reflected in the lightweight, open skeleton (left).

SPRINGBOK

S-shaped horns

upper incisors absent

shearing molars

The molar teeth of ruminants are specially designed to cope with cutting through and crushing tough, fibrous vegetation. Neatly shaped cusps on the teeth provide shearing edges for this purpose.

SUGAR GLIDER

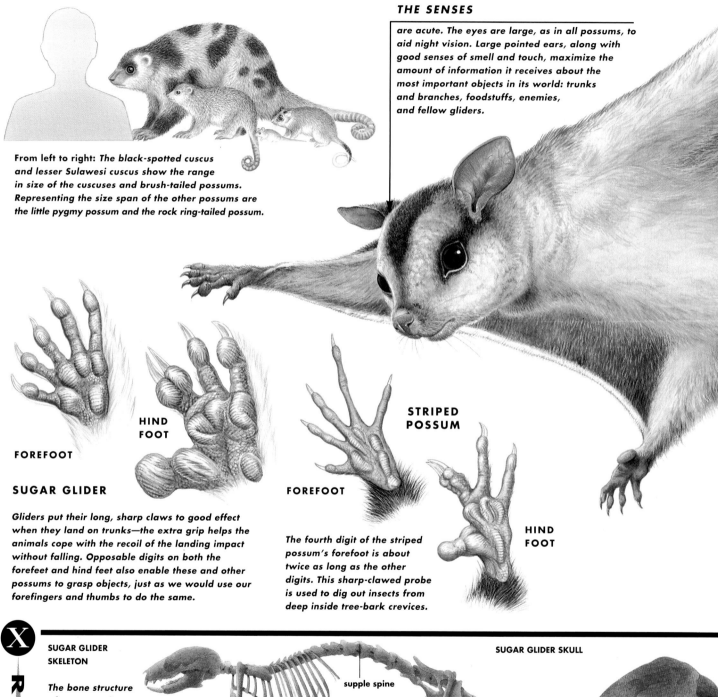

From left to right: *The black-spotted cuscus and lesser Sulawesi cuscus show the range in size of the cuscuses and brush-tailed possums. Representing the size span of the other possums are the little pygmy possum and the rock ring-tailed possum.*

THE SENSES

are acute. The eyes are large, as in all possums, to aid night vision. Large pointed ears, along with good senses of smell and touch, maximize the amount of information it receives about the most important objects in its world: trunks and branches, foodstuffs, enemies, and fellow gliders.

FOREFOOT

HIND FOOT

SUGAR GLIDER

STRIPED POSSUM

FOREFOOT

HIND FOOT

Gliders put their long, sharp claws to good effect when they land on trunks—the extra grip helps the animals cope with the recoil of the landing impact without falling. Opposable digits on both the forefeet and hind feet also enable these and other possums to grasp objects, just as we would use our forefingers and thumbs to do the same.

The fourth digit of the striped possum's forefoot is about twice as long as the other digits. This sharp-clawed probe is used to dig out insects from deep inside tree-bark crevices.

X RAY

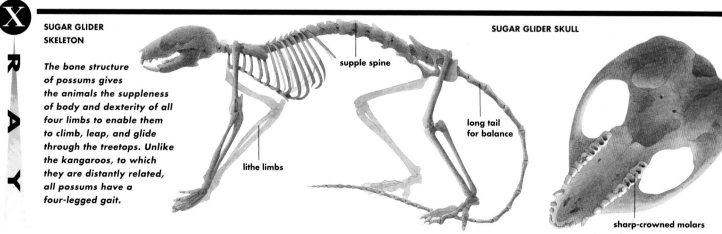

SUGAR GLIDER SKELETON

The bone structure of possums gives the animals the suppleness of body and dexterity of all four limbs to enable them to climb, leap, and glide through the treetops. Unlike the kangaroos, to which they are distantly related, all possums have a four-legged gait.

supple spine

long tail for balance

lithe limbs

SUGAR GLIDER SKULL

sharp-crowned molars

X-ray illustrations Elisabeth Smith

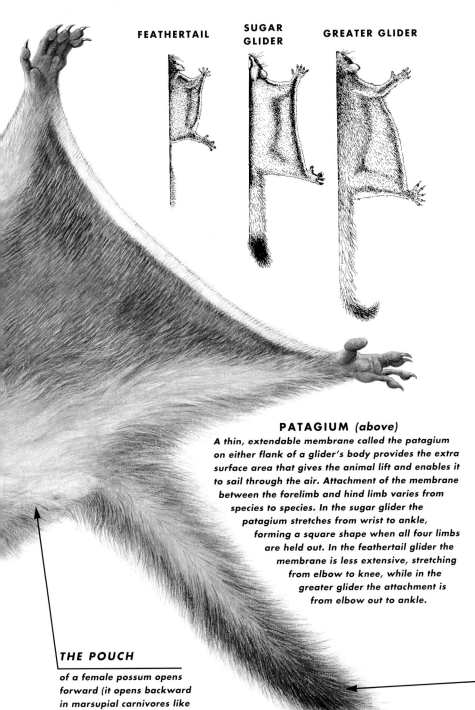

FEATHERTAIL

SUGAR GLIDER

GREATER GLIDER

SUGAR GLIDER

LOCATION: SE, E, NW, N AUSTRALIA
& NEW GUINEA

CLASSIFICATION

GENUS: *PETAURUS*

SPECIES: *BREVICEPS*

SIZE

HEAD–BODY LENGTH: 6.3–8.3 IN (16–21 CM)

TAIL LENGTH: 6.5–8.3 IN (16.5–21 CM)

WEIGHT: 3.4–5.6 OZ (95–160 G)

COLORATION

PALE GRAY ABOVE, CREAM TO PALE GRAY BELOW;
DARK STRIPE FROM FOREHEAD TO BACK AND
SOMETIMES WHITE NOSE TO TAIL

FEATURES

LARGE EYES

LARGE POINTED EARS

SUPPLE BODY

EXTENDABLE GLIDING MEMBRANES ON FLANKS

OPPOSING FIRST OR FIRST AND SECOND DIGITS

LONG BUSHY TAIL

DARK DORSAL STRIPE AND PATCHES BEHIND EARS

PATAGIUM *(above)*

A thin, extendable membrane called the patagium on either flank of a glider's body provides the extra surface area that gives the animal lift and enables it to sail through the air. Attachment of the membrane between the forelimb and hind limb varies from species to species. In the sugar glider the patagium stretches from wrist to ankle, forming a square shape when all four limbs are held out. In the feathertail glider the membrane is less extensive, stretching from elbow to knee, while in the greater glider the attachment is from elbow out to ankle.

THE POUCH

of a female possum opens forward (it opens backward in marsupial carnivores like the dunnarts and the Tasmanian devil). The pouch is basically a fold of skin that encloses the mother's teats and the newborn infants that attach themselves to them.

THE TAIL

is long and well furred. It tends to be held straight when the animal is gliding, and, along with the curvature of the gliding membranes, it probably helps control the direction of flight.

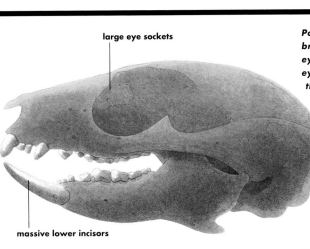

large eye sockets

massive lower incisors

Possums typically have a rather broad, flattened skull, with large eye sockets to house the prominent eyes. The foremost incisors in the lower jawbone are large, stout, and forward-pointing.

TEETH OF A LEAF-EATER
The molar teeth of leaf-eating possums are well suited for grinding fibrous food. Sharp ridges on the crowns of these teeth break the food down into a more readily digestible form.

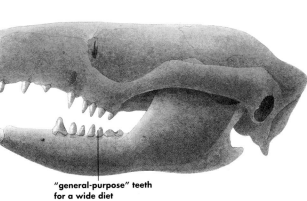

BRUSH-TAILED POSSUM SKULL

"general-purpose" teeth
for a wide diet

Main illustration Peter David Scott/Wildlife Art Agency. Color detail illustrations Wayne Ford/Wildlife Art Agency

TASMANIAN DEVIL

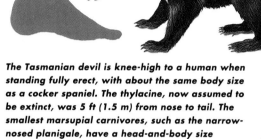

The Tasmanian devil is knee-high to a human when standing fully erect, with about the same body size as a cocker spaniel. The thylacine, now assumed to be extinct, was 5 ft (1.5 m) from nose to tail. The smallest marsupial carnivores, such as the narrow-nosed planigale, have a head-and-body size barely greater than a man's thumb.

Barry Croucher/Wildlife Art Agency

THE SNOUT

is long, with plenty of sensitive whiskers for feeling the way in the dark, and well-developed olfactory organs inside for the keen sense of smell.

THE EYES

are small and beady, not large like many night-active animals, since the devil chiefly uses its sense of smell to locate food and assess its surroundings.

JAWS

The jaws gape widely. Powerful muscles give a terrific biting force to crunch up gristle and bones.

X RAY

four incisors each side

UPPER JAW DENTITION

cheek teeth

Most marsupial carnivores have four pairs of upper incisors and three pairs of lower incisors. Some have five upper pairs. The canine teeth are long and pointed, as in many carnivores, for stabbing and tearing the meaty meal. The cheek teeth are large and ridged, for shearing gristle and cracking bone.

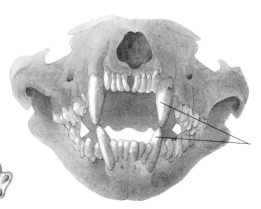

The head is large in proportion to the body, to accommodate the heavily built jaws, large teeth, and highly developed jaw muscles.

large canines

X-ray illustrations Elisabeth Smith

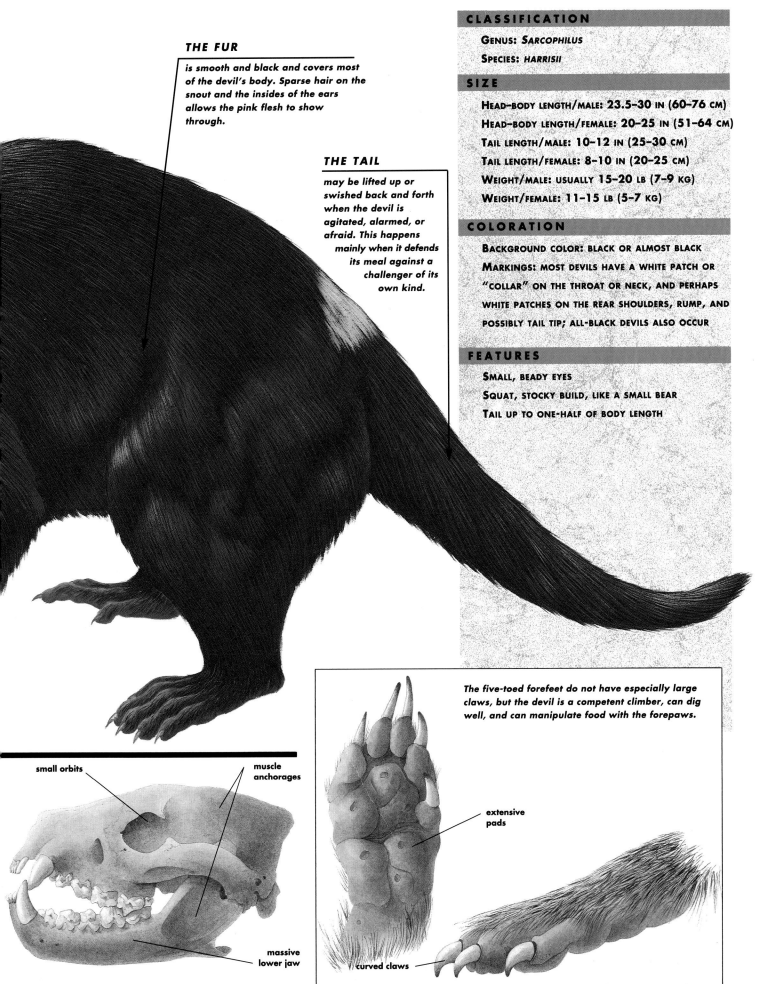

THE FUR

is smooth and black and covers most of the devil's body. Sparse hair on the snout and the insides of the ears allows the pink flesh to show through.

THE TAIL

may be lifted up or swished back and forth when the devil is agitated, alarmed, or afraid. This happens mainly when it defends its meal against a challenger of its own kind.

TASMANIAN DEVIL
LOCATION: TASMANIA

CLASSIFICATION

GENUS: *SARCOPHILUS*

SPECIES: *HARRISII*

SIZE

HEAD–BODY LENGTH/MALE: **23.5–30** IN (60–76 CM)

HEAD–BODY LENGTH/FEMALE: **20–25** IN (51–64 CM)

TAIL LENGTH/MALE: **10–12** IN (25–30 CM)

TAIL LENGTH/FEMALE: **8–10** IN (20–25 CM)

WEIGHT/MALE: USUALLY **15–20** LB (7–9 KG)

WEIGHT/FEMALE: **11–15** LB (5–7 KG)

COLORATION

BACKGROUND COLOR: BLACK OR ALMOST BLACK

MARKINGS: MOST DEVILS HAVE A WHITE PATCH OR "COLLAR" ON THE THROAT OR NECK, AND PERHAPS WHITE PATCHES ON THE REAR SHOULDERS, RUMP, AND POSSIBLY TAIL TIP; ALL-BLACK DEVILS ALSO OCCUR

FEATURES

SMALL, BEADY EYES

SQUAT, STOCKY BUILD, LIKE A SMALL BEAR

TAIL UP TO ONE-HALF OF BODY LENGTH

The five-toed forefeet do not have especially large claws, but the devil is a competent climber, can dig well, and can manipulate food with the forepaws.

small orbits

muscle anchorages

extensive pads

massive lower jaw

curved claws

THREE-TOED SLOTH

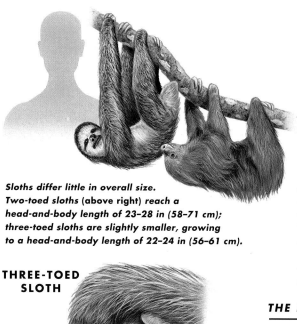

Sloths differ little in overall size. Two-toed sloths (above right) reach a head-and-body length of 23–28 in (58–71 cm); three-toed sloths are slightly smaller, growing to a head-and-body length of 22–24 in (56–61 cm).

THREE-TOED SLOTH

FINGERS

Curved, hooked claws give the sloth a tenacious grip. Rather confusingly, the clawed fingers are referred to as toes. In all species, the hind limbs have three toes. These illustrations show the forepaws of the two sloth types.

THREE-TOED SLOTH

TWO-TOED SLOTH

THE FACE

is nearly naked, with a rigid expression. The facial muscles are much reduced except for those used for chewing. Hard, horny lips help in grasping leaves.

THE EYES

are small and directed forward. They apparently give the sloth color vision.

THE COAT

has two layers. The underfur is short and fine, while the overcoat consists of longer and coarser hairs. The green hue of the fur results from the color of two species of blue-green algae that grow along grooves in the hair shafts. The long hair of the overcoat is an adaptation to conserve body heat.

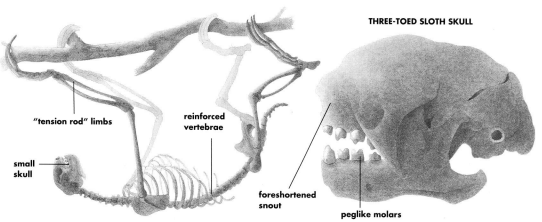

X-RAY

SLOTH SKELETON

The skeleton of the sloth reflects its exclusively arboreal lifestyle, with the skeleton used to support the hanging body weight. The limbs are long and used as tension rods rather than pillars of support, as is usual in most other mammals. As in other edentates, the vertebrae are reinforced by bony structures called xenarthrales, which give support to the back.

"tension rod" limbs

small skull

reinforced vertebrae

THREE-TOED SLOTH SKULL

foreshortened snout

peglike molars

X-ray illustrations Elisabeth Smith

THE FORELIMBS

are longer than the hind limbs, particularly in three-toed sloths.

FUR

The sloth's coat looks shaggy and moth eaten. In fact, it is often full of tiny moths. The green tinge derives from algae that find the damp, warm fur ideal; they also provide camouflage.

PALE-THROATED SLOTH

LOCATION: TROPICAL NORTHERN SOUTH AMERICA

CLASSIFICATION

GENUS: *BRADYPUS*

SPECIES: *TRIDACTYLUS*

SIZE

HEAD-BODY LENGTH: 16-24 IN (40-60 CM)

TAIL LENGTH: 0.8-3.5 IN (2-9 CM)

WEIGHT: 5-12 LB (2.2-5.5 KG)

WEIGHT AT BIRTH: 7-8.8 OZ (200-250 G)

COLORATION

GENERALLY GRAY-BROWN, SLIGHTLY DARKER ON THE HEAD AND FACE. ON THE SHOULDERS THERE IS USUALLY A PALE AREA WITH BROWN MARKINGS. OFTEN THE COAT COLOR APPEARS GREEN, DUE TO THE ALGAE GROWING IN THE FUR. THERE IS CONSIDERABLE VARIATION IN COAT COLOR AMONG SOME INDIVIDUALS OF CERTAIN SPECIES

FEATURES

CURVED CLAWS

ROUNDED HEAD WITH FLATTENED FACE

THREE DIGITS ON EACH FOREFOOT AND HIND FOOT

LONG ARMS

STUMPY TAIL

SMALL EYES

SMALL, INCONSPICUOUS EARS

COARSE, SHAGGY FUR COAT

THE TAIL

is short and stumpy and looks rather an afterthought. It is in fact redundant, since the sloth does not need to balance while moving through the trees.

SLOTH SKULLS

The three-toed sloth's skull is block shaped with a flattened snout, whereas the two-toed sloth has a slightly more elongated skull. In both genera the zygomatic arch (a cheek-bone) is not complete. There are no canine or incisor teeth; the simple, peglike cheek teeth grow throughout the animal's life. They have high cusps and form efficient surfaces for grinding down leaves.

TWO-TOED SLOTH SKULL

eye socket

simple teeth

open-ended cheekbones

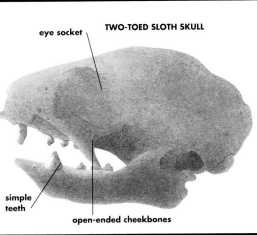

hooklike claws

FOOT

first and fifth digits

second, third, and fourth digits

highly mobile ankle

HANDS AND FEET

The hooklike hands and feet are specially adapted to an arboreal life. In the foot (left), the first and fifth digits barely exist. The central digits are mostly bound within the foot, and the claws are reinforced within by a toe bone. The outer digits of the hand (below) are also reduced. With tendons in the rest position (shown) the claw makes an angle of 90° with the hand.

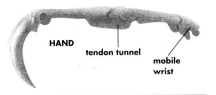

HAND

tendon tunnel

mobile wrist

Main illustration Steve Kingston

T I G E R

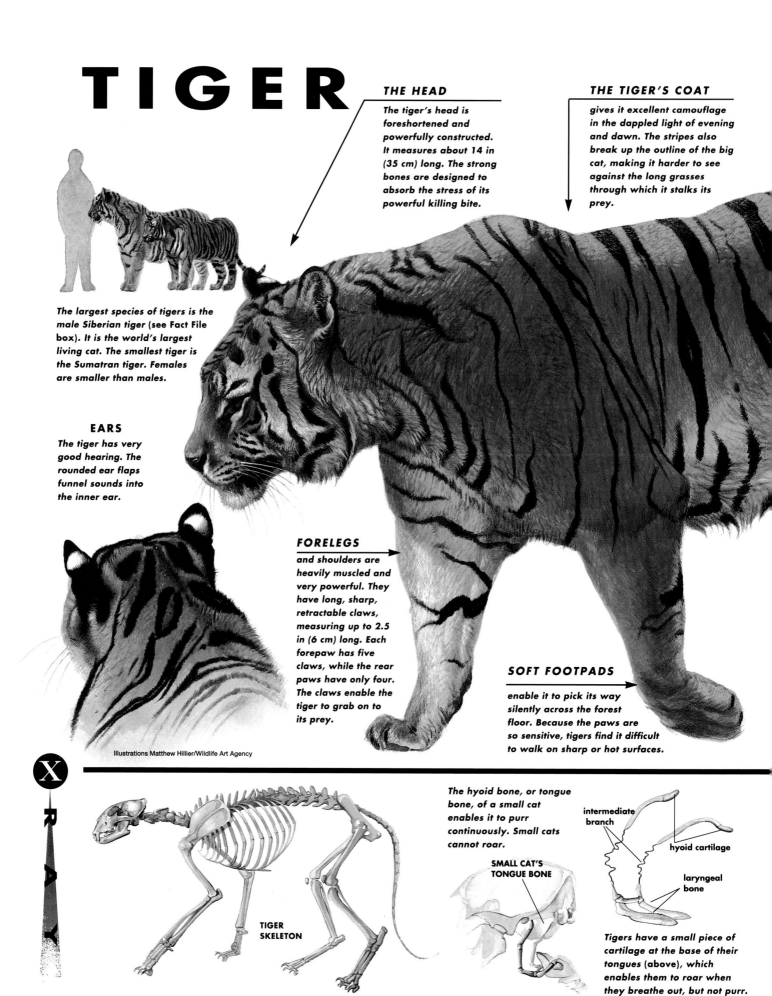

THE HEAD

The tiger's head is foreshortened and powerfully constructed. It measures about 14 in (35 cm) long. The strong bones are designed to absorb the stress of its powerful killing bite.

THE TIGER'S COAT

gives it excellent camouflage in the dappled light of evening and dawn. The stripes also break up the outline of the big cat, making it harder to see against the long grasses through which it stalks its prey.

The largest species of tigers is the male Siberian tiger (see Fact File box). It is the world's largest living cat. The smallest tiger is the Sumatran tiger. Females are smaller than males.

EARS

The tiger has very good hearing. The rounded ear flaps funnel sounds into the inner ear.

FORELEGS

and shoulders are heavily muscled and very powerful. They have long, sharp, retractable claws, measuring up to 2.5 in (6 cm) long. Each forepaw has five claws, while the rear paws have only four. The claws enable the tiger to grab on to its prey.

SOFT FOOTPADS

enable it to pick its way silently across the forest floor. Because the paws are so sensitive, tigers find it difficult to walk on sharp or hot surfaces.

Illustrations Matthew Hillier/Wildlife Art Agency

The hyoid bone, or tongue bone, of a small cat enables it to purr continuously. Small cats cannot roar.

SMALL CAT'S TONGUE BONE

TIGER SKELETON

intermediate branch

hyoid cartilage

laryngeal bone

Tigers have a small piece of cartilage at the base of their tongues (above), which enables them to roar when they breathe out, but not purr.

X-ray illustrations Gary Martin/Wildlife Art Agency

SUMATRAN   **SIBERIAN**   **WHITE TIGER**

SIBERIAN TIGER

LOCATION: SIBERIA

CLASSIFICATION

GENUS: *PANTHERA*

SPECIES: *TIGRIS*   **SUBSPECIES:** *ALTAICA*

SIZE

HEAD–BODY LENGTH/MALE: 106–150 IN
(270–380 CM). FEMALES ARE SMALLER

SHOULDER HEIGHT/MALE: 41–43 IN (105–110 CM)

TAIL LENGTH: 39 IN (100 CM)

WEIGHT: 550–675 LB (250–306 KG)

WEIGHT AT BIRTH: 27–53 OZ (785–1,500 G)

COLORATION

REDDISH GOLDEN COAT WITH BLACK STRIPES

WHITE UNDERSIDE

BENGAL TIGER

CLASSIFICATION

GENUS: *PANTHERA*

SPECIES: *TIGRIS*

SUBSPECIES: *TIGRIS*

SIZE

HEAD–BODY LENGTH/MALE: 74–87 IN (189–220 CM)

SHOULDER HEIGHT/MALE: 35–37 IN (90–95 CM)

TAIL LENGTH: 32–35 IN (81–90 CM)

WEIGHT: 400–575 LB (180–260 KG)

WEIGHT AT BIRTH: 33–42 OZ
(925–1,195 G)

COLORATION

COAT IS USUALLY FAWN TO ORANGY RED, WITH
LIGHTER FUR ON ITS BELLY

DARK STRIPES

Illustration Matthew Hillier/Wildlife Art Agency

The tiger's teeth are well adapted to killing. The long canines, which can be up to 5 in (13 cm) long, pierce the flesh of the prey, allowing the tiger to secure a firm hold. The carnassials are used to slice through the muscles and tendons of the prey.
Similar to the blades on a pair of scissors, these teeth are ideal for this purpose. The shape and length of the tiger's skull add to the leverage of its jaws, making it difficult for prey to wriggle free.

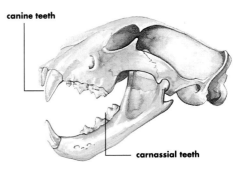

canine teeth

carnassial teeth

VAMPIRE BAT

THE WING MEMBRANE

consists of a double layer of skin enclosing muscles and elastic fibers. These control its stiffness, making it taut for flight but relaxed and easy to roll up when not in use.

THE FUR

or pelage of cave-dwelling bats such as the vampire is quite short, but species that roost in more exposed sites have longer fur for better insulation against cold winds and rain.

EARS

are large, complex, and folded. They are used to receive the vibrations that help the bat to find its prey.

The vampire (top) is, perhaps, much smaller than people think: With wings folded, it can easily fit into the palm of a hand. Its wingspan averages 8 in (20 cm), while that of the bulldog bat (bottom) measures about 11.5 in (29 cm).

COZUMEL SPEAR-NOSED BAT

TOME'S LONG-EARED BAT

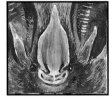

SEBA'S SHORT-TAILED BAT

WRINKLE-FACED BAT

Bats have a variety of outgrowths from their snout or lips, which may take the form of lance-shaped projections or strange flaps of skin (left). These nose leaves are used to modify or focus the echolocation calls that bats emit. The bizarre wrinkle-faced bat has, as well as a nose leaf, a fold of skin on its chin that acts as a kind of mask when it is extended upward, covering the bat's face when it is roosting.

THE FLAT FACE

and short, broad snout of the vampire bat enable it to sink its teeth into its prey. Its eyes are relatively large but, probably, unable to perceive colors.

 Illustrations John Cox/Wildlife Art Agency

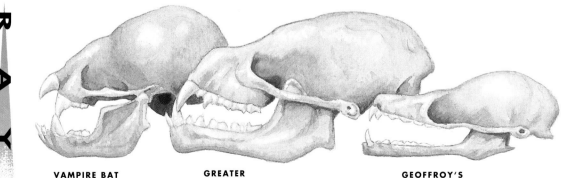

VAMPIRE BAT

GREATER SPEAR-NOSED BAT

GEOFFROY'S LONG-NOSED BAT

The greater spear-nosed bat, which has a broad diet that includes small vertebrates, insects, and fruit, has a strong skull and generalized teeth that can be used for crushing or grinding. Geoffroy's long-nosed bat has a more delicate skull and poorly developed

X-ray illustrations Elisabeth Smith

All bats have a large ear flap called the pinna, and some insect-eating bats have a tragus, or earlet—a smaller projection made of cartilage—in front. The size and shape of the tragus vary considerably among the species.

TOME'S LONG-EARED BAT

SHORT-FACED BAT

VAMPIRE BAT

BULLDOG BAT

COMMON VAMPIRE BAT

LOCATION: MEXICO TO NORTHERN ARGENTINA

CLASSIFICATION

GENUS: *DESMODUS*

SPECIES: *ROTUNDUS*

SIZE

HEAD–BODY LENGTH: 3–3.5 IN (70–90 MM)

WEIGHT/MALE: 0.5–2 OZ (15–50 G)

WINGSPAN: 6.5–10 IN (160–250 MM)

WEIGHT AT BIRTH: 0.25 OZ (5–7 G)

COLORATION

DARK GRAY/BROWN ON UPPER PARTS, PALER (OFTEN WHITISH OR BUFF) ON THE UNDERSIDE

YOUNG: PINK

FEATURES

DARK BROWN EYES

FORWARD-FACING, POINTED EARS

ENLARGED, RAZOR-SHARP UPPER INCISOR AND CANINE TEETH

LONG, GROOVED TONGUE

SHORT, NAKED SNOUT WITH PROMINENT GROOVES

THE FINGER BONES

are enormously elongated to support the wing membrane; the length of the bones varies, though, from one family to another.

STRONG THUMBS

Vampires have strong, hook-shaped thumbs that they use to pull themselves forward when they crawl and that provide thrust when they hop or jump.

---

teeth. It has little need for powerful jaws or strong teeth, as it feeds primarily on nectar and pollen. The vampire bat, by contrast, has a strong jaw for biting into flesh and a short but broad snout, making room for enlarged and highly specialized teeth.

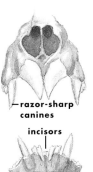

razor-sharp canines

incisors

VAMPIRE BAT

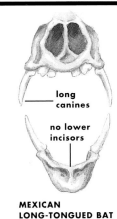

long canines

no lower incisors

MEXICAN LONG-TONGUED BAT

The vampire's upper canines and incisors are sharp for slicing through skin; its cheek teeth have few crushing surfaces, since it subsists on a liquid diet.

The Mexican long-tongued bat extracts nectar by extending its tongue into flowers. It has no lower incisors, which means it has less chance of biting its tongue.

STOMACH

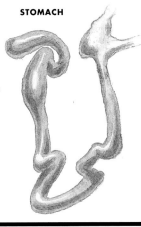

The stomach of the vampire bat is built to allow the animal to take in large quantities of blood quickly. One end of the tubular stomach is folded into a U shape that can swell up to four times in diameter and expand in length when the bat feeds.

WEASEL

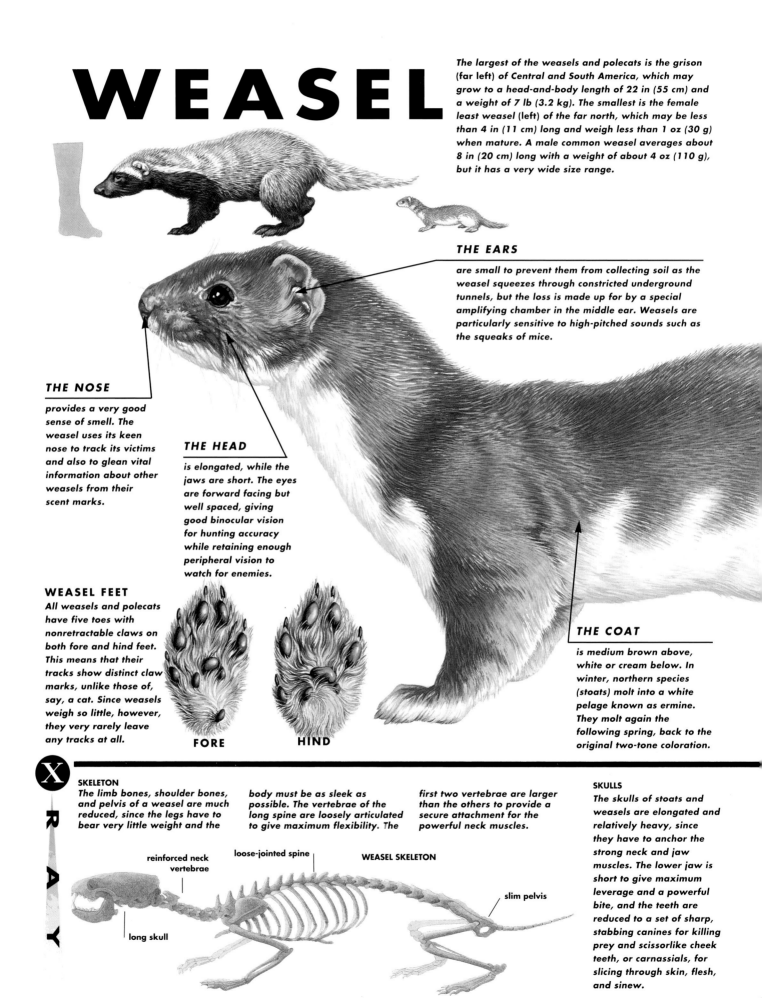

The largest of the weasels and polecats is the grison (far left) of Central and South America, which may grow to a head-and-body length of 22 in (55 cm) and a weight of 7 lb (3.2 kg). The smallest is the female least weasel (left) of the far north, which may be less than 4 in (11 cm) long and weigh less than 1 oz (30 g) when mature. A male common weasel averages about 8 in (20 cm) long with a weight of about 4 oz (110 g), but it has a very wide size range.

THE EARS

are small to prevent them from collecting soil as the weasel squeezes through constricted underground tunnels, but the loss is made up for by a special amplifying chamber in the middle ear. Weasels are particularly sensitive to high-pitched sounds such as the squeaks of mice.

THE NOSE

provides a very good sense of smell. The weasel uses its keen nose to track its victims and also to glean vital information about other weasels from their scent marks.

THE HEAD

is elongated, while the jaws are short. The eyes are forward facing but well spaced, giving good binocular vision for hunting accuracy while retaining enough peripheral vision to watch for enemies.

WEASEL FEET

All weasels and polecats have five toes with nonretractable claws on both fore and hind feet. This means that their tracks show distinct claw marks, unlike those of, say, a cat. Since weasels weigh so little, however, they very rarely leave any tracks at all.

FORE

HIND

THE COAT

is medium brown above, white or cream below. In winter, northern species (stoats) molt into a white pelage known as ermine. They molt again the following spring, back to the original two-tone coloration.

X RAY

SKELETON

The limb bones, shoulder bones, and pelvis of a weasel are much reduced, since the legs have to bear very little weight and the body must be as sleek as possible. The vertebrae of the long spine are loosely articulated to give maximum flexibility. The first two vertebrae are larger than the others to provide a secure attachment for the powerful neck muscles.

SKULLS

The skulls of stoats and weasels are elongated and relatively heavy, since they have to anchor the strong neck and jaw muscles. The lower jaw is short to give maximum leverage and a powerful bite, and the teeth are reduced to a set of sharp, stabbing canines for killing prey and scissorlike cheek teeth, or carnassials, for slicing through skin, flesh, and sinew.

reinforced neck vertebrae

loose-jointed spine

WEASEL SKELETON

slim pelvis

long skull

X-ray illustrations Elisabeth Smith

STOAT FEET

Each foot has five toes, complete with stout, sharp claws. At 1.6 in (42 mm) long and 1 in (25 mm) wide, the hind foot is about twice the size of the forefoot. When the stoat is moving at high speed, the space between each set of four prints is about 12–20 in (30–50 cm).

STOAT

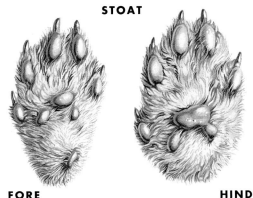

FORE   **HIND**

POLECAT FEET

The polecat rarely leaves tracks, since it travels mainly in dense cover. It does, however, tend to use regular pathways where the tracks can be seen. The prints are a little larger than those of the stoat; the stride is correspondingly longer.

POLECAT

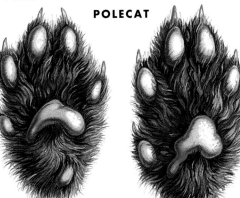

COMMON WEASEL

LOCATION: EUROPE (NOT IRELAND)

CLASSIFICATION

GENUS: *MUSTELA*

SPECIES: *NIVALIS*

SIZE

HEAD–BODY LENGTH: 6–9 IN (17–24 CM)

TAIL LENGTH: 1–3 IN (3–9 CM)

WEIGHT: 1.5–9 OZ (40–250 G)

WEIGHT AT BIRTH: 0.03–0.1 OZ (1–3 G)

COLORATION

CHESTNUT BROWN UPPER PARTS AND WHITE OR CREAM BENEATH, WITH A DISTINCT BUT IRREGULAR BORDER LINE BETWEEN THE TWO

FEATURES

VERY SMALL BODY

ELONGATED, SINUOUS FORM

SHORT LEGS

SHORT TAIL

TRIANGULAR FACE WITH SHORT MUZZLE

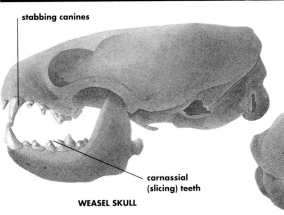

THE SPINE

is extremely flexible, allowing the weasel to loop and coil like a snake. Powerful back muscles enable it to subdue its prey by curling around it and pinning it down.

THE TAIL

has little function and has become relatively short to minimize heat and energy losses through the skin.

THE LEGS

are short but powerful to give freedom of movement and maneuverability in confined burrows.

---

stabbing canines

carnassial (slicing) teeth

WEASEL SKULL

POLECAT AND FERRET SKULLS
Hybrid polecat-ferrets look much like the wild polecat parent. To identify a dead animal, look at its skull: Ferrets and, to some extent, hybrids have a constriction in the skull behind the eyes.

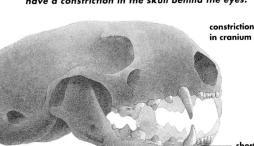

STOAT SKULL

short, heavy jaw

constriction in cranium

FERRET   **POLECAT**

Color illustrations Rachel Lockwood/Wildlife Art Agency

WILD BOAR

Smallest of the pigs and peccaries is the pygmy hog. It is 23–26 in (58–66 cm) long and weighs 13–20 lb (6–9 kg). The largest is the giant forest hog, which measures 51–83 in (130–210 cm) and weighs 628–1,333 lb (285–605 kg).

IDENTIFYING BOARS AND SOWS

The boar's head (top) has a long muzzle with well-developed canines. The sow's head (bottom) is much smaller and the teeth are not nearly as powerful as the boar's.

SKIN AND COAT ↑

Very thick skin with coarse bristles. Some individuals grow long hairs on the face, and/or a fairly thick mane of hair. In summer the boar's bristles are rather sparse; in winter they grow closer together.

FEET

Each of the four toes ends in a hoof. The first toe is missing; the third and fourth toes normally bear the animal's full weight. The second and fifth toes have smaller hooves, situated higher up the leg.

Illustrations Wayne Ford/Wildlife Art Agency

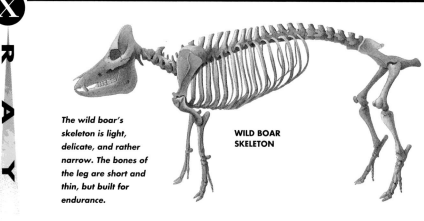

X
R
A
Y

The wild boar's skeleton is light, delicate, and rather narrow. The bones of the leg are short and thin, but built for endurance.

WILD BOAR SKELETON

The foot bones are separate, rather than fused, with the middle two being the longest. The small hooves on the second and fifth toes only touch the ground when the pig walks on marshy or soft ground.

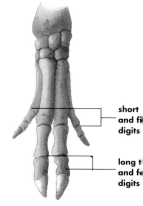

short and fi digits

long t and fe digits

WILD BOAR

EYES

The warthog's eyes are small but bright. It does not have particularly good vision; smell and hearing are its more developed senses.

GS

*spite of its short legs,
wild boar can run
t when necessary. Its
rmal gait is a trot but it
n gallop over short
tances when
rsued or when
pursuit of
ey.*

CLASSIFICATION

GENUS: SUS

SPECIES: SCROFA

SIZE

HEAD–BODY LENGTH: 35.5–71 IN (90–180 CM)

TAIL: 11.8–15.8 IN (30–40 CM)

SHOULDER HEIGHT: 35.5 IN (90 CM)

WEIGHT: 110–440 LB (50–200 KG)

WEIGHT AT BIRTH: UNDER 2.2 LB (1 KG)

COLORATION

PALE GRAY TO BLACK; BROWNISH GRAY BRISTLES
YOUNG ARE STRIPED FAWN AND DARK BROWN

FEATURES

EARS ARE VERY MOBILE AND EXPRESSIVE AND ARE USUALLY KEPT PRICKED

TAIL, WHICH HAS A THICK TASSEL OF HAIR AT THE END, HANGS DOWN WHEN THE ANIMAL IS AT REST BUT IS HELD STRAIGHT OUT WHEN MOVING ABOUT. IT IS NOT COILED, AS IN THE DOMESTIC PIG

THE WILD BOAR'S BEST DEVELOPED SENSES ARE HEARING AND SMELL. IT CAN LOCATE THE POSITION OF FOOD THAT IS DEEP UNDERGROUND

SCENT GLANDS AND WARTS

The skin on the nostrils and rump contains scent glands for marking territory and identifying other individuals. Unlike many other wild pigs, the wild boar does not have warts on its face.

The skull bones are large and bulky. The upper and lower jawbones are elongated and equipped with teeth adapted for grinding food. A long prenasal bone supports the nose.

WILD BOAR SKULL
(side view)

grinding teeth

The wild boar has two tusks in the lower jaw—actually the lower canine teeth that have developed into hollow, tubelike structures. They grow out of the side of the jaw, straight up outside the mouth, then curve backward until they point toward the eyes. The curved upper canines fit inside the lower incisors.

lower-jaw tusk

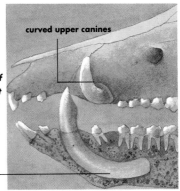

curved upper canines

WILD CAVY

Cavylike rodents vary dramatically in size. Largest of the superfamily—and indeed of all the world's rodents—is the capybara, with a head-and-body length of 42–53 in (107–135 cm) and a maximum weight of 141–146 lb (64–66 kg). Smaller representatives of the caviomorphs include the degus, which have a head-and-body length of 5–8 in (13–20 cm). Chinchilla rats and tuco-tucos are also tiny.

THE EYES

are sensitive and the animal is constantly on the lookout for danger, even when eating with its head down.

THE LARGE EARS

are positioned well to the sides of the head, and can pick up the faintest sounds.

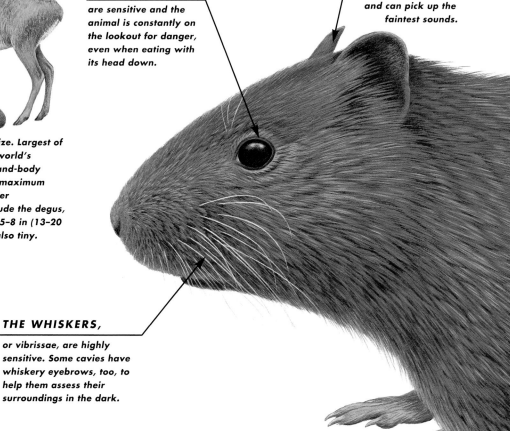

THE TEETH

A cavy's incisor teeth, like those of all rodents, are designed for gnawing. However, unlike a rat's teeth, which are a yellow-brown color, a cavy's teeth are white.

THE WHISKERS,

or vibrissae, are highly sensitive. Some cavies have whiskery eyebrows, too, to help them assess their surroundings in the dark.

SHARP CLAWS

on all four feet help the cavy clamber around. They grow continually, but are worn down on the rough ground.

X RAY

The cavy sits and walks with its legs tucked under its body. Its skeleton reveals this hunched posture. There are only five to seven caudal (tail) vertebrae tucked under the pelvic girdle, hence the lack of any visible tail. The cavy's body forms a contrast with that of the Patagonian hare, which has longer legs and a more upright stance.

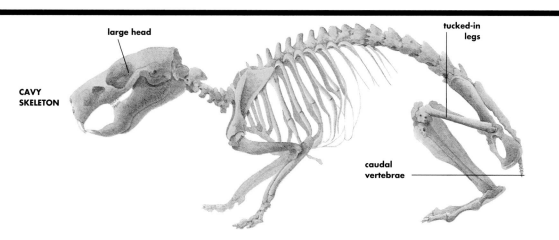

large head

tucked-in legs

CAVY SKELETON

caudal vertebrae

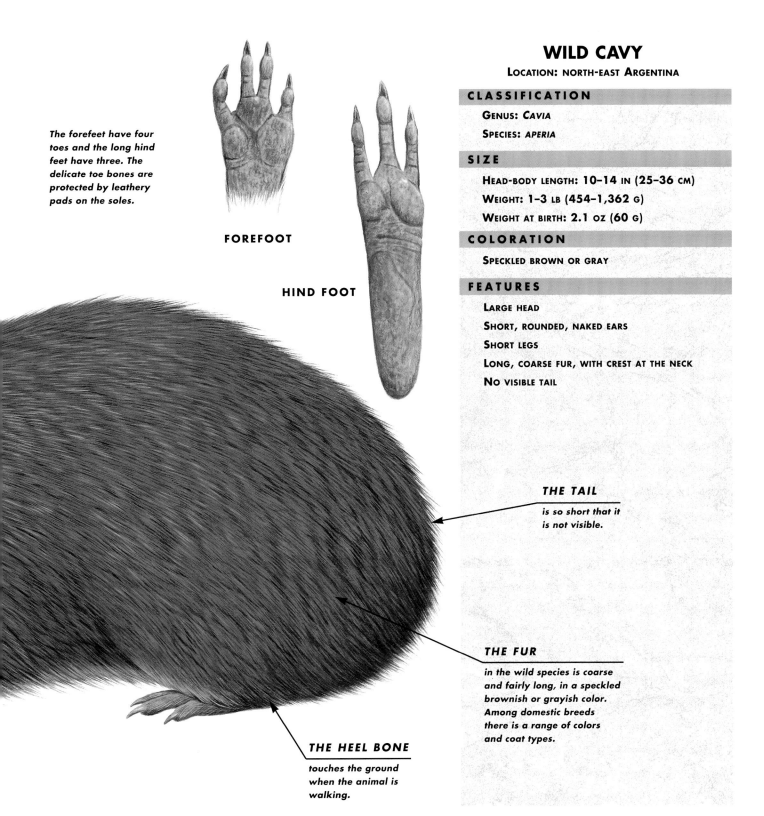

The forefeet have four toes and the long hind feet have three. The delicate toe bones are protected by leathery pads on the soles.

FOREFOOT

HIND FOOT

WILD CAVY
LOCATION: NORTH-EAST ARGENTINA

CLASSIFICATION

GENUS: *CAVIA*

SPECIES: *APERIA*

SIZE

HEAD-BODY LENGTH: 10–14 IN (25–36 CM)

WEIGHT: 1–3 LB (454–1,362 G)

WEIGHT AT BIRTH: 2.1 OZ (60 G)

COLORATION

SPECKLED BROWN OR GRAY

FEATURES

LARGE HEAD

SHORT, ROUNDED, NAKED EARS

SHORT LEGS

LONG, COARSE FUR, WITH CREST AT THE NECK

NO VISIBLE TAIL

THE TAIL
is so short that it is not visible.

THE FUR
in the wild species is coarse and fairly long, in a speckled brownish or grayish color. Among domestic breeds there is a range of colors and coat types.

THE HEEL BONE
touches the ground when the animal is walking.

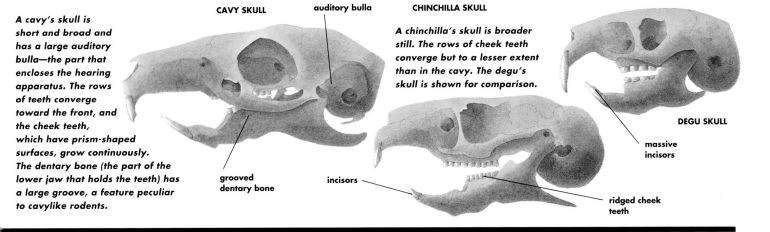

A cavy's skull is short and broad and has a large auditory bulla—the part that encloses the hearing apparatus. The rows of teeth converge toward the front, and the cheek teeth, which have prism-shaped surfaces, grow continuously. The dentary bone (the part of the lower jaw that holds the teeth) has a large groove, a feature peculiar to cavylike rodents.

CAVY SKULL auditory bulla

grooved dentary bone

CHINCHILLA SKULL

A chinchilla's skull is broader still. The rows of cheek teeth converge but to a lesser extent than in the cavy. The degu's skull is shown for comparison.

incisors

ridged cheek teeth

DEGU SKULL

massive incisors

WILDEBEEST

An adult male blue wildebeest or brindled gnu (above left) is one of the largest antelope (see Fact File). The mountain reedbuck, however, (above right) is the smallest of the reedbuck and has a shoulder height of up to 23 in (76 cm) and a weight of 66 lb (30 kg).

SITATUNGA   HARTEBEEST   KLIPSPRINGER

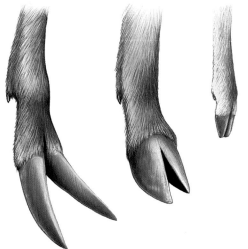

Artiodactyls have cloven hooves with two toes. The mountain-dwelling klipspringer, a dwarf antelope, has small, pointed hooves for balance. The larger hartebeest and sitatunga have splayed hooves to support their weight on soft ground.

THE MANE

of the wildebeest is long and tufted and very distinctive. The animal often shakes its mane vigorously during ritual displays.

THE HEAD

is massive with a broad muzzle. There are scent glands on the face that are rubbed on the rumps of other wildebeest during social interaction.

THE EARS

are large. Hearing is acute as this animal is the favorite prey of many predators. During courtship the ears are turned downward.

THE HOOVES

are even and slightly splayed in proportion to the weight of this large animal. Wildebeests are always on the move.

WILDEBEEST SKELETON
Short in the back and extraordinarily long in the leg, the skeleton of the wildebeest is a classic example of an open-plains grazer. Although it lacks the graceful gait of, for example, the horse, the wildebeest is nevertheless built for speed and stamina. The dorsal vertebrae are dramatically extended to produce the characteristic forequarter "hump."

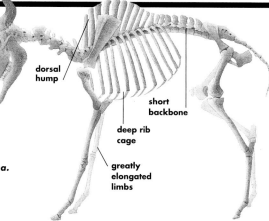

dorsal hump

short backbone

deep rib cage

greatly elongated limbs

In the wildebeest's skull the lower incisors bite against the hard pad that replaces the upper incisor teeth. The cheek teeth are high-crowned and ridged for grinding

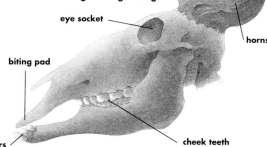

eye socket

horns

biting pad

incisors

cheek teeth

X-ray illustrations Elisabeth Smith. B/W Ruth Grewcock

SABLE   KUDU   FOUR-HORNED

Antelope have evolved different types of horn for varying reasons. The long, curved-back horns of the sable are a means of self-defense, while the spiral horns of the kudu are used in social interaction. The four-horned antelope, the most primitive antelope, has two pairs of horns, one at the front and one at the rear of its head.

BLUE WILDEBEEST

LOCATION: NORTHERN S AFRICA & ZAMBIA

CLASSIFICATION

GENUS: *CONNOCHAETES*

SPECIES: *TAURINUS*

SIZE

HEAD–BODY LENGTH: 60–96 IN (150–240 CM)

TAIL LENGTH: 14–22 IN (35–56 CM)

WEIGHT/MALE: 397–606 LB (180–275 KG)

WEIGHT/FEMALE: 309–353 LB (140–160 KG)

COLORATION

GRAYISH SILVER, WITH BROWNISH BANDS ON THE FOREQUARTERS AND NECK

THE FACE AND SCRAGGY MANE ARE BLACK, EXCEPT IN TWO SUBSPECIES, WHICH HAVE VERY OBVIOUS WHITE BEARDS

CONSPICUOUS BLACK TAIL

FEATURES

OXLIKE AND MISLEADINGLY FEROCIOUS IN APPEARANCE

BOTH SEXES HAVE HORNS, WHICH ARE HEAVY AND CURVED

THE HEAD IS MASSIVE WITH A BROAD MUZZLE

THE FEMALES HAVE FOUR MAMMAE

FORELEGS MUCH HEAVIER THAN HIND LEGS

THE BODY

appears clumsy and "front heavy," giving it the appearance of a buffalo. Wildebeests rub their heads on each other's rumps as a form of scent marking.

THE TAIL

is black and highly visible. The wildebeest is often described as the clown of the plains, as it cavorts about, lashing its tail vigorously. This may help to attract the attention of females, and certainly is an efficient flyswatter.

THE LEGS

are long and elegant. As in most antelopes, this streamlining means that wildebeest are fast runners.

BUSHBUCK SKULL

This typical spiral-horned antelope has a long, narrow face. The lower incisors project forward, and the cheek teeth have ridges of enamel on the crown.

narrow skull

projecting incisors

horns

high-crowned cheek teeth

ANTELOPE FORELIMBS

An antelope's legs have evolved to provide speed and endurance. Have a look at your hand and feel the bones between the wrist and knuckles; these are the metatarsals. On an antelope, the outer two metatarsals have been lost, while the central two have fused to become the single, long "cannon bone." The splayed hooves sit at the tips of the "fingers."

humerus

elbow joint

ulna (forearm)

wrist

"cannon bone" (central two metatarsals)

cloven hoof with two "fingers"

WOLF

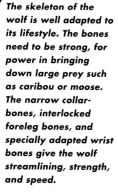

The gray wolf is larger than the red wolf and considerably larger than most domestic dogs. Its nearest domestic likeness is the German shepherd dog.

HEARING

With its large, pointed ears, the wolf is able to hear very faint sounds made by prey from a considerable distance—the equivalent of being able to hear a watch ticking 33 ft (10 m) away. The wolf relies on its hearing for hunting, much more than on its eyesight, which is not particularly good.

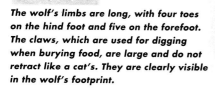

The wolf's limbs are long, with four toes on the hind foot and five on the forefoot. The claws, which are used for digging when burying food, are large and do not retract like a cat's. They are clearly visible in the wolf's footprint.

SENSE OF SMELL

All dogs are noted for their acute sense of smell, which has been put to good use by humans— German shepherd dogs are trained to sniff out drugs and explosives, for example. The wolf is no exception and relies heavily on its sense of smell for tracking prey and recognizing other wolves and their territory.

WALKING/RUNNING

Wolves walk with a trotting pace and leave a single line of paw prints. Other wolves walk along the leader's tracks in single file. Wolves are good runners and, with their great stamina, can keep up their loping style of running over long distances, managing speeds of up to 28 mph (45 km/h) in shorter bursts.

Color illustrations Guy Troughton/Wildife Art Agency

X R A Y

The skeleton of the wolf is well adapted to its lifestyle. The bones need to be strong, for power in bringing down large prey such as caribou or moose. The narrow collarbones, interlocked foreleg bones, and specially adapted wrist bones give the wolf streamlining, strength, and speed.

WOLF SKELETON

The wrist bones of the wolf are fused together for extra strength. When closed, the toes are rugged and strong. Splaying the toes allows the wolf to grip on to slippery, uneven, and steep surfaces.

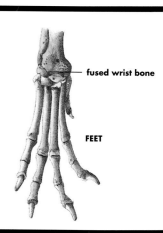

fused wrist bone

FEET

X-ray illustrations Elisabeth Smith

GRAY WOLF

CLASSIFICATION

GENUS: *CANIS*

SPECIES: *LUPUS*

SIZE

HEAD–BODY LENGTH: 39–59 IN (100–150 CM)

TAIL LENGTH: 12–20 IN (30–50 CM)

WEIGHT: 60–150 LB (27–68 KG)

FEMALE IS SLIGHTLY SMALLER THAN THE MALE, WEIGHING ABOUT 11 LB (5 KG) LESS

WEIGHT AT BIRTH: 1 LB (0.5 KG)

COLORATION

COLOR: USUALLY GRAY/YELLOWISH BROWN. VARIES BY REGION FROM WHITE TO SANDY REDDISH, BROWNISH, OR BLACK

COLOR OF NEWBORNS: SOOTY BROWN, EXCEPT IN ARCTIC WHERE FUR IS LIGHT BLUE OR DULL SLATE

The broad head and long muzzle of the wolf contain strong jaws and teeth. The pointed canine teeth can be up to 2 in (5 cm) long. Powerful face muscles hold the teeth locked together and help the wolf hang on to its prey.

STREAMLINED SHAPE

The wolf is built for speed as it travels in pursuit of prey, often under cover through dense woodland and undergrowth: pointed muzzle, head, and ears; narrow chest; long, slim legs; smooth fur; slender, tapering body; and long, pointed tail.

FUR

Soft, thick underfur keeps the wolf warm and dry, and long "guard" hairs keep snow and water out. Pale underparts, blotchy darker markings on the body, ears, and tail, and color to match habitat, give the wolf the advantage of camouflage as it moves up on its prey.

FEATURES

EYE COLOR: YELLOWISH

EARS: ERECT, BLACK EDGES

TAIL: LONG, BUSHY, DROOPING

FEET: FOREFEET HAVE FIVE TOES

HIND FEET HAVE FOUR TOES

CLAWS: CANNOT BE RETRACTED

An open mouth reveals the contents of the long muzzle—a set of 42 fearsome-looking teeth made up of 6 incisors, 2 canines, 8 premolars, and 6 molars in the lower jaw. The upper jaw has 2 fewer molars.

The elongated shape of the skull is typical of the dog family.

WOLF SKULL (side view)

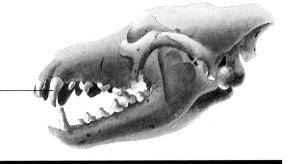

canine teeth

WOLVERINE

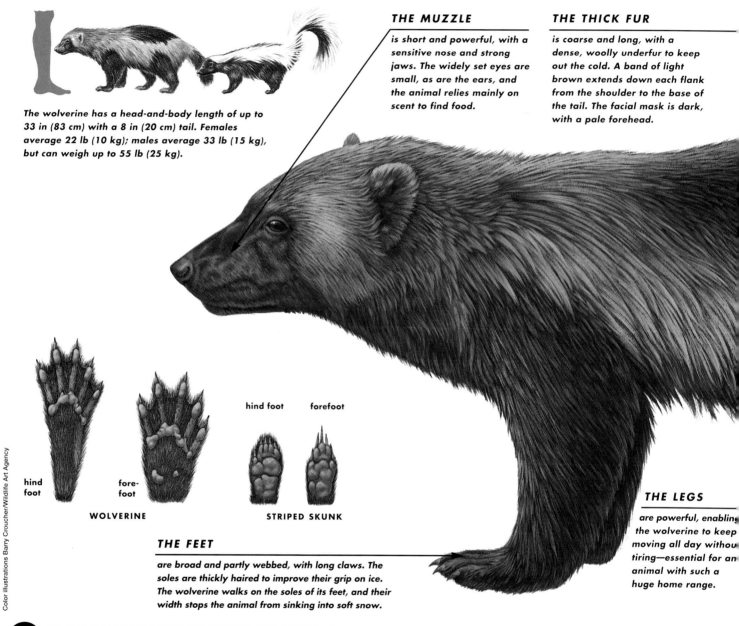

The wolverine has a head-and-body length of up to 33 in (83 cm) with a 8 in (20 cm) tail. Females average 22 lb (10 kg); males average 33 lb (15 kg), but can weigh up to 55 lb (25 kg).

THE MUZZLE

is short and powerful, with a sensitive nose and strong jaws. The widely set eyes are small, as are the ears, and the animal relies mainly on scent to find food.

THE THICK FUR

is coarse and long, with a dense, woolly underfur to keep out the cold. A band of light brown extends down each flank from the shoulder to the base of the tail. The facial mask is dark, with a pale forehead.

hind foot   forefoot

hind foot   fore-foot

WOLVERINE

STRIPED SKUNK

THE LEGS

are powerful, enabling the wolverine to keep moving all day without tiring—essential for an animal with such a huge home range.

THE FEET

are broad and partly webbed, with long claws. The soles are thickly haired to improve their grip on ice. The wolverine walks on the soles of its feet, and their width stops the animal from sinking into soft snow.

Color illustrations Barry Croucher/Wildlife Art Agency

X RAY

The wolverine's skeleton reflects its heavy, muscular build. The neck is stout, and the general proportions are more bearlike than mustelid. The bones in the hind feet are greatly elongated.

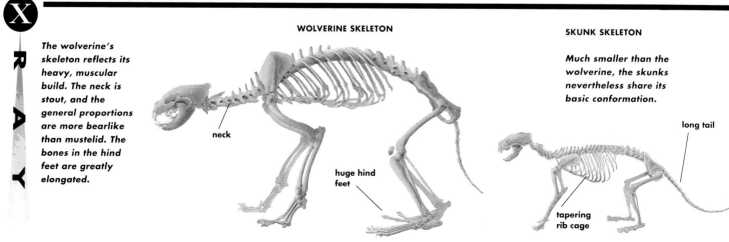

WOLVERINE SKELETON

neck

huge hind feet

SKUNK SKELETON

Much smaller than the wolverine, the skunks nevertheless share its basic conformation.

long tail

tapering rib cage

X-ray illustrations Elisabeth Smith

SPOTTED SKUNK
Black with white stripes on the back and sides, plus smaller stripes and spots on the rump.

HOG-NOSED SKUNK
Black except for a white "cape" from brow to tail. Alternatively, black with two white stripes.

STRIPED SKUNK
Black with a varying degree of white areas, among which there are no stray black hairs.

WOLVERINE

LOCATION: ALASKA, CANADA & NORTHERN EURASIA

CLASSIFICATION

GENUS: *GULO*

SPECIES: *GULO*

SIZE

HEAD–BODY LENGTH: UP TO 33 IN (83 CM)

TAIL LENGTH: 8 IN (20 CM)

AVERAGE WEIGHT/MALE: 33 LB (15 KG)

AVERAGE WEIGHT/FEMALE: 22 LB (10 KG)

WEIGHT AT BIRTH: 3.5 OZ (100 G)

FEMALES ARE ABOUT 10 PERCENT SHORTER THAN MALES AND 30 PERCENT LIGHTER IN WEIGHT

COLORATION

DUSKY BROWN WITH DARK MASK AND PALE BROWN BROW; DISTINCT PALE BAND EXTENDING FROM SHOULDER TO RUMP ON EACH FLANK, JOINING OVER BASE OF TAIL

CUBS: WHITE TO SANDY YELLOW

FEATURES

POWERFUL, BEARLIKE BUILD

BUSHY TAIL

BROAD, STRONGLY CLAWED FEET

AWKWARD GAIT

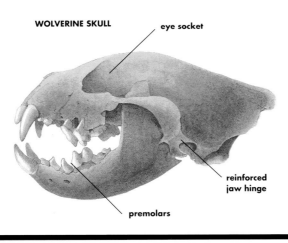

THE BUSHY TAIL
distinguishes the wolverine from the bears, which it otherwise resembles. The tail is usually carried low.

The powerful jaw muscles of the wolverine are anchored to the prominent crest on its skull, providing the leverage to crack the limb bones of reindeer and reach the rich marrow within. The big, bladelike premolar teeth, called the carnassials, are principally adapted for shearing flesh and sinew, but they are also strong enough to crush even the thickest of bones.

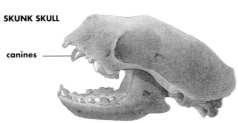

WOLVERINE SKULL

eye socket

reinforced jaw hinge

premolars

SKUNK SKULL

canines

The skunk's skull is typical of mustelids, with a heavy, strongly hinged jaw, blunt nasal area, and long, sharp canines.

WOMBAT

The common wombat (above left) is the largest of the wombats (see Fact File). The giant bandicoot (above right) reaches a head-and-body length of 15–22 in (39–56 cm) with a tail 4.7–13.4 in (12–34 cm) long, while the mouse bandicoot (above center) measures only 6–7 in (15–17.5 cm) from head to rump, with a tail 4.3 in (11 cm) long.

FEET

The wombat walks on the flats of its feet, rather like humans and bears. The broad feet are armed with long, sturdy claws: five on each forefoot, four on each hind foot. The second and third digits on the foot are partially joined together to make a double-claw, which is used in grooming. When burrowing, the forefeet cut away fresh soil, and the hind feet kick the freshly excavated debris back up the newly dug tunnel.

HIND FOOT   **FOREFOOT**

THE EYES

give fairly poor vision—typical of a burrowing animal that relies heavily on scent and hearing.

THE EARS

are small and rounded, with dense fur on the outer surface. The sense of hearing is good.

THE NOSE

is naked with granular skin, like that of a bear or dog. Hairy-nosed wombats have soft, velvety fur between the nostrils. In all species, sense of smell is excellent. The split upper lip enables the wombat to bring its incisors close to the ground to crop low-growing grass.

THE BODY

is squat and barrel-like, showing the compact form possessed by many burrowers.

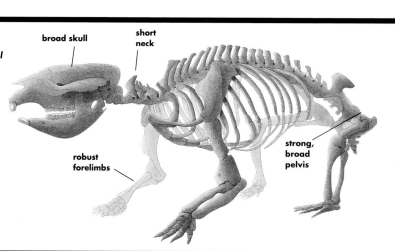

X-RAY

SKELETON

The wombat's short, stocky legs and powerful shoulders are built for burrowing. The animal walks on the soles, not the toes of its feet, and cannot run particularly fast, but it compensates by having a greater spread of muscle on the limb bones. Stout bones are a feature of many marsupials, since they help support the weight of a full pouch.

broad skull

short neck

robust forelimbs

strong, broad pelvis

TEETH

Unlike other marsupials, wombats have rootless, ever-growing incisor teeth (right). This adaptation to gnawing tough grasses is also found in rodents. Another rodentlike feature is the diastema, a large gap between the incisors and the grinding cheek teeth. This space allows large chunks of food to be moved about in the mouth.

X-ray illustrations Elisabeth Smith

BANDICOOT

BILBY

EAR LENGTHS
Bandicoots and bilbies have long, finely tapering snouts, the length of which varies between species. Most bandicoots, except for the pig-footed species, have fairly short ears. By comparison, bilbies have spectacularly long ears—part of the reason for their alternative name of "rabbit-eared bandicoot."

COMMON WOMBAT

CLASSIFICATION

GENUS: *VOMBATUS*

SPECIES: *URSINUS*

SIZE

HEAD–BODY LENGTH: **35–45** IN **(90–115 CM)**

TAIL LENGTH: ABOUT **1** IN **(2.5 CM)**

HEIGHT: **14.2** IN **(36 CM)**

WEIGHT: **48.5–86** LB **(22–39 KG)**

WEIGHT AT BIRTH: **0.07** OZ **(2 G)**

COLORATION

COAT IS BLACK OR MOUSE BROWN–GRAY, AND COARSE IN TEXTURE

BROWN SNOUT

FEATURES

SQUAT, THICKSET BODY WITH A ROUNDED RUMP "OVERHANGING" THE HIND LIMBS

BROAD HEAD

SNUB MUZZLE AND SMALL, ROUNDED EARS

LONG, STOUT CLAWS ON ALL FEET

THE LIMBS
are not built for running but for burrowing. The short, stout legs enable brief but powerful digging thrusts.

THE TAIL
is tiny and stubby; a long tail would be a hindrance when burrowing.

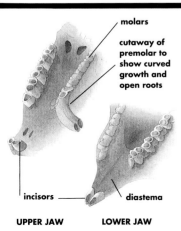

molars

cutaway of premolar to show curved growth and open roots

incisors

diastema

UPPER JAW   **LOWER JAW**

SKULL
The zygomatic arches of a wombat's skull (near right) flare sideways to make room for enlarged masseter muscles that move the jaws in the side-to-side motion required for grinding tough plant food. Bandicoots (far right) have teeth suited to a diet of both plant and animal matter, with sharp canines and pointed premolars.

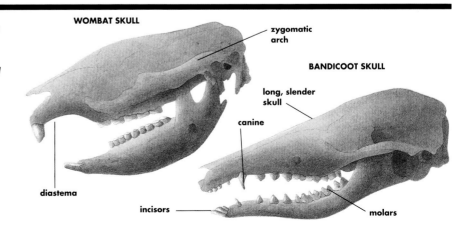

WOMBAT SKULL

zygomatic arch

BANDICOOT SKULL

long, slender skull

canine

diastema

incisors

molars

CLASSIFICATION

The following lists the genuses of the mammals detailed in this book.

ARTIODACTYLA	african buffalo, american bison, camel, giraffe, hippopotamus, ibex, pronghorn, red deer, springbok, wild boar, wildebeest
CARNIVORA	african civet, african wild dog, arctic fox, badger, black bear, cheetah, dhole, eurasian wildcat, giant panda, golden jackal, grizzly bear, hyena, jaguar, leopard, lion, maned wolf, meerkat, otter, pine marten, polar bear, puma, raccoon, red fox, serval, spectacled bear, tiger, weasel, wolf, wolverine
CETACEA	blue whale, dolphin, killer whale, sperm whale
CHIROPTERA	gray-headed fruit bat, greater horseshoe bat, common pipistrelle bat, vampire bat
EDENTATA	armadillo giant anteater, three-toed sloth
INSECTIVORA	european mole, hedgehog, shrew
LAGOMORPHA	brown hare, rabbit
MARSUPIALIA	kangaroo, koala, oppossum, rat kangaroo, sugar glider, tasmanian devil, wombat
MONOTREMATA	platypus
PERISSODACTYLA	plains zebra, przhevalski's horse, rhino
PINNIPEDIA	common seal, fur seals
PRIMATES	capuchin chimpanzee, gibbon, gorilla, lesser galago, mandrill, marmoset, orang utan, red colobus
PROBOSCIDEA	elephant
RODENTIA	brown rat, canadian beaver, capybara, deer mouse, hamster, lemming, naked mole rat, porcupine, prairie dog, red squirrel, wild cavy
SIRENIA	manatee
TUBULIDENTATA	aardvark